DATE DUE

MAY 4 1992		

CRITERION-REFERENCED MEASUREMENT

CRITERION-REFERENCED MEASUREMENT: THE STATE OF THE ART

EDITED BY

RONALD A. BERK

THE JOHNS HOPKINS UNIVERSITY PRESS
Baltimore and London

Manufactured in the United States of America

The Johns Hopkins University Press, Baltimore, Maryland 21218
The Johns Hopkins Press Ltd., London

Library of Congress Catalog Card Number 79-18194
ISBN 0-8018-2264-5

Library of Congress Cataloging in Publication data will be found on the last printed page of this book.

To Marion

CONTENTS

PREFACE

THIS BOOK PROVIDES a comprehensive assessment of the state of the art of criterion-referenced measurement and evaluation. It is a product of the first annual Johns Hopkins University National Symposium on Educational Research (NSER), held in Washington, D.C., in October 1978.

The Symposium

The idea for a symposium was first suggested to me by Gilbert B. Schiffman. The state-of-the-art concept applied to the symposium was stimulated by the divisional state-of-the-art addresses presented at the 1978 American Educational Research Association Conference. The need for a "research symposium" with a practical orientation became obvious as I observed that much of the research generated year after year did not seem to be reflected in classroom and school district practices. Consequently, despite the sophisticated research dissemination methods available, a gap between research findings and their implementation in practice was evident. The symposium was seen as one possible vehicle to bridge that gap.

Purposes. The symposium was conceived as a mechanism for assembling research scholars on an issue of national concern to educational researchers and practitioners. The scholars selected to participate in the first symposium have contributed significantly to the advancement and understanding of criterion-referenced measurement through their publications, through presentations at national conferences, and through the workshops and training sessions they have conducted for teachers and evaluators. Their task was to synthesize the research on the topic that has been amassed over the past decade and translate the results into forms that practitioners and researchers can use. The presentations provided a state-of-the-art assessment of the methodological underpinnings of criterion-referenced measurement in terms of what has been done, what should be done, and what still needs to be done.

Advisory Board. The annual theme and invited speakers for the symposium are chosen according to the recommendations of the NSER

Advisory Board. I gratefully acknowledge the valuable contributions of the 1978 board members: Joan Bollenbacher, Robert L. Brennan, Lois E. Burrill, Ronald K. Hambleton, David J. Kleinke, James M. McPartland, William B. Michael, and Lorrie A. Shepard.

Audience. The symposium was designed to attract researchers from universities, private corporations, and R & D laboratories, and practitioners at the federal, state, and local levels of research and evaluation. The response to the 1978 symposium was enthusiastic. More than 260 distinguished educators from thirty-eight different states, Canada, Mexico, Bermuda, and the Netherlands attended the symposium.

Acknowledgments

The symposium and this book represent the culmination of a tremendous amount of work by numerous individuals. I am delighted to mention the contributions of a few who deserve special credit. First, I extend my deepest appreciation to the five speakers/authors and to Victor R. Martuza (University of Delaware) and Samuel A. Livingston (Educational Testing Service), who served as discussants at the symposium, for sharing their expertise and exhibiting rare patience and cooperation. The administrative and financial support given by Dean Roman J. Verhaalen and Elaine C. Davis of the Evening College of The Johns Hopkins University made it all possible. Margaret B. Lamb (Educational Testing Service) supplied valuable input in the early stages by helping me structure an idea into the form of a symposium. Joan S. Millison and Sharon D. Custis coordinated the symposium with alacrity. Jessie H. Rodner offered many helpful comments on the development of the symposium and preparation of my manuscript. Henry Tom, social sciences editor of The Johns Hopkins University Press, provided useful suggestions throughout the publication process. Finally, I thank Ilse M. Harrop and Betty C. Vaughan for their typing and assistance related to both the symposium and this book.

CRITERION-REFERENCED MEASUREMENT

INTRODUCTION

AMONG THE MANY CHANGES that have occurred in the area of educational measurement and evaluation during the past decade, the shift from norm-referenced to criterion-referenced testing has been the most dramatic. An increasing emphasis on mastery-proficiency-competency is permeating all levels of education and other professions, particularly medicine and the allied health fields. The recent back-to-basics trend and the state mandates for minimum competency testing for high school graduation certification and grade-to-grade promotion have provided additional impetus to the movement. Commercial test publishers have also committed substantial resources to the production of criterion-referenced testing systems and diagnostic-prescriptive instructional packages.

The current momentum for generating tests that are designed expressly for interpreting an individual's performance in terms of what he or she can and cannot do irrespective of the performance of other students has a rather sporadic history. The concept of an absolute versus relative standard of measurement can be traced to the work of Thorndike (1913), Flanagan (1951), Nedelsky (1954), and Ebel (1962). The term *criterion-referenced* was first coined in 1962 (cf. Glaser & Klaus 1962). The distinction between a *criterion-referenced* and a *norm-referenced* test was most clearly defined in Glaser's seminal essay (1963). He stated:

> The scores obtained from an achievement test provide primarily two kinds of information. One is the degree to which the student has attained criterion performance, for example, whether he can satisfactorily prepare an experimental report, or solve certain kinds of word problems in arithmetic. The second type of information that an achievement test score provides is the relative ordering of individuals with respect to their test performance, for example, whether Student A can solve his problems more quickly than Student B. The principal difference between these two kinds of information lies in the standard used as a reference. What I shall call criterion-referenced measures depend upon an absolute standard of quality, while what I term norm-referenced measures depend upon a relative standard. (P. 519)

For the remainder of the 1960s there was a sparsity of major research activity on the topic. An article by Popham and Husek in 1969, however, seemed to provide the stimulation needed to arouse the measurement community. It not only amplified Glaser's distinction between

3

criterion-referenced and norm-referenced measurement, but also enumerated the advantages and disadvantages of the two approaches in instructional decision making. The explosion of interest that followed in the decade of the 1970s has not yet abated.

Since 1970, there has been a proliferation of research on the psychometric properties of criterion-referenced tests. The published research has appeared in a variety of journals, monographs, and books. The proportionately greater number of unpublished papers consisting of conference presentations and reports by school districts and R & D laboratories are generally accessible through the ERIC abstracting and document retrieval system.

Unfortunately, much of the research proceeded independently with little regard for potentially comparable work. This can be illustrated by the confusion over terminology in the titles and contents of the articles. Although some researchers consistently use the label "criterion-referenced test", it is not uncommon to find the terms *domain-referenced test, objectives-referenced test, competency-based test, proficiency test,* and *mastery test* used interchangeably in the literature. When this problem is coupled with the diverse forms in which the research exists, one is confronted with a body of research that is published, unpublished, redundant, and fragmented. From this perspective, it is hardly surprising to find that the quality of available criterion-referenced tests developed by teachers, evaluators, and test publishers is not commensurate with the magnitude of the efforts to produce them (cf. Hambleton & Eignor 1978).

Purposes of the Book

This book attempts to determine the state of the art of criterion-referenced measurement. Its contribution to the measurement field will depend largely on how well it accomplishes the following purposes: (1) to clarify the terminology and jargon related to criterion-referenced tests; (2) to synthesize the research that has accumulated over the past decade; (3) to translate the research results into forms meaningful and useful for practitioners and researchers; and (4) to bring into sharp focus the major issues in criterion-referenced measurement that have been resolved and those that need resolution.

Probably any volume that claims to present a state-of-the-art assessment of any research domain is doomed to the flaw of some omission. The topics chosen for review in this volume have been judged crucial for the proper construction, interpretation, and use of criterion-referenced tests. Admittedly, other important topics germane to criterion-referenced measurement such as test length, matrix sampling, and latent trait theory applications were omitted or only partially treated. This was primarily due to the time constraints of the symposium from which the chapters originated. For those omissions, the editor assumes responsibility.

Definition of a Criterion-Referenced Test

Since the term *criterion-referenced measurement* was first applied to proficiency assessment by Glaser and Klaus (1962), more than fifty descriptions of a criterion-referenced test have appeared in the research. Various comparisons of these descriptions suggest there is general agreement that the test is intended to reference an individual's score to a well-defined domain of behaviors (cf. Gray 1978; Hambleton, Swaminathan, Algina, & Coulson 1978; Livingston 1977; Millman 1974). Popham's (1978, p. 93) definition most accurately captures that conceptualization: *"A criterion-referenced test is used to ascertain an individual's status with respect to a well-defined behavioral domain."* Such tests are often referred to as *domain-referenced*. The principal concern in their development is obtaining rigorous and precise domain specifications to maximize the interpretability of an individual's domain score.

An alternative conceptualization of criterion-referenced measurement derived from mastery learning theory (Block & Burns 1976; Bloom 1968; Carroll 1963, 1970; Mayo 1970) is represented by the *mastery test*. It is used to classify students as masters and nonmasters of an objective in order to expedite individualized instruction. Empirical item analysis procedures are recommended to determine whether the items are instructionally sensitive or discriminate between instructed and uninstructed groups. Methods for setting absolute performance standards for mastery and the estimation of classification errors are particularly important.

The characteristics of the domain-referenced and mastery conceptualizations of a criterion-referenced test are outlined in table I.1. Given the familiar objectives-based framework and item analysis requirements of the mastery test, it has become the most frequently used criterion-referenced test in practice. Satisfying the domain specification criteria for clarity in the domain-referenced approach has been considerably more difficult.

Organization of the Book

The book is divided into three sections with a total of six chapters. Each section is preceded by introductory remarks and highlights of the chapters in that section. The topics addressed by the chapters

TABLE I.1. Characteristics of Domain-Referenced and Mastery Conceptualizations of a Criterion-Referenced Test

Stages of Development	Alternative Conceptualizations	
	Domain-Referenced	Mastery
Content domain specification (chapters 1 & 2)	Possible strategies: (1) Amplified objectives (2) IOX test specifications (3) Mapping sentences (4) Item transformations (5) Item forms (6) Algorithms	Instructional and behavioral objectives
Item construction (chapter 2)	Generation rules	Traditional rules
Item domain specification (chapter 3)	Infinite or finite (contingent upon precision of domain specification strategy)	Infinite
Item analysis (chapter 3)	. . .	Item-objective congruence Item statistics
Item selection (chapter 3)	Random	Nonrandom
Cut-off score selection (chapter 4)	Optional	Required
Validity (chapter 4)	Content Construct Decision	Content Criterion-related Construct Decision
Reliability (chapters 5 & 6)	Possible approaches: (1) Decision-consistency estimate ($\hat{p}_o$ or $\hat{\kappa}$) (2) Index of dependability ($\Phi(\lambda)$) (3) Error of measurement or estimate around domain score using Φ or other indices	Decision-consistency estimate ($\hat{p}_o$ or $\hat{\kappa}$)
Score interpretation[a]	Reference score to domain Reference score to cut-off score for mastery-non-mastery decisions	Reference score to cut-off score for mastery-non-mastery decisions

[a]While score interpretation is not a stage or issue in test development per se, it is a major consideration in all of the preceding eight stages.

correspond to the stages of development listed in table I.1 and the characteristics of both types of criterion-referenced tests. A brief summary of the contents follows.

Part One. Content Domain Specification/Item Generation

This section reviews strategies for defining the domain of content or behaviors that the test is to measure (chapter 1) and computer-based procedures for generating sets of items from the domain definition (chapter 2). Both chapters stress the domain-referenced conceptualization.

Part Two. Item and Test Validity

The two chapters in this section describe several analyses to furnish judgmental and empirical evidence that the test functions effectively. Chapter 3 examines methods to determine item validity and revise those items identified as invalid. It emphasizes the mastery conceptualization. Chapter 4 extends some of the item analysis methods to the appraisal of content and construct validity. A survey of procedures for setting cut-off scores is also included. That presentation is applicable to both types of criterion-referenced tests.

Part Three. Reliability

Three major approaches to estimating criterion-referenced test reliability are presented in this section. The first approach deals with the consistency of mastery-nonmastery classifications across parallel test forms (chapter 5). This decision-consistency model is most appropriate for the mastery test. The second and third approaches, which are derived from generalizability theory, pertain to the consistency of squared deviations of individual scores from the cut-off score and the consistency of individual scores across randomly parallel test forms, respectively (chapter 6). Both of these were designed exclusively for the domain-referenced conceptualization.

For ease of use by practitioners and researchers, each chapter is organized into four main parts: (1) "Introduction," which defines the topic and explains its significance in criterion-referenced measurement; (2) "Review," which provides a critical survey of all major strategies, methods, conceptualizations, and formulations related directly to the topic; (3) "Suggestions for Future Research," which list the specific types and areas of research that still need attention; and (4) "Guidelines for Practitioners," which discuss the implications of the recommended strategy(s) for tests developed by classroom teachers and by evaluators at the district, state, and national levels.

Intended Uses of the Book

Consistent with its structure, contents, and orientation, this volume should be used as a handbook for evaluators charged with developing criterion-referenced and minimum competency tests. The treatment of the topics in parts one and two presumes the reader has had at least one basic course in measurement. Some of the technical material in part three also requires a working knowledge of analysis of variance for the reader to derive its full benefit.

The book can also serve as a text and reference for courses or workshops for teachers on criterion-referenced measurement and second- and third-level graduate courses in measurement. Researchers should use the book as a guide for conducting future investigations in the field.

References

Block, J. H., and Burns, R. B. 1976. Mastery learning. In *Review of research in education,* ed. L. S. Shulman. Vol. 4. Itasca, Ill.: F. E. Peacock.

Bloom, B. S. 1968. Learning for mastery. *Evaluation Comment* 1, no. 1.

Carroll, J. B. 1963. A model of school learning. *Teachers College Record* 64: 723-33.

_____. 1970. Problems of measurement related to the concept of learning for mastery. *Educational Horizons* 48: 71-80.

Ebel, R. L. 1962. Content standard test scores. *Educational and Psychological Measurement* 22: 15-25.

Flanagan, J. C. 1951. Units, scores, and norms. In *Educational measurement,* ed. E. F. Lindquist. Washington, D.C.: American Council on Education. Pp. 659-763.

Glaser, R. 1963. Instructional technology and the measurement of learning outcomes: Some questions. *American Psychologist* 18: 519-21.

Glaser, R., and Klaus, D. J. 1962. Proficiency measurement: Assessing human performance. In *Psychological principles in systems development,* ed. R. M. Gagné. New York: Holt, Rinehart and Winston. Pp. 419-74.

Gray, W. M. 1978. A comparison of Piagetian theory and criterion-referenced measurement. *Review of Educational Research* 48: 223-49.

Hambleton, R. K., and Eignor, D. R. 1978. Guidelines for evaluating criterion-referenced tests and test manuals. *Journal of Educational Measurement* 15: 321-27.

Hambleton, R. K.; Swaminathan, H.; Algina, J.; and Coulson, D. B. 1978. Criterion-referenced testing and measurement: A review of technical issues and developments. *Review of Educational Research* 48: 1-47.

Livingston, S. A. 1977. Psychometric techniques for criterion-referenced testing and behavioral assessment. In *Behavioral assessment: New directions in clinical psychology,* ed. J. D. Cone and R. P. Hawkins. New York: Brunner/Mazel. Pp. 308-29.

Mayo, S. T. 1970. Mastery learning and mastery testing. *Measurement in Education* 1: 1-4.

Millman, J. 1974. Criterion-referenced measurement. In *Evaluation in education: Current applications,* ed. W. J. Popham. Berkeley, Calif.: McCutchan. Pp. 311-97.

Nedelsky, L. 1954. Absolute grading standards for objective tests. *Educational and Psychological Measurement* 14: 3-19.

Popham, W. J. 1978. *Criterion-referenced measurement.* Englewood Cliffs, N.J.: Prentice-Hall.

Popham, W. J., and Husek, T. R. 1969. Implications of criterion-referenced measurement. *Journal of Educational Measurement* 6: 1-9.

Thorndike, E. L. 1913. *Educational psychology.* Vol. 1. New York: Teachers College, Columbia University.

PART ONE

CONTENT DOMAIN SPECIFICATION/ ITEM GENERATION

THE FIRST STEP IN THE DEVELOPMENT of a criterion-referenced test is to define operationally the domain of content or behaviors the test is to measure. It is also the most important step. The validity and interpretability of the test scores are contingent upon the precision of the domain specifications. Therefore, it is essential that the relationship of the scores to the domain be planned deliberately and systematically into the test design to assure meaningful results.

The leading proponents of criterion-referenced tests contend that the traditional approach to defining a body of content that includes a content outline, a list of objectives, and a table of specifications or similar "blueprint" tends to produce an *ambiguous* domain definition. The arguments focus on the subjectivity involved in composing those specifications. That is, the selection of content topics and objectives is quite arbitrary, typically representing only one test maker's conceptualization of the domain. Such specifications would be open to different interpretations by different test makers. Given this ambiguity, the specifications are felt to be inadequate for item writing.

Coupled with this criticism is the charge that traditional item construction procedures used to write items from the specifications are also ambiguous. It is argued that employing those procedures results in a set of items that reflects the biases and idiosyncrasies of each test maker. Consequently, different test makers would probably develop different items from the same specifications.

The domain specification strategies devised over the past decade for building criterion-referenced tests are intended to overcome the aforementioned deficiencies of the traditional approach. The strategies strive to provide an *unambiguous* definition of a domain and implicitly or explicitly constitute sets of rules for generating the items, such that any two test makers would construct identical items from the same specifications. The extent to which any of the strategies can actually supply an unambiguous link between a behavioral domain and the corresponding test items is addressed in chapters 1 and 2.

Professor W. James Popham, as Director of the Instructional Objectives Exchange (IOX) at UCLA, offers his insights and experiences in wrestling with four different strategies since 1968. In chapter 1, he traces the developments related to behavioral objectives beginning in 1968, item forms in 1971, amplified objectives in 1973, and IOX test specifications in 1978. The most recent scheme represents the con-

13

fluence of ideas from ten years of work on the three earlier IOX projects. It consists of five components: (1) a general description of the behavior(s) to be measured, (2) a sample test item, (3) the stimulus attributes that constrain the composition of the items, (4) the response attributes (selected or constructed responses), and (5) an optional specification supplement to include additional item content where necessary. Professor Popham assesses the precision of the various strategies in achieving descriptive clarity in terms of a specificity-interpretability continuum. While he acknowledges that the latest IOX effort falls short of total specificity, he points out that it yields substantial clarity dividends over the less descriptive schemes. The discussion of this issue is presented from the perspective that a certain degree of imprecision will always characterize domain specifications, at least until humans start functioning like computers.

In chapter 2, Professor Jason Millman concentrates his attention on the next logical step in the test development process—the generation of items from the domain specifications. Since both authors agree that writing domain specifications is much more of an art than a science, the role of computers in facilitating test construction cannot be considered seriously until the specifications have been completed. That role is the subject of Professor Millman's presentation. He first explores the potential of computers for item banking, test assembly, and test administration. Then he describes mechanical procedures for applying particular algorithmic and linguistic strategies to generate criterion-referenced test items via computer. Professor Millman indicates that the technology exists for generating items, tests, and randomly parallel forms of the same test. The implications for practice in an area such as minimum competency testing are numerous. The feasibility of the computer-based strategies, however, has yet to be demonstrated effectively.

1

DOMAIN SPECIFICATION STRATEGIES

W. James Popham

Introduction

Creativity is a uniformly cherished commodity. Hence, what self-respecting test development agency would not want its item-writing staff to be simply brimming with Faulkner-like folks or Hemingway clones? After all, almost all test items hinge on the way writers use words, and creatively woven words make for better reading than stodgy ones.

But, contrary to the common adoration of creativity in any form, there is a phase in the development of criterion-referenced tests when freewheeling creativity is to be shunned, and that is when item writers are actually nutsing and boltsing out a pile of test items. The remainder of this analysis will constitute an effort to demonstrate why we should wish to put a clamp on such creativity and how we might go about effectively stifling the fervor of the inventive item writer.

To realize why anyone would have the affrontery to rail against creativity, it is requisite to look hard at criterion-referenced tests and decide why they were spawned in the first place. Unlike their norm-referenced predecessors, which rely chiefly on the relative status of an examinee's performance in relationship to the performances of those in a normative group, criterion-referenced tests are supposed to tell us what it is that examinees can or can't do. The phrase, "What examinees can or can't do," is deceptively simple, since it fails to communicate all that vividly just how much difficulty is actually embedded in the task of spelling out even a run-of-the-mill "can or can't do," much less a really complicated one.

If a criterion-referenced test doesn't unambiguously describe just what it's measuring, it offers no advantage over norm-referenced measures. And therein comes the crunch, since to describe the set of behaviors ostensibly being measured by a criterion-referenced test we are almost totally dependent on verbal symbols—on words.

Although it's true that in certain fields, such as the hard sciences, for example, people can describe phenomena by employing sophisticated measuring instruments and tons of numbers, we do not have that luxury when describing an examinee's performance on an educational test. Think about the process of educational measurement for a moment and you'll see why we must depend totally upon verbal precision if we ever hope to describe satisfactorily what it is that an examinee's performance really means.

In the typical case, a student attempts to answer a flock of test items; some he answers correctly and some he doesn't. A raw score of, say, forty-five correct out of sixty items is obtained. What does that score mean? In what conceivable way does it signify what the examinee "can or can't do"? Well, in a norm-referenced world, of course, we'd quickly consult our norm table and discover that a raw score of forty-five is equivalent to the eighty-sixth percentile; hence, all would be well. All would be well, that is, if we only wanted to know how a person scoring forty-five on the test stacked up against other people. But if we want to know what the forty-five scorer "can or can't do," norm tables don't offer much solace.

To get a fix on what our student's score really means, of course, we could say that raw score of forty-five represented a 75 percent mastery of the sixty possible items. And that kind of an assertion would make good sense *if* (a) the sixty items represented a relatively homogeneous collection of instances for the student to exhibit a *single* skill, and (b) the nature of those sixty items has been described well enough that we really know what they're trying to measure. Those are truly substantial *ifs*.

Let's start off with condition (b), a reversal of the traditional alphabetic sequence. Note that one condition requisite for rendering an accurate interpretation of what an examinee's test performance signifies is a lucid description of the nature of the items on the test. It is because we know how an examinee responds to particular stimuli that we can infer something about what those responses signify. The more clearly we understand what the stimuli are to which the examinee responds, the more accurate our inferences are apt to be. Thus, an indispensible element necessary to render accurate interpretations of examinees' test performances is a carefully crafted description of the type of test item being employed to measure a particular skill, attitude, etc. (The bulk of this analysis will be devoted to a scheme for providing such descriptions.)

Now let's return to condition (*a*), since it is here where unbridled creativity will get us in a peck of trouble. Assume that we have carved out a decent description of what a test's items are supposed to be like, that is, we've in essence set forth the rules that govern the creation of the test items. In other words, we have explicated a set of *test specifications*. Now, if those specifications are going to convey with veracity what's being measured, then it is necessary for the test items to be totally congruent with the limits that constitute those specifications. If all of the items on the test are, in fact, congruent with the test's specifications, then those items will be sufficiently homogeneous to allow us to make sense of an assertion that "Johnny has mastered 75 percent of the items measuring this competency."

We can represent such a blissful situation pictorially, as seen in figure 1.1, where a tight descriptive scheme (test specifications) plus congruent test items yields an unerring interpretation of what an examinee's test performance means, and permits us to characterize that test performance according to the proportion of items that the examinee can answer correctly. Since the items on the test constitute a sample of the possible items that could be generated to assess the behavior in question, we can place considerable confidence in the legitimacy of our interpretation.

On the other hand, if either or both of these elements are missing, as seen in figure 1.2, then the interpretations we make of an examinee's test performance are likely to be meaningless. A fuzzy set of test specifications makes all sensible test interpretations impossible. Incongruent items further muddy the interpretive waters. Put them both together, as in figure 1.2, and you will surely have nonsensical interpretations.

Where we do need creativity is in the development of highly communicative descriptive schemes that lay out the rules for item writers.

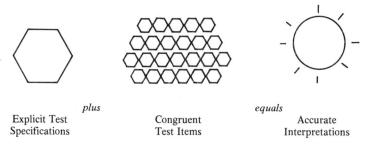

	plus		*equals*	
Explicit Test		Congruent		Accurate
Specifications		Test Items		Interpretations

FIGURE 1.1. The requisite elements for an accurate interpretation of examinee performance on a criterion-referenced test.

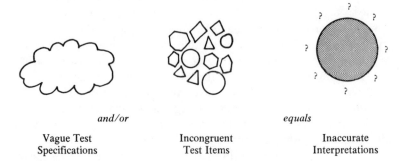

	and/or	equals
Vague Test	Incongruent	Inaccurate
Specifications	Test Items	Interpretations

FIGURE 1.2. Elements accounting for an inaccurate interpretation of examinee performance on a criterion-referenced test.

These descriptive schemes, deftly fashioned, will simultaneously (1) constrain item writers so that they can produce congruent items and (2) communicate to those who must interpret examinees' test performances.

Where we do *not* need creativity is in the writing of items that match those descriptive constraints. Item writers need to be bright. This is not a setting where dullards will shine. But they need to employ their brightness in dutifully cleaving to the admonitions set forth in the test's specifications. Creative departures from the rules in the specifications will create items that, albeit innovative, fail to mesh with those specifications and thus contribute to interpretive confusion. It is to forestall the generation of incongruent, or runaway, test items that so much attention must be given to the generation of test specifications.

Once truly constraining test specifications have been devised, then a necessary but not sufficient condition for accurate test interpretation is present. An additional necessary condition is that the item writers follow those specifications to the letter. Following-to-the-letter writing of items is inconsistent with creative writing of items.

If you cannot quell an item writer's zest for invention, send that individual scurrying to more congenial pursuits, such as sculpture, gymnastics, or erotic dance.

Review of Specification Strategies

How, then, can we head off the incongruent test item? Assuming that we have rounded up a staff of bright but compliant item writers, how do we deter them from generating aberrant items?

Let's turn, therefore, to a consideration of how we can best prepare item-writing rules, that is, test specifications, that truly aid item writers in the construction of congruent items. To deal with this problem it would be delightful if we could consult the research literature and draw upon the pioneering efforts of empirically oriented investigators who have engaged in hand-to-hand, but experimental, combat with test specifications—and won.

But, sadly, research dealing with the particulars of test specifications is almost totally nonexistent. To illustrate, in their recent comprehensive review of research dealing with criterion-referenced measurement, Hambleton et al. (1978) cite only the work of Ebel (1962) and Hively, Patterson, and Page (1968) when the topic of test specifications is discussed. Neither the Ebel nor the Hively analysis is actually an empirical investigation of, for example, the efficacy of varying forms of test specification. They are, instead, conceptual observations regarding how one might design constraints so that more readily interpretable test performance is possible. Even so, however, since Hively and his colleagues actually applied measurement insights in the creation of many test instruments, his observations (1968, 1973) have been particularly useful to a number of individuals working with criterion-referenced test construction.

Lacking solid research bases for out work with criterion-referenced test specifications, it seems necessary to rely on our best experience-based hunches about what sorts of test specification will prove serviceable. The reader will, it is hoped, be lenient since from this point forward I must draw heavily on my personal experiences in attempting to stumble on a salubrious test specification strategy. These experiences extend over a ten-year period and are chiefly drawn from projects carried out by the Instructional Objectives Exchange (IOX), a Los Angeles agency specializing in the development of criterion-referenced tests.

Behavioral Objectives. When IOX was born in 1968, it was intended that it serve as a clearinghouse for behavioral objectives so that busy educators who needed such objectives would not have to engage in wheel reinvention. Contained in the booklets of behavioral objectives that IOX tossed forth upon an eagar flock of educators were scores of behaviorally stated objectives and sample test items to illustrate how each objective might be measured. Sometimes we included a half dozen sample items per objective, sometimes fewer.

Although I was spending a major chunk of my professional time attempting to drum up educator acceptance of behavioral objectives, particularly as a vehicle for curriculum and instructional planning, it did not take the IOX staff long to realize that as delimiting devices for item writers, behavioral objectives were inadequate. Given their typically terse form, behavioral objectives left far too many decisions to the item writer.

Different IOX staff members who were attempting to come up with sample items for the same objective would usually whip up items that bore scant resemblance to one another. It was clear—behavioral objectives, whatever their virtues for curriculum and instruction, were too abbreviated to constrain item writers.

Item Forms. When IOX decided to expand its development work to include criterion-referenced tests, we sought out the advice of the best persons we could find to tell us how to build the specifications to govern our test development efforts. Those individuals, in our view, were Wells Hively, then of the University of Minnesota, and Jason Millman, then and forever of Cornell University. During the summer of 1971, Wells and Jay offered our staff wise counsel on how to whomp up winning criterion-referenced testing devices.

At first we tried to employ the *item form* scheme that Hively, Patterson, and Page (1968) had used in their Minnesota efforts. The item form was a highly detailed set of rules for creating test items of what was hoped to be a homogeneous nature. Although Wells had used item forms almost exclusively in connection with the assessment of mathematics and science skills, he was convinced that his approach could not be employed in the measurement of more elusive quarries.

We gave item forms a solid try. They were detailed and, when well formulated, quite constraining. But working with the kinds of examinee behavior that we were attempting to measure, we ended up with too many item forms and, even worse, two few item writers who were willing to pay attention to them.

In retrospect, it is now quite obvious that we were working with classes of behavior that were too miniscule. Although the size of our behavior domains approximated those used by Wells and his cohorts in Minnesota, the "chunks" of examinee behavior that we were attempting to measure were just too small. We were overwhelming ourselves with hyperspecificity.

Amplified Objectives. The experience with Wells and Jay had proved illuminating in a number of ways, one of which was that we needed far more delimiting detail than we were able to squeeze out of the objectives in our behavioral objectives collections. The guidance of Millman and Hively also led us to move toward fewer, larger scope objectives. As a consequence, we tried developing criterion-referenced tests for, say, Reading Comprehension Grades 4-6, and measured the key skills in that grade range with, for example, only thirty to forty separate criterion-referenced tests. In our previous collections of behavioral objectives we might have had as many as 100-200 objectives to cover that same grade range.

Because we wanted to maintain some continuity with our major efforts prior to that time, namely, serving as a brokerage for behavioral objectives, and yet recognizing that we needed more detailed constraints for our criterion-referenced item writers, we adopted the descriptive phrase *amplified objectives.*

An amplified objective was, as its title suggests, a more elaborate version of a behavioral objective. Our amplified objectives hovered in specificity somewhere between (*a*) our previous telegraphic behavioral objectives and (*b*) Hively's item forms. An example of an IOX amplified objective is included in appendix A. Amplified objectives represented an IOX attempt at compromise. We wanted to add more specificity, but not too much. We were shooting for just the right balance between clarity and conciseness. We missed.

As it turned out, although the IOX amplified objectives did tie down item writers considerably, there was far too much slack still remaining. The amplified objectives, with the possible exception of those in mathematics, allowed item writers—and test interpreters—too much latitude. Although as an effort in test specification the IOX amplified objectives represented a valiant attempt, they fell short on the delimitation scale.

A Limited-Focus Strategy. Given our less than lustrous success in subduing the problem of appropriate specificity level, the IOX staff spent at least a year or so in wound licking and allied endeavors. The more we pondered the dilemma, the bigger the dilemma seemed to be. The crux of the problem was that as we ladled in additional spoonfuls of specificity, we were simultaneously reducing the likelihood that our item writers, and, by the same token, classroom teachers, would ever pay attention to the resulting superspecific descriptions.

We had tried the terseness of behavioral objectives; they were not sufficiently constraining. We had tried item forms; they were too detailed. We had attempted to take the middle ground with amplified objectives; they had proved to be insufficiently precise. We were troubled.

But after rumination, not to mention desperation, we bumbled our way toward what currently seems to be a viable hope of hopping our dilemma's horns. We concluded that if we could only retain the descriptive rigor of item forms, yet figure out a way to get item writers and teachers to heed that heightened specificity, we would have a winner. Our discussions led us in the direction of limiting our measurement focus to a smaller number of assessed behaviors, but to conceptualize these behaviors so that they were larger scale, important behaviors that subsumed lesser, en route behaviors.

By using a *limited focus* measurement strategy (Popham 1978), we were able to create a small enough number of test descriptors so that item writers and teachers would attend to them. We could employ a level of descriptive detail requisite to foster precise communication with item writers as well as those who must make sense out of an examinee's test performance.

Although we are not measuring all of the good things that should be measured in the world, and make no pretense at doing so, we are at least confident that we're doing a good job of measuring what we say we're measuring. Limited focus is the key element in the current efforts of IOX to develop criterion-referenced tests that are both (1) sufficiently specific to communicate properly to test users and (2) sufficiently targeted to be of utility to busy classroom teachers.

IOX Test Specifications. The current effort of IOX to delimit the class of behaviors being assessed by a criterion-referenced test we refer to as *test specifications*. We have adopted the more general descriptive phrase, test specifications, to permit us over time to sharpen our approach to circumscribing a set of measured behaviors.

Our current versions of test specifications have greatly benefited from Hively's item form strategies, only applying that approach to more substantial lumps of examinee behavior. An example of a current IOX set of test specifications is provided in appendix B. There are four (and sometimes five) components of a set of IOX test specifications.

General description. The initial component of a set of IOX criterion-referenced test specifications is a one- or two-sentence general description of what it is that the test measures. The purpose of the general description is to provide a succinct overview of the set of behaviors to be described more fully later in the specifications.

In some criterion-referenced test specifications this component is referred to as an "objective." Yet, because many criterion-referenced tests will be used as preinstruction status determiners, not necessarily as measures of whether instructional intentions have been achieved, the phrase "general description" appears to be more defensible.

It should be apparent that a test specifier would have to possess the gift of prophecy in order to anticipate with certainty what a complete set of test specifications, particularly the subsequent stimulus-attributes and response-attributes sections, will look like. Accordingly, the general description statement is often phrased tentatively when one commences a set of test specifications. Indeed, it usually ends up looking quite different as a consequence of the more detailed analysis that occurs as the remaining components of the test specification are explicated.

Sample item. The next component in a set of IOX test specifications is a sample item, complete with directions to the student, that might be used in the test itself. Such illustrative items are usually easy to supply, since the test frequently consists of a number of relatively short items. Therefore, it is a simple matter to select one of these items for illustrative purposes. Sometimes, when the test is more complicated and the items more lengthy, it becomes difficult to supply a sample item. Nonetheless, an illustrative item is always provided as the second component of each set of test specifications.

There are two reasons for providing a sample item. First, some people using the specifications, particularly busy individuals, may find their need for test description satisfied with the general description statement and the illustrative item alone. Such people, if forced to read the entire set of specifications, might avoid it completely. But they can be abetted by the communication, albeit incomplete, provided by the specification's general description plus sample item.

The second purpose of the sample item is to provide format cues for those who must generate the items that will constitute the test. Of course, it often makes little difference what the format of a given type of test is. For instance, is it really important whether a true/false item presents the examinee with T/F or F/T options? Undoubtedly not. Yet, there are instances when format variations do seem to be important. In such cases an illustrative item can go a long way toward setting forth the preferred form in which items are to be constructed.

Stimulus attributes. In a test an examinee is presented with some sorts of stimuli that, in general, are designed to yield a response. In the third component of IOX criterion-referenced test specifications, the attributes of this stimulus material are set forth.

In the stimulus-attributes section of the test specifications we must set down all the really influential factors that constrain the composition of a set of test items. This means that we must first think through exactly what those factors are and how they can be most accurately and succinctly described. We have to decide how to cope with content considerations. Just how should a range of eligible content be most effectively circumscribed? Anything less than the most rigorous standards of intellectual scrutiny will result in specifications that are imprecise or, worse, misleading.

Response attributes. The final component of a set of IOX test specifications focuses on the examinee's response to the elements generated according to the stimulus-attributes section. Only two types of response on the part of the examinee exist. The examinee can either *select* from response options presented in the test—for example, as in true/false or multiple-choice questions—or the examinee can *construct* a response—for example, as in essay, short-answer, or oral presentations. Thus, only *selected responses* or *constructed responses* will be encountered, and in the response-attributes section of the specifications the rules regarding these two response possibilities will be treated.

If the test involves a selected response, then rules must be provided for determining not only the nature of the correct response, but also the nature of the wrong-answer options. For instance, in a multiple-choice test it would be imperative to state first the guidelines for creating the correct answer. Next, the test specifier must spell out the various classes of wrong-answer option that might constitute any item's distractors. It is not appropriate merely to indicate that such distractors will be "incorrect." Instead, the precise nature of these wrong answers must be carefully explicated.

But although the difficulties of delineating the response-possibilities section for selected response sorts of test are considerable, they become almost trivial when a test specifier attempts to spell out the response-attributes section of specifications for tests involving constructed responses. Here the task is to explain the criteria that permit reliable judgment of the adequacy of examinees' constructed responses. Ideally, these criteria would be so well formulated that to determine the acceptability of any constructed response would be simple. Realistically, however, criteria possessing such precision can rarely be created. The test specifier will have to think as lucidly as possible about such criteria, and even then there may be more slack in this section of the specifications than we would like.

Specification supplement. There are instances in which our IOX test specifications deal with sets of content—for example, a series of rules or a list of important historical figures. If we included this content information in either the stimulus-attributes or the response-attributes section, we would have created a set of specifications too voluminous for the typical reader. Beyond that, by being obliged to wade through such lengthy content citations, a reader of the specifications might actually be distracted from some of the important noncontent-specification statements. In such cases it is often convenient to include a supplement at the close of the specifications that sets forth such information. Such a supplement is obviously optional.

Suggestions for Future Research

Given the essentially anecdotal nature of the foregoing remarks, it is more than apparent that we need research, and lots of it, dealing with the procedures for spelling out test specifications and subsequently generating test items that mesh with those specifications.

Chiefly, we need to assess the efficacy of varied procedures for constraining criterion-referenced item writers. The approach to test specifications used at IOX constitutes only one way to play that game. There may be other, markedly better specification strategies that should be tried out, then empirically honed. Berk (1979) has described six strategies for specifying content domains and items with criterion-referenced tests. The adequacy of these and other such strategies must be investigated without delay.

We need to abandon the intuitively derived, experience-based schemes for generating criterion-referenced tests. We must move toward an experimentally tested technology of criterion-referenced test construction.

Guidelines for Practitioners

This analysis will be terminated by a series of observations, some even related to each other, regarding the rigors of rapping out test specifications for criterion-referenced tests. As will soon be apparent to the reader, these musings will be a far piece from anything even mildly definitive.

Realistic Expectations. When we use a phrase like *test specifications,* some folks naively assume that we're really tying down all the loose ends in a domain of examinee behaviors. It isn't so.

It would be glorious if we could so precisely circumscribe a domain of important examinee behaviors that we would know with complete and all-consuming clarity just what it is that the examinee "can or can't do." But to create a set of specifications that captured that much detail would surely force us to create a major opus of several hundred pages in length. Remember, we're talking about an *important,* hence undoubtedly complex, examinee behavior. As it is, many IOX test specifications run five or more single-spaced pages in length. And specifications of that length begin to tax severly the item writer's, and certainly the classroom teacher's, patience.

With respect to the degree of constraint that any test specification of reasonable length can exert, it probably makes sense to think of a continuum something like that seen in figure 1.3, where we have a range of specificity that at the left is little more detailed than a behavioral objective and, accordingly, permits multiple interpretations. At the right we have a voluminous (almost inconceivably detailed) set of test specifications. The rigor of interpretability increases, of course, as one moves from left to right. Even with the descriptive detail currently contained

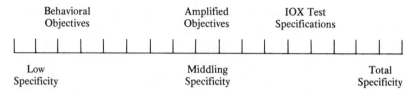

FIGURE 1.3. A range of specificity for the descriptive schemes employed with criterion-referenced tests.

in the IOX test specifications, there is still a certain degree of imprecision associated with the interpretation of test performance. Until humans start functioning like computers, there probably always will be.

But even though the efforts of criterion-referenced testing specialists, for the foreseeable future, will fall short of total delimitation, there are clearly substantial clarity dividends over the less descriptive schemes represented at the left of the specificity continuum.

Homogeneity. Once upon a time, when I was younger and foolisher, I thought we could create test specifications so constraining that the test items produced as a consequence of their use would be *functionally homogeneous*, that is, essentially interchangeable. But if we use the difficulty of an item as at least one index of the item's nature, then it becomes quite obvious that even in such teensy behavior domains as measuring the student's ability to multiply pairs of double-digit numbers, the task of $11 \times 11 = ?$ is lots easier than $99 \times 99 = ?$

About the only way we can ever attain functional homogeneity is to keep pruning the nature of the measured behavior so that we're assessing ever more trifling sorts of behavior. That would be inane. We can, however, if we do a smashing job in creating test specifications, achieve sets of items that are *derivatively homogeneous*, that is, that can be judged as having been derived from the same set of specifications. We can apply something akin to a test specification paternity test in order to show that the behavioral domain delimited by the test specifications, a domain that include items of differing difficulty levels, is the legitimate home of all the items on the test.

Art with a Capital A. At no point in the test development process for criterion-referenced measures is it more apparent that we are employing art, rather than science, than when the general nature of the behavioral domain to be tested is initially conceptualized.

Particularly in view of our current predilection toward larger behavioral domains that (1) effectively coalesce smaller, en route behaviors yet (2) maintain sufficient descriptive rigor to communicate effectively, these conceptualizations become artistic endeavors of no small shakes. I am constantly distressed that so few of our staff members seem to possess the ability to corral apparently diverse, yet related, sets of subskills, then blend them into a new, subsuming skill that serves as the focus for the measurement.

I am even more distressed that I am unable to teach people how to go about this conceptualization process. I can explain how I personally do it, and I can get a few other staff members to engage in similar introspection, but I have been completely unable to reduce the process to a form that is directly teachable—complete with practice exercises, etc.—to others.

With respect to the conceptualizing of such behavioral domains, as well as a galaxy of other phases of criterion-referenced test development, it is so apparent that we're still nibbling on a cake whose frosting may be technology but whose many layers are art, art, and more art.

Appendix A

An Illustrative IOX Amplified Objective for a
Third-Grade Level Reading Comprehension Skill

DETERMINING SEQUENCE FROM TENSE
AND WORDS THAT SIGNAL ORDER

Objective:

The student will correctly identify the sequence of three sentences by determining order from tense and words that signify order.

Sample Item:

Directions. Read the three sentences. Then mark an "X" next to the answer that arranges the sentences in the proper order.

Example:

A. Once there were only candles for lighting the home.
B. Later there were dim electric lights.
C. Tesla thought of a way to make the electric lights brighter.
____a) A,C,B   ____b) A,B,C   ____c) C,A,B

Amplified Objective:

Testing Situation.

1. The student will be given three sentences and will identify their proper sequence on the basis of verb tenses and signal words.

2. Three sentences containing signal words and/or changes in verb tense will be provided.
3. Vocabulary will be familiar to the third grader.

Response Alternatives.

1. Three possible orderings of the sentence will be given.
2. At least one distractor should *not* consist of a random ordering. It should maintain the first event as first, varying only the second and third events.
3. The other distractor may be any other incorrect ordering of the events.

Criterion of Correctness.

The correct answer will be the order that can be determined on the basis of one of the following:

1. Words that signify sequence, e.g., afterwards, finally, then, before, during, now, next, lastly, later, earlier, meanwhile, long ago, once
2. Verb tense (future, past, present)

Appendix B

An Illustrative Set of Criterion-Referenced Test Specifications for a High School Minimum Competency Test in Reading

DETERMINING MAIN IDEAS

General Description

The student will be presented with a factual selection such as a newspaper or magazine article or a passage from a consumer guide or general-interest book. After reading that selection, the student will determine which one of four choices contains the best statement of the main idea of the selection. This statement will be entirely accurate as well as the most comprehensive of the choices given.

Sample Item

   Directions. Read the selections in the boxes below. Answer the questions about their main ideas.

THE COLD FACTS

Had you lived in ancient Rome you might have relieved the symptoms of a common cold by sipping a broth made from soaking an onion in warm water. In Colonial America you might have relied on an herbal concoction made from sage, buckthorn, goldenseal, or bloodroot plants. In Grandma's time, lemon and honey was a favorite cold remedy, or in extreme cases, a hot toddy laced with rum. Today, if you don't have an old reliable remedy to fall back on, you might take one of thousands of drug preparations available without prescription. Some contain ingredients much like the folk medicines of the past; others are made with complex chemical creations. Old or new, simple or complex, many of these products will relieve some cold symptoms, such as a stopped-up nose or a hacking cough. But not a single one of them will prevent, cure, or even shorten the course of the common cold.

Reproduced with permission from *Test Specifications, IOX Basic Skill Tests: Secondary Level, Reading* (Los Angeles: The Instructional Objectives Exchange, 1978), pp. 21-24.

1. Which one of the following is the best statement of the main idea of the article you just read?
   a. Old-fashioned herbal remedies are more effective than modern medicines.
   b. There are many kinds of relief, but no real cures, for the common cold.
   c. Some of today's cold preparations contain ingredients much like those found in folk remedies of the past.
   d. Americans spend millions of dollars a year on cold remedies.

Stimulus Attributes

1. Each item will consist of a reading selection followed by the question "Which one of the following is the best statement of the main idea of the (article selection) you just read?" Eligible reading selections include adaptations of passages from factual texts such as general-interest books and consumer guides and pamphlets. Care should be taken to pick selections of particular interest to young adults and to avoid selections which may in the near future appear dated. Each reading selection will be titled, will be at least one paragraph long, and will contain from 125-250 words. Not more than 1,000 words of reading material can be tested in any set of five items. At least two of the five items in any set of five items must contain reading selections that are more than one paragraph long.
2. If necessary, the following modifications may be made to a selection used for testing:
   a. A title may be added if the selection does not have one, or if the selection represents a section of a longer piece whose title would not be applicable to the excerpt. If a title is added, it should be composed of a brief, interest-getting and/or summarizing group of words.
   b. A selection may be shortened, but only if the segment which is to be used for testing makes sense and stands as a complete unit of thought without the parts which have been omitted. If necessary, minor editing can be done to a reading selection which represents a shortening of a longer piece, but this editing should be for the purposes of clarity and continuity only, and not for the purposes of increasing or decreasing the difficulty level, or changing the content, of the text.
3. Reading selections used for testing should not exceed a 9th grade reading level, as judged by the Fry readability formula.

Response Attributes

1. A set of four single-sentence response alternatives will follow each reading selection and its accompanying question. All of these statements must plausibly relate to the content of the reading selection, either by reiterating or paraphrasing portions of that selection or by building upon a word or idea contained in the selection.

2. The three incorrect response alternatives will each be based upon a lack of one of the two characteristics needed by a correct main idea statement: *accuracy* and *appropriate scope*. A correct main idea statement must be accurate in that everything it states can be verified in the text it describes. It must have appropriate scope in that it encompasses all of the most important points discussed in the text that it describes.

3. A distractor exemplifies a *lack of accuracy* when it does any one or more of three things:
   a. Makes a statement contradicted by information in the text.
   b. Makes a statement unsupported by information in the text. (Such a statement would be capable of verification or contradiction if the appropriate information were available.)
   c. Makes a statement incapable of verification or contradiction; that is, a statement of opinion. (Such statements include value judgments on the importance or worth of anything mentioned in the text.)

4. A distractor exemplifies a *lack of appropriate scope* when it does one of two things:
   a. Makes a statement that is too narrow in its scope. That is, the statement does not account for all of the important details contained in the text.
   b. Makes a statement that is too broad in its scope. That is, the statement is more general than it needs to be in order to account for all of the important details contained in the text.

5. The important points which must be included in a main idea statement are those details which are emphasized in the text by structural, semantic, and rhetorical means such as placement in a position of emphasis, repetition, synonymous rephrasing, and elaboration. Whether any given main idea statement contains all of the important points that it should is always debatable rather than indisputable. The nature of the question asked on this test, i.e., select the *best* main idea statement from among those given, attempts to account for this quality of relative rather than absolute correctness.

6. The distractors for any one item must include at least one statement that lacks accuracy and one statement that lacks appropriate scope. On a given test, between 10 and 20 percent of the distractors should be sentences taken directly from the text.

7. The correct answer for an item will be that statement which is both entirely accurate and of the most appropriate scope in relation to the other statements given. If a sentence in the text itself qualifies as the best main idea statement which can be formulated about the selection, that sentence may be reiterated as a response option. No more than 20 percent of the items on a

given test may have as their correct answer a main idea statement which is a direct restatement of a sentence in the text.

References

Berk, R. A. 1979. A critical review of content domain specification/item generation strategies for criterion-referenced tests. Paper presented at the annual meeting of the American Educational Research Association, April 1979, San Francisco.

Ebel, R. L. 1962. Content standard test scores. *Educational and Psychological Measurement* 22:15-25.

Hambleton, R. K.; Swaminathan, H.; Algina, J.; and Coulson, D. B. 1978. Criterion-referenced testing and measurement: A review of technical issues and developments. *Review of Educational Research* 48:1-47.

Hively, W.; Maxwell, G.; Rabehl, G.; Sension, D.; and Lundin, S. 1973. *Domain-referenced curriculum evaluation: A technical handbook and a case study from the MINNEMAST Project.* CSE Monograph Series in Evaluation, no. 1. Los Angeles: Center for the Study of Evaluation, University of California.

Hively, W.; Patterson, H. L.; and Page, S. A. 1968. A "universe-defined" system of arithmetic achievement tests. *Journal of Educational Measurement* 5:275-90.

Popham, W. J. 1978. *Criterion-referenced measurement.* Englewood Cliffs, N.J.: Prentice-Hall.

2

COMPUTER-BASED ITEM GENERATION

Jason Millman

Introduction

Regardless of your predisposition toward criterion-referenced measurement—pro or con, don't know or don't care—the movement has deposited at least one noteworthy nugget in the fields of the test makers. The importance of specifying clearly the content coverage of the test has been reinforced. As long as I remember, there have been, at least for achievement tests, tables of specifications, blueprints, test plans, or other organizing schemes that represented the areas the test maker decided to measure and from which the test user could glean some feeling for the scope of the examination. But Jim Popham and others have said, "That is not enough." Knowing that there is, for example, an item on a history test that measures a fact about economic depressions does not help us very much to appreciate what is being assessed. Nor does the specification, "Produce a factual question about economic depressions," tell an item writer exactly how to write the question. Should the question be easy or hard, about the 1929–33 U.S. depression or some other, about the causes or effects of the depression, or about what a depression is?

From my perspective, the heart of criterion-referenced measurement is that it provides additional meaning from scores by referencing the test outcome to a clearly specified body of test content, from which the items are generated. (This is in contrast to norm-referenced testing, in which the meaning of a test score derives from its comparisons to other scores.) For a criterion-referenced test to have meaning in some absolute sense, the content domain must be well explicated.

The importance of clearly specifying the domain of tasks from which the test items will be drawn cannot be overestimated. As Linn (1979) reminds us, even seemingly straightforward domains like the addition of single-digit numbers can benefit from further description. How many numbers are to be added? Can they be negative as well as positive, base eight as well as base ten? How are they to be placed on the page—horizontally as well as vertically? Are oral as well as written administration, speeded as well as unspeeded presentation, and multiple-choice as well as constructed response formats permitted?

Without a clear statement of the range of items that can be used to measure mastery, it is not possible to judge whether the test items actually employed are representative or merely a restricted subset. Whether or not students have demonstrated mastery will clearly depend upon which items are used in the test. Different conceptions of item domains will yield different items and different decisions about students. And test writers need guidance concerning what is and is not permissible to ask; otherwise the tests will reflect the idiosyncracies of the particular writers employed. The presence of a domain definition, then, permits everyone to judge the content validity of achievement tests. Test users and writers can determine whether the items match the range of relevant tasks admissible as test items, exceed the limits, or represent too narrow a test of the competency.

Communicability of test content provides other benefits. The existence of clear test specifications makes it easier to establish mastery standards or passing scores. Although the setting of passing scores always involves an element of judgment, the task can be made seemingly less arbitrary when the population of tasks is clearly specified.

Explicitly stated and public test specifications make it clear to all—to instructors, to students, to the community—what learnings are expected. Teaching can be targeted to those explicitly stated skills thought to be particularly important. Clear test specifications can broaden the teacher's conception of the skill area and increase the diversity of supporting examples. How this may be done with concept learning has been discussed by Tiemann and Markle (1978).

Popham (see chapter 1) recounted attempts to specify domains and write criterion-referenced test items in an articulated and meaningful manner. Popham, more than anyone, has both led us and pushed us in this direction. I'll not discuss these item-writing approaches further, in part because Popham has done an excellent job in this respect and in part because there are other sources where this material can be found. Early attempts to discuss in one place such item-writing procedures are Millman (1974) and Hsu (1975).

There now exist two excellent sources that summarize the state of the art for developing criterion-referenced tests. I'm referring to a book by

Popham (1978) and the AERA preconference workshop materials by Hambleton and Eignor (1979). Other detailed, but less helpful, statements of how to make criterion-referenced tests have been provided by Shaycoft (1976) and by Swezey and Pearlstein (1974). The paper by Anderson (1972) and the introductory chapters in a book by Hively (1974) are also instructive. Finally, inspection of the standards used to judge the adequacy of criterion-referenced tests can assist the would-be criterion-referenced test constructor. Such standards may be found in the Walker et al. reference (1979), in the Popham (1978) book, and in a Hambleton and Eignor (1978) paper.

Once the test domain is defined, a reasonable next step is to let the computer generate the test items and, with the inclusion of a test design, the test itself. First I'll mention some objections to using the computer to make tests and then I will provide a review of efforts to test by computer.

Making tests by computer, critics protest, is too restricting, too hard, too expensive, and too mechanical. Granted, each of these concerns has at least an element of truth. Let's consider them one at a time.

It is too restricting (with respect to what can be tested). Chief Jim Popham challenged me to produce by computer items from a more elusive area of inquiry. I beat my feathers and sweated off my war paint in a partially successful attempt. I am speaking much less boldly these days about the applicability of computerized item-generating techniques to all subject matter fields. The time is not yet here. However, for many fields, including the basic skills and minimum competency subject matter domains, the technology is within our grasp.

It is too hard. It is difficult to specify test content specifically enough that item generation can be done by computer. But later in this chapter I'll describe some present schemes and proposed undertakings that should reduce the hassle involved.

It is too expensive. Item writing and test making are, at present, labor intensive, and people are expensive. The one-time development costs can be heavy; however, the computer-generating schemes to be mentioned here are economically feasible and may even save money.

It is too mechanical. So are cars, food processors, and dental drills. Perhaps what is at issue is not that a machine produced the test, but the legitimate fear that the best interests of the examinee will not be served if the testing system is too rigid. I feel, however, that testing by computer celebrates, rather than retards, opportunities for the individual.

Review of Computer-Based Strategies

Computers are marvelous record-keeping devices. As such, they have been used to monitor student progress and evaluate programs by scheduling and scoring tests and by organizing and storing test data. Brennan (1973) has provided a good statement about such applications of computers. My focus here, however, is on using computers for test construction rather than for test management.

Computers are used to make tests in two general ways. In the more frequent method, test items are stored in the computer in exactly the same way they are to appear on the test. The computer is then used to select, assemble, and present these items to test takers, either in a predetermined way or in an interactive mode in which the item that is chosen depends upon the performance of the examinee on previous items.

In the second method, rules for generating the test items, rather than the items themselves, are stored in the computer. Because this algorithmic approach to testing by computer appears to have the greater applicability for criterion-referenced testing, the bulk of this chapter will discuss this method of use. But first, a brief discussion of the uses of computers to produce tests when the items have already been written and stored.

Item Banking. For many years, several individuals have been producing tests by computers at their schools or colleges. A number of these efforts are described by Lippey (1974). These systems tend to work the same way. The test items for a course are typed into the computer. More items are typically stored than will be used on any one test. In the more elaborate versions, items are categorized by subject matter content and item difficulty level. The computer is then programmed to produce a test having a specified number of questions and, in the more sophisticated versions, a desired distribution of items across subject matters and item difficulty levels.

Since there are more items stored in the computer than appear on any one test, it is possible to produce multiple tests having different items arranged in different orders. The frequency with which any two tests will contain some items in common depends upon the size of the pool of items and the length of the test. Some applications of the ability to produce multiple tests of this type, called randomly parallel tests, will be discussed later.

Although in this procedure a population of items exists, it would be stretching the concept of criterion-referencing or domain-referencing to call tests generated from such a population criterion-referenced tests. That is because the population of items cannot be clearly described without telling about each of the items. When a student obtains a score of

80 percent, for example, it is not very descriptive to say that we estimate the student knows 80 percent of the items stored in the computer, or even to say that we estimate the student knows 80 percent of the test items about unit 2 that are stored in the computer. Missing are the domain definitions, the amplified objectives, the item forms, or other test descriptions about which Popham wrote.

One large computer company (Westinghouse) offers a service in which the user picks the objectives to be referenced on the test and the computer selects items associated with the chosen objectives. Although far more extensive in number of objectives and number of items available to the user than the systems I was referring to above, the principles and weaknesses are the same. Knowing that a student answered correctly two questions out of three on objective 4.7 doesn't tell us all that much about the student's competence with respect to that objective because the objective alone is not an adequate test description. Without knowing more about the particular three items that were used—whether they were hard or easy, what exactly their content was, how the questions were asked, and so forth—we are hard pressed to evaluate the student's competence.

Adaptive Testing. Another variation in which computers are employed to make tests using a pool of stored items as the raw materials is called adaptive testing. This is the general term used to describe several procedures in which the particular items administered to the examinee at one point in time depend upon the examinee's performance on items administered at a previous time. Although a computer is not required (see, e.g., Lord 1971), the interactive feature between item administration and the individual can be faciliated by use of the computer. Weiss and Betz (1973) offer a good introduction to adaptive testing.

In one form of adaptive testing, the *number* of test items administered to each person varies. Examinees who are clearly above or below some passing score or other standard can be assessed with relatively few items. Examinees functioning at a level close to the standard are administered more items so that their status with respect to the standard can be evaluated with greater accuracy.

In the second form of adaptive testing, the *difficulty level* of the test items administered to each person varies. Examinees who are doing well on the earlier items are administered harder items later on; examinees who are missing many items are later given easier items to answer. By continually adapting the difficulty level of items to the examinee's performance, the examinee's true status can be more accurately identified.

In neither form of adaptive testing is a clearly specified domain used. Depending upon how the population of items was created, the score derived from such testing procedures might be a good estimate of the student's performance with respect to some construct, like mathematics ability. But without a reference to the specific tasks that are included, no criterion-referenced interpretation is possible.

Let me now turn to what is important from a criterion-referenced perspective, that is, to the situation in which we do have adequate test description. One procedure for delineating test item content from which items can be produced is to list all possible variations. Thus, for example, for a world history objective dealing with knowledge of the principal adversaries in major wars, a list of all major wars and the adversaries could be produced and placed in the specification supplement Popham mentioned. Items that would be constructed would then be required to reference only the wars appearing on the list.

Algorithms. Algorithms are another way to produce items from a domain. This method involves a rule that is employed to generate an item and is often used in conjunction with the exhaustive listing technique. Fremer and Anastasio (1969) were among the first to use the computer to generate items by algorithm. Facet theory is obviously relevant to the listing and algorithmic approaches, and a review article by Berk (1978) is a good introduction to potential applications.

Figure 2.1 consists of an item program written in a special language that a colleague and I devised for the purpose (see Millman & Outlaw 1978). The item-generation process follows the rule to ask for the cube of an integer between 4 and 7 and to produce four possible answers. (The computer command, MULTCHOICE, automatically letters the options and randomizes their order of appearance.) The algorithm shown in line 40 generates the correct answer and will automatically be used in the item and printed as the answer. Three of the remaining six options will be selected for any given execution of the item-generating program. An ex-

```
 10 A = RANDOM(4,7)
 20 A, SUPER(3), "equals:"
 30 FROM
 40 A*A*A
 50 A*3
 60 A+3
 70 A+30
 80 A*10+3
 90 A*A
100 (A+1)*A*A
110 MULTCHOICE 4
120 RIGHT 1
130 WRONG CHOOSE AT RANDOM
```

FIGURE 2.1. An item program that illustrates the use of algorithms for generating items.

5^3 equals:

A. 53
B. 125
C. 8
D. 150

Answer: B

FIGURE 2.2. An example of a possible item that could be produced from the item program shown in figure 2.1.

ample of a possible item using the algorithms contained in figure 2.1 is shown in figure 2.2.

Each item program represents a small domain of items. In the case of figure 2.1, there is a clear specification of the permissible numbers to be cubed, the format of the test items, and the distractors to be used.

Under the system being described, item programs like that in figure 2.1 instead of the items themselves are stored in the computer. To make a test, one or more item programs are executed one or more times each. If a skill development exercise sheet is desired, for example, maybe only one or few item programs are used, each one being executed several times. If a survey test is desired covering, say forty different skill domains, then each of forty different item programs will be selected and each executed only once. Because each item program is capable of producing a large number of variations in the content of a specific item, it is unlikely that any given two tests will contain exactly the same items.

More complicated item programs than the one shown in figure 2.1 are usually written. Typically, these programs combine both the use of algorithms and extensive listings of possible content to give variety to the various items that are produced. Figure 2.3 represents some of the items that were generated from a single, albeit extensive, program that represented my attempt to meet Popham's challenge to computer generate items representing a more elusive domain. My work was made considerably easier because Popham had already prepared an excellent set of test specifications that I was able to use for my prototype development.

Linguistic Transformations. A different way to describe a domain has led to another way to routinize the item-writing task. The domain consists of a passage of instructional text and permissible ways of transforming sentences in that text into questions. Bormuth (1970) and later Anderson (1972) offer examples of classes of specific linguistic transformations that can unambiguously produce test questions. For example, the sentence, Jim Popham lassos elusive lovelies, could, using the noun deletion transformation, be converted into the questions Who lassos elusive lovelies? and What does Jim Popham lasso? As Bormuth (1970) puts it:

> [These] operations should be capable of being systematically applied to an instructional program in such a way that all items of the type derivable by those operations will be produced. When this requirement is met by a set of operations, not only does it insure the definability of item populations but it also insures that tests made by these operations will be independently reproducible given only a knowledge of what operations were used to derive the items and their responses. (P. 35)

Finn (1975) has developed algorithms for creating items from passages that build upon Bormuth's work. When the passage is entered into the

Mother to daughter whose dog, Sneaker, has just died: YOU CAN'T FEEL THAT BADLY.

   A. moralizing
   B. denying experience
   C. belittling
   D. condescension

ANSWER: B.

Son: Cathy has broken up with me
Mother: DO YOU FEEL VERY BADLY ABOUT THAT?

   A. recognizing feeling
   B. taking responsibility for the feeling
   C. being receptive
   D. describing results

ANSWER: C.

Mother to daughter whose best friend, Shirley, is moving away: IT ISN'T THAT TERRIBLE.

   A. indirect attack
   B. sarcasm
   C. belittling
   D. denying experience

ANSWER: D.

Mother to son whose dog, Hecate, has just died: SO WHAT ELSE IS NEW?

   A. contradictory messages
   B. condescension
   C. sarcasm
   D. indirect attack

ANSWER: C.

FIGURE 2.3. Computer-generated test items referencing a higher level cognitive skill. Student is asked to identify the parent response according to Haim Ginott.

computer, together with computer tapes of word frequency counts, the computer can be used to identify target words and their sentences, which can then be converted into questions through transformations specified in the algorithms. Practical examples are supplied by Stevens and O'Neill (1974*a*, 1974*b*) and in the research of Roid and Finn (1977). Roid and Finn recommend transforming sentences containing "high information" nouns and adjectives, defined as words that are relatively rare in American textbooks and that only appear a single time in a passage.

Suggestions for Future Research

One area of further investigation involves applying the technology we already possess to produce multiple versions of randomly parallel tests and evaluating its utility. It is my belief that schemes like those we have developed at Cornell can be of great value in a number of practical applications.

Recall that the computer scheme produced different versions of items generated from one or more domains. Test users have at their disposal a stack of randomly parallel tests, all different. Lord (1977) has shown that compared to conventional testing, computer-generated repeatable testing, as he calls it, is equally effective in estimating examinee ability and more effective (because of greater item sampling) in estimating group performance.

Availability of these multiple forms permits the retesting of students, since the different questions insure that the student needs to learn the generalizable skill rather than the answers to specific items. I have employed the testing scheme for my statistics course. It was ideal, since the course is organized in a mastery learning format. The students are extremely positive about having several opportunities to achieve mastery in a given area of study.

The scheme is also useful in situations where testing is scheduled at the convenience of the examinee. In my opinion, states that have minimum competency testing requirements should allow students to attempt to pass the tests frequently. The scheme permits this, alleviates the test security problem, and, through the domain specifications, can make the scope of the test content public. Remedial instruction can be more targeted when the general class of skills is known.

A second area worth exploring is the development of higher level computer languages that would facilitate writing diverse items from standard domain specifications. In an advanced stage of development, the item writer would supply a prototype item and answers to some computer-initiated questions. The computer would then be capable of generating a population of items referencing a domain defined by the prototype item, the item writer's answers to the computer's questions, and the computer algorithms.

Two intermediate development efforts seem more feasible at this time. One consists of a different computer algorithm for each of several classes of questions. It may be possible to write a high-level computer program that first asks the item writer some specific questions and then takes over and constructs its own item-generating scheme. For example, many problems in the sciences and mathematics involve substituting known values into a formula (such as distance equals rate times time) and solving for the one unknown. With guidance, the item writer could supply such information as the relevant equation, the permissible units of measure and allowable conversions, possible contexts or applications, and so forth. This input and the general computer program would be sufficient to produce the item-generating scheme needed to make actual test items.

A second way of letting the computer do more of the item writing would involve using the properties of transformational grammar to produce variety in how a question is asked. The user, in this envisioned scheme, would enter a prototype item into the computer together with the identification of the structural elements (noun phrases, modifiers, etc.). The computer would return a number of possible linguistic transformations of the original question. The user would check them out for semantic appropriateness before they become part of the item pool.

Perhaps the most important area for further investigation is that of improving our ability to write domain specifications. Popham stressed how writing test descriptions is largely an art. I agree and feel we need to make criterion-referenced test construction more of a science. One way to do this is to learn more about important content and format variables that should be explicitly stated and systematically manipulated during the item-writing process. Some empirical work (Millman 1978) suggests that it may be difficult to find such variables applicable for a wide range of content areas, examinee populations, and instructional histories.

The test specification task is, in many respects, similar to that faced by taxonomy builders, and the taxonomic literature may be of value. The methodology followed by the University of Wisconsin project on conceptual abilities (Harris & Harris 1973) or by the Institute for Research on Teaching at Michigan State University (see, e.g., Schmidt et al., 1978) might be instructive and should be considered.

Guidelines for Practitioners

How should the practitioner construct items while the needed research and development activities are being performed? Teachers might best spend their limited time attempting to broaden and clarify their test content domains. They would continue to make tests by hand, but it is hoped that their examinations and the corresponding instruction will more fully capture the extensiveness and richness of the subject matter domain.

We have seen that when criterion-referenced test interpretations arc desired and examinees are not being compared, there is much to be gained by permitting different students to take different forms of a test. The technology is now available to produce such tests with the aid of computers, and test makers with more resources than teachers should begin to explore these opportunities.

References

Anderson, R. C. 1972. How to construct achievement tests to assess comprehension. *Review of Educational Research* 42: 145-70.

Berk, R. A. 1978. The application of structural facet theory to achievement test construction. *Educational Research Quarterly* 3: 62-72.

Bormuth, J. R. 1970. *On the theory of achievement test items.* Chicago, Ill.: University of Chicago Press.

Brennan, R. L. 1973. Computer-assisted achievement testing in instruction. *Journal of Educational Technology Systems* 2: 3-16.

Finn, P. J. 1975. A question writing algorithm. *Journal of Reading Behavior* 7: 341-67.

Fremer, J. J., and Anastasio, E. J. 1969. Computer-assisted item writing: I, Spelling items. *Journal of Educational Measurement* 6: 69-74.

Hambleton, R. K., and Eignor, D. R. 1978. Guidelines for evaluating criterion-referenced tests and test manuals. *Journal of Educational Measurement* 15: 321-27.

_____. 1979. *A practitioner's guide to criterion-referenced test development, validation, and test score usage.* Laboratory of Psychometric and Evaluative Research Report no. 70. Amherst, Mass.: School of Education, University of Massachusetts.

Harris, M. L., and Harris, C. W. 1973. *A structure of concept attainment abilities.* Madison, Wis.: Wisconsin Research and Development Center for Cognitive Learning, University of Wisconsin.

Hively, W., ed. 1974. *Domain-referenced testing.* Englewood Cliffs, N.J.: Educational Technology Publications.

Hsu, T. C. 1975. Approaches to the construction of achievement test items. *The Researcher* 14: 31-50.

Linn, R. L. 1979. Issues of validity in measurement for competency-based programs. In *Practices and problems in competency-based measurement,* ed. M. A. Bunda and J. R. Sanders. Washington, D.C.: National Council on Measurement in Education. Pp. 108-23.

Lippey, G., ed. 1974. *Computer-assisted test construction.* Englewood Cliffs, N.J.: Educational Technology Publications.

Lord, F. M. 1971. The self-scoring flexilevel test. *Journal of Educational Measurement* 8: 147-51.

_____. 1977. Some item analysis and test theory for a system of computer-assisted test construction for individualized instruction. *Applied Psychological Measurement* 1: 447-55.

Millman, J. 1974. Criterion-referenced measurement. In *Evaluation in education: Current applications,* ed. W. J. Popham. Berkeley, Calif.: McCutchan. Pp. 311-97.

_____. 1978. *Determinants of item difficulty: A preliminary investigation.* Technical Report, no. 114. Los Angeles: Center for the Study of Evaluation, University of California.

Millman, J., and Outlaw, W. S. 1978. Testing by computer. *AEDS Journal* 11: 57-72. (Also available as an extension publication of the New York State College of Agriculture and Life Sciences, Building 7, Research Park, Cornell University, Ithaca, New York 14853. Price: $1.75.)

Popham, W. J. 1978. *Criterion-referenced measurement.* Englewood Cliffs, N.J.: Prentice-Hall.

Roid, G., and Finn, P. J. 1977. *Algorithms for developing test questions from sentences in instructional materials.* Interim Technical Report for Contract MDA 903-77-C-0189. Monmouth, Ore.: Teaching Research Division, Oregon State System of Higher Education.

Schmidt, W. H.; Porter, A. C.; Floden, R. E.; and Freeman, D. J. 1978. *Training manual for the classification of the content of fourth grade mathematics.* Research Series no. 4. East Lansing, Mich.: Institute for Research on Teaching, Michigan State University.

Shaycoft, M. F. 1976. *Guide to the development, evaluation, and use of criterion-referenced tests.* Palo Alto, Calif.: American Institutes for Research.

Stevens, J. D., and O'Neill, H. F. 1974a. *Suggestions for development of test items.* Austin, Tex.: Computer-Assisted Instruction Laboratory, University of Texas.

_____. 1974b. *Suggestions for generating multiple-choice items at the comprehension, application, and analysis levels.* Austin, Tex.: Computer-Assisted Instruction Laboratory, University of Texas.

Swezey, R. W., and Pearlstein, R. B. 1974. *Developing criterion-referenced tests.* 287-AR18(2)-IR-0974-RWS-RBP. Reston, Va.: Applied Science Associates, Army Research Institute for the Behavioral and Social Sciences.

Tiemann, P. W., and Markle, S. M. 1978. Domain-referenced testing of conceptual learning. Paper presented at the annual meeting of the American Educational Research Association, March 1978, Toronto.

Walker, C. B.; Dotseth, M.; Hunter, R.; Smith, K. O.; Kampy, L.; Strickland, G.; Neafsey, S.; Garvey, C.; Bastone, M.; Weinberger, E.; and Yohn, K. 1979. *CSE criterion-referenced test evaluation.* Los Angeles: Center for the Study of Evaluation, University of California.

Weiss, D. J., and Betz, N. E. 1973. *Ability measurement: Conventional or adaptive?* Research Report 73-1. Minneapolis: Psychometric Methods Program, Department of Psychology, University of Minnesota.

PART TWO

ITEM AND TEST VALIDITY

THE VALIDITY OF a criterion-referenced test is concerned with the intent or purposes for which the test is designed and the scores are used. It can be analyzed at both the item and test levels. The analyses furnish judgmental and empirical evidence that the test functions effectively consistent with its purposes. Item validity focuses on how well each item measures its respective objective (item-objective congruence) and differentiates between masters and nonmasters of that objective (item discrimination). Test validity that is based on the clusters of items corresponding to the objectives pertains to the representativeness of the item samples in relation to the domain specifications (content/descriptive validity), the meaning of the test scores in relation to the initial test structure (construct validity), and the decisions for which the scores are used (decision validity). The evidence obtained to assess item validity contributes greatly toward establishing the validity of the total test and score interpretations.

The validity of decisions based on cut-off scores is perhaps the most important, controversial, and misunderstood validity issue in criterion-referenced measurement. The decision maker must confront the accuracy of mastery-nonmastery classification decisions sooner or later. Either the decision maker can use estimates of the probabilities of correct and incorrect classifications and consider the consequences of the two types of error (false mastery and false nommastery) to adjust the cut-off score a priori or those consequences may need to be explained a posteriori by the decision maker in the classroom, school board room, or courtroom without the benefit of any prior evidence of decision validity (see 1978 winter issue of *Journal of Educational Measurement*). Furthermore, it seems pointless even to compute a reliability index (see part 3) unless the cut-off score has been validated. A high reliability index based on an invalid standard, for example, might indicate that a test can consistently classify students incorrectly across parallel test forms. Certainly the methodological problems involved in assuring the validity of mastery or competency inferences are complex. That does not diminish the theoretical and practical significance of the task; it just augments the challenge.

In chapter 3, Professor Ronald A. Berk addresses the first topic of item validity within the framework of a criterion-referenced test item analysis. Four types of analysis are examined: (1) item-objective congruence, (2) item statistics, (3) item selection, and (4) item revision. The procedures for field testing the items and interpreting difficulty, discrimination, and homogeneity statistics receive special attention. Seventeen different statistics reported in the literature are critiqued in the form of a "consumers' guide." It was recommended that the difficulty index and one of the simpler discrimination indices provide sufficient information for most applications. Item selection criteria are then delineated using both the judgmental and empirical information. A decision to accept, revise, or discard an item according to the criteria is tantamount to determining which items are valid and which items are not. Finally, for those items identified for revision, a further analysis is described that scrutinizes the internal structure of an item to provide insight into what parts need to be revised. Professor Berk concludes that a firm conceptual foundation and substantial evidence exist to support the use of the item analysis procedures for current practices.

Professor Ronald K. Hambleton extends many of the preceding methods to the appraisal of content and construct validity. In chapter 4, he first reviews techniques for establishing content validity. The techniques relate to item validity, the technical quality of the items, and the representativeness of the items. The development of domain specifications and the systematic collection and analysis of content specialists' ratings are strongly recommended. The variety of rating forms devised by Professor Hambleton and the utility of the interrater agreement measures suggest that the rating techniques hold considerable promise for practitioners. In contrast to the characteristic of content validity that is essentially invariant over time and across different groups of students, construct validity is perceived as dependent upon the intended score interpretations, which may vary markedly from one application to another. Two empirical approaches for conducting construct validity studies are explicated: Guttman scalogram analysis and factor analysis. A listing of nine potential sources of invalidity in regard to test score interpretation and discussions of criterion-related and decision validity complete Professor Hambleton's survey of validity issues.

A second major review devoted to the topic of setting standards or cut-off scores for mastery-nonmastery decision making constitutes the remainder of chapter 4. A rationale for why cut-off scores should be used and some guidelines for selecting an appropriate method are offered first. The subsequent review encompasses sixteen different methods of determining cut-off scores for criterion-referenced tests. For purposes of convenience and clarity, Professor Hambleton grouped the methods into three categories: (1) judgmental, (2) empirical, and (3) judgmental-empirical combination. His critical assessment of the various methods led to two sets of procedural guidelines for setting standards: one for classroom testing and a second for basic skills testing for grade-to-grade promotion and high school graduation certification.

ITEM ANALYSIS

RONALD A. BERK

Introduction

The set of items generated from the domain specifications needs to undergo a review process to identify structural flaws and determine whether the items function or "behave" consistently with the purposes for which they were constructed. Depending upon the rigor and precision of the specifications, the process may be quite short or rather lengthy. The nature of the item analysis relates to how the item domain is conceptualized. When items are written from objectives-based specifications using traditional item-construction rules, those items, viewed collectively, constitute a *sample* from a theoretical domain of "all possible items" that could be written for the objective. This domain can be thought of as an *infinite item domain*. For example, a 5-item sample may be developed for an objective where the domain could conceivably contain 50 or even 500 items. This notion contrasts with a *finite item domain*, where all possible items can actually be enumerated and generated. Proponents of item transformations, item forms, and algorithms claim this is possible (cf. Berk 1979a). The items to be included on a test are then selected from the domain using a random or stratified random sampling plan. This would assure representation of the item domain and, hence, the interpretability of individual domain scores.

These two concepts of item sampling have distinctly different implications for an item analysis. The item sample associated with a theoretical domain requires a comprehensive review. Each item must be scrutinized to appraise whether it (1) measures its respective instructional and behavioral objectives and (2) differentiates among masters and non-masters of those objectives. In addition, it must be free of structural flaws that could cue or confuse the student. The extent to which the items are *valid* for these purposes depends on the outcomes of two analyses. The first is concerned with the establishment of item-objective congruence or the degree of relationship between each item and the objective it is intended to measure. The second involves statistical procedures designed to express the degree of relationship between the intent of each item and the responses of students to each item.

Such item analyses are unnecessary and, in fact, undesirable when the item sample is actually drawn from a finite domain or pool of items. It has been argued that in "domain-referenced testing" the use of item statistics for refining and selecting the items would theoretically destroy the defining character of the test, thereby weakening the interpretability of the domain score (Hambleton, Swaminathan, Algina, & Coulson 1978; Millman 1974; Millman & Popham 1974). Furthermore, given the precision of the strategies that can be employed to generate the item domain, the need to assess congruence between the items and the domain specifications or to search for flaws in the items seems questionable.

Therefore, an item analysis should be conducted for criterion-referenced test items produced from the relatively less rigorous objectives-based specifications where item sampling from a finite domain is not possible. This would apply to most tests developed by teachers and evaluators, since the manual (as opposed to computer) generation of a domain of *quality* items for the purpose of sampling is difficult, time comsuming, and quite expensive. The potential utility of even computer assistance for item banking, item sampling, and test construction (Barcikowski & Patterson 1972; Gorth, Allen, & Grayson 1971; Gorth & Grayson 1969; Hamer & Young 1978; Lippey 1974; Menne 1977; Millman [see chapter 2]; Wood & Skurnik 1969; Woodson 1968) has yet to be realized. Consequently, practitioners should seriously consider the use of the item analysis techniques described in the following sections.

Review of Item Analysis Procedures

Several item-analysis procedures have been devised expressly for criterion-referenced tests. They pertain to four topics: (1) item-objective congruence, (2) item statistics, (3) item selection, and (4) item revision. While most of the research has focused on item statistics, guidelines for the other three areas have recently been proposed. This review will critically examine the various methodologies according to the steps by which a teacher or evaluator would conduct an item analysis.

Item-Objective Congruence. The most important item characteristic is item-objective congruence. It is concerned with the extent to which an item measures the objective it is intended to measure. Congruence is determined by a judgmental process. The items are reviewed in relation to the list of instructional and behavioral objectives and the table of domain specifications. Three criteria are employed to determine the congruence or match between the items and objectives: (1) behavior, (2) content, and (3) hierarchical classification.

Since the items are generated from the statements of objectives, the behavioral (verb) and content components of the objectives should be reflected in the format and content of the items. Agreement in terms of the first two criteria is typically built in during the item construction phase. These aspects of congruence, however, still merit attention before administering the test. Occasionally, verbs in the behavioral objectives suggesting essay questions (e.g., explain) are mismatched with complex multiple-choice items. Either the objectives should be corrected or the items rewritten.

The time devoted to establishing congruence should be concentrated on the third criterion. More disagreements seem to occur regarding item and objective classifications in the cognitive, affective, and psychomotor taxonomies than with the preceding criteria. When the items are examined according to those hierarchial schemes, it is not uncommon to find discrepancies, particularly at the middle and upper levels of the cognitive domain. The discrepancies can be identified by using the test draft as an item checklist against which the classification categories can be compared. An item-by-item analysis can be conducted to ascertain whether the initial intent of each objective is, in fact, realized in each item. Teachers tend to construct items at lower levels of cognition than the specifications originally indicated. For an objective classified at the application level, for example, it is not surprising to find the corresponding item to have been written at the knowledge level. This may be due to confusion over what constitutes measures at the different levels of the hierarchy or to the process by which the objectives are developed.

If the item is the predominant consideration when the objective is being written, the type of behavioral outcome is often restricted by the teacher's knowledge of test items. To the extent that the domain specifications are defined in the context of some preconceived notion of what the items should look like, the resulting objectives and their classifications are developed to fit the items rather than the reverse. This creates problems in maintaining the link with the content domain. The assessment of congruence will usually reveal inconsistencies between the items and the specifications. Under those conditions the test maker has two choices: either modify the objectives and their classifications to correspond with the items or rewrite the items to correspond with the existing classifications.

The foregoing procedures can be extended to items developed at the district and state levels. The difference lies in the number of persons judging the characteristic. Instead of individual teacher judgment at the classroom level, the collective judgment of a panel of content specialists is required (Dahl 1971). Three approaches to assessing congruence using content specialists have been described by Rovinelli and Hambleton (1977): (1) an index derived from Hemphill and Westie's (1950) index of homogeneity of placement, (2) a rating scale in the format of a semantic differential, and (3) a matching task that is analyzed using the chi-square test for independence. The empirical comparison among the methods revealed that the index that quantifies the degree of agreement among the individual judgments provide the most meaningful measure of congruence. For specific guidelines on this procedure and several others, the reader is referred to Hambleton's discussion of content validity (chapter 4).

Regardless of the method employed to determine item-objective congruence, however, it is crucial that when discrepancies occur, the appropriate corrections are made. That property is a *necessary but not sufficient condition for test validity.* If it cannot be stated unequivocally that the items measure the objectives, then any other characteristic becomes meaningless. The interpretability of the test results in terms of objectives hinges on the congruence between the items and objectives.

Item Statistics. Once the items have been judged congruent with the objectives, the teacher/evaluator should plan to field test them with groups of students. The response data obtained from the students can be used to evaluate the effectiveness of the items in terms of whether they function in the manner in which they were intended. The steps in the process include the selection of criterion groups, gathering informal student feedback, and computing difficulty, discrimination, and homogeneity statistics. The following presentation is based largely on the comprehensive survey of item statistics by Berk (1978).

Selection of criterion groups. The first consideration in the use of item statistics is the selection of the students to whom the items should be administered. The majority of the statistics are based on pretest-posttest repeated measurements from one group to two independent measurements from two different groups. Only four statistics are computed from one set of data gathered from group (Brennan 1972, Engel & LaDuca 1977, Epstein 1977, Pettie & Oosterhof 1976).

The choice of which groups to use depends upon their availability and the purpose of the test. Since a criterion-referenced test is employed in most instances to identify masters and nonmasters of a set of objectives, the question a teacher/evaluator needs to answer is *Who should be able to answer the items correctly and who should not*? Two categories of student are of interest—those who would be *successful* (masters) and those who would be *unsuccessful* (nonmasters) on the items. For the majority of instructional programs for which tests are developed, these groups will consist of students who have and students who have not been exposed to the instruction. It is likely that most if not all students prior to instruction will perform poorly on the items. If this level of performance is not obtained, either the items are failing to function as expected or the objectives have been taught previously. When the latter appears to be the explanation, the justification for the instruction needs to be examined. In the case of the second group, which is tested after the instruction has been completed, performance should be quite high. That is, most if not all of these students should answer the items correctly.

The two groups of students chosen for the item analysis are often referred to as *criterion groups*. Their selection is based on some criterion of current or future performance. This may be success in the instructional program in which the test will be used or success in a subsequent program, i.e., unit, course, grade level. The former often suggests summative decision making at one point in time, whereas the latter denotes placement decision making within a predictive context. Placement in a program that contains sequentially arranged units each represented by an instructional objective presumes that a student's success in any single unit is prerequisite for success in the following unit. Therefore, students who have successfully completed the entire program can serve as one of the criterion groups for validating the placement test items. The same group may also be employed in the validation of items used for summative decisions about individual mastery at the conclusion of the program.

A clear definition of the criterion is essential. Two approaches for identifying criterion groups are described below: (1) preinstruction-postinstruction measurements and (2) uninstructed-instructed groups. Both are applicable to criterion-referenced tests designed for placement, formative, and summative decision making. The advantages and disadvantages of the approaches are noted.

The *preinstruction-postinstruction measurements* method has been an integral part of mastery learning and diagnostic-prescriptive teaching for several years (Block 1971; Block & Burns 1976; Carroll 1963, 1970). It involves *testing one group of students twice*, before instruction (preinstruction) and after instruction (postinstruction). Students are commoly tested with the same set of items on the two occasions. Alternatively, a parallel or equivalent set of items can be used on the second administration.

The advantage of measuring students before and after instruction is that it permits the teacher to examine individual as well as group gains. This can be particularly useful in assessing progress from one unit to the next. Information on gains cannot be obtained from any other type of design.

One major disadvantage of the approach, however, pertains to the *impracticality of administering the posttest.* It precludes the item analysis from being conducted before the instruction is completed. Hence, any instructional application of the measure would likely be deferred until the following year. A second disadvantage concerns the amount of time allowed between the pretest and posttest. When the administrations are in close succession, it is possible for the students' performance on the pretest to influence their performance on the posttest. One way to obviate this problem of *testing effect* would be to develop an equivalent set of items. If this is unfeasible due to practical constraints or the nature of the behavioral objectives (e.g., extreme specificity), it is recommended that the intervening period between the administrations be extended a reasonable length of time so that the carry-over effect of memory from the initial testing can be minimized. This extension should not be as long as four months or longer, to avoid incurring the effect of *maturation.* It is well known that simply growing older can improve a student's achievement performance. This would confound the measurement of gain to which the teacher wishes to attribute the effect of instruction. Improvement as a result of instruction and maturation become inextricably mixed when several months pass before the posttest is administered. The item analysis is designed to focus only on the change in item responses due to instruction.

In order to expedite computation of the item statistics, the results of the two measurements should be displayed in the form of a student × item matrix. This format is shown in table 3.1. The table consists of the item scores (0, 1) of ten students who were administered five items both before and after instruction. The students were assigned a score of 1 for a correct response and 0 for an incorrect response or no response (omit). The rationale for scoring an omit as 0 relates to the purpose of the test. Since a criterion-referenced test assesses how much a student knows unaffected by speed of response, no time limit is imposed. Therefore, when students are given ample time to complete the test, it can be assumed that if a student did not respond to an item, it was because he or she did not know the correct answer.

The *uninstructed-instructed groups* approach is a form of the known-groups technique employed for many years in the validation of personality tests (Cronbach & Meehl 1955, Edwards 1970, Wiggins 1973). Only recently has the technique been applied to criterion-referenced measure-

TABLE 3.1. Student X Item Matrix for Preinstruction-Postinstruction Measurements

| | Preinstruction | | | | | Postinstruction | | | | |
| | Item | | | | | Item | | | | |
Student	1	2	3	4	5	1	2	3	4	5
1	0	0	1	1	1	1	0	1	1	1
2	0	1	1	1	0	1	1	1	1	1
3	0	1	0	1	1	1	1	1	1	1
4	0	0	0	1	1	1	1	0	1	1
5	0	0	1	1	0	1	0	0	1	1
6	0	0	0	1	0	1	1	0	1	0
7	0	1	1	1	1	1	0	0	1	1
8	0	0	1	1	0	1	0	1	1	0
9	0	0	0	1	0	1	1	0	1	1
10	0	0	1	1	0	1	1	1	1	1

ment (Henrysson & Wedman 1974, Jackson 1970, Klein & Kosecoff 1976, Millman 1974, Zieky 1973). It involves *testing two separate groups of students at the same point in time*, one group that has not received instruction (the uninstructed group) and a second group that has received instruction (the instructed group).

The known-groups technique compares one group of persons known by independent means to possess more of the specified trait/attribute with a second group known to possess much less. In the validation of a criterion-referenced test, the trait of interest is *knowledge*. The acquisition of knowledge in most content domains is a continuous process. Learning to read, write, and solve mathematical problems occurs gradually throughout a person's formal schooling. Improvement in these areas is frequently accompanied by improvement in the other subject areas. Since students learn at different rates, at any given time the students within a single classroom would vary in the amount of knowledge they possess. Therefore, in general, it can be expected that students in an instructed group will possess *more knowledge* related to a set of instructional objectives and an uninstructed group will possess *much less*. There are only two special cases where a group might know all or nothing. They will be discussed shortly.

The uninstructed-instructed groups approach requires that the two groups be identified on the basis of *independent, informed teacher judgment*. Students in one or more classrooms who have not received instruction or who are known to be deficient on the objectives to be assessed may serve as the uninstructed group. Conversely, students in other classrooms who have received "effective" instruction on the objectives may comprise the instructed group. This group, in the judgment of the teacher, should have demonstrated *success* in the instructional unit. Whether this success pertains to a current or subsequent unit depends on the orientation of the test. Student performance on written assignments, quizzes, and other classroom tasks is often the available information a teacher must rely upon for guidance in making the judgment.

The students chosen for the instructed group should be as similar as possible to those in the uninstructed group in ability level and all other relevant characteristics. Although the groups will often be unequal in size, the proportional distributions of the characteristics should be equivalent. For example, if one group has 60 percent boys and 40 percent girls, this balance should be maintained in the second group. The only real difference that should exist between the uninstructed and instructed groups is exposure to the instructional treatment.

While the approach is applicable in most testing situations, there are two instances where possessing or not possessing the knowledge necessary to master objectives will be characterized as *all or nothing*: (1) where minimum essential skills or competencies are being measured and (2) where no prior knowledge on objectives can be expected due to the nature of the content domain. The former is concerned with the "all"; the latter emphasizes the "nothing."

When basic skills or *minimum competencies* are to be assessed, complete mastery by the instructed group is desirable. If a test is designed to identify children who cannot succeed or function at a minimum level, the criterion *successful* group that is chosen must unequivocally by definition perform at least at that level and most likely could perform at a higher level. This means the group should be able to demonstrate total mastery, or 100 percent performance, on the set of minimum skills. If this does not occur, it is possible that the skills may not be "minimum." The criterion *unsuccessful* group should perform at less than total mastery. The actual performance could be expected to range from 0 to less than 100 percent. This group should consist of the type of children to be identified by the test.

The item validation of a placement test to determine reading readiness, for example, would require the selection of children who clearly can and cannot read. In other programs, such as learning disabilities and English as a second language, the criterion groups would consist of children who possess and do not possess specific disabilities and those who are native English speakers and speakers of English as a second language (e.g., Hispanic Americans), respectively. Evidence of these different attributes can often be found in school records. Again, teacher judgment plays a significant role in locating the children.

The procedure has implications for other competency-based decisions in course placement, grade level placement, high school graduation certification, and functional literacy. All extensions of the validation model must confront the same crucial issue—*operationally defining the criterion of success* in terms of the designated target groups.

Dissimilar to the above, where 100 percent mastery is desirable for the instructed group, is the case where *no prior knowledge* can be expected for the uninstructed group. This occurs in courses that introduce the student to completely unfamiliar content, e.g., an introductory foreign language course. A test administered prior to the instruction would yield results that unequivocally demonstrate nonmastery, or 0 performance. For the purposes of validation there is no need to administer the test to uninstructed students who are expected to know nothing about the content; item and test performance can be assumed to equal 0. The test must be administered, however, to an instructed group.

The advantage of the uninstructed-instructed group approach is one of *practicality.* The item analysis can be conducted at one point in time, prior to instruction, if an instructed group of students is concurrently available. This can facilitate the immediate use of the test for mastery-nonmastery decisions during the program being taught.

One disadvantage is the difficulty of *defining suitable criteria* for identifying the groups. The more objectivity that can be incorporated into the process, the better. "Informed" judgment as described previously is one step in that direction. At present, this seems to be an intuitively sound procedure for performing item analyses at the classroom level. Another disadvantage that is inherent in the approach is the problem of *assuring group equivalence.* Since randomly assigning students to instructed and uninstructed groups is generally unfeasible and inappropriate, the test maker may need to explain differences in group performance that may not be attributable to the instructional treatment, e.g., age, sex, ability levels, socioeconomic background. Realistically, the best strategy to avert this charge from arising would be deliberately to control for possible extraneous factors in the initial selection of the groups and to exhibit caution in interpreting the item analysis results.

The scoring and presentation of the item data for the uninstructed and instructed groups is identical to the preinstruction-postinstruction approach. Table 3.2 displays a student × item matrix with item scores on five items administered to one group of ten uninstructed students and a second group of ten instructed students.

Informal student feedback. Immediately following the administration of the items to the criterion groups, informal student feedback on the items can be obtained. This constitutes a nonstatistical aspect of item

TABLE 3.2. Student X Item Matrix for Uninstructed and Instructed Groups

| | Uninstructed Group | | | | | | Instructed Group | | | | |
| | Item | | | | | | Item | | | | |
Student	1	2	3	4	5	Student	1	2	3	4	5
1	0	0	1	1	1	1	1	1	1	1	1
2	0	1	1	1	0	2	1	1	0	1	1
3	0	1	0	1	1	3	1	1	1	1	1
4	0	0	0	1	1	4	0	0	1	1	1
5	0	0	1	1	0	5	1	0	1	1	0
6	0	0	0	1	0	6	1	1	1	1	1
7	0	1	1	1	1	7	1	0	0	1	1
8	0	0	1	1	0	8	0	1	0	1	0
9	0	0	0	1	0	9	1	0	1	1	0
10	0	0	1	1	0	10	1	1	1	1	1

analysis. Frequently, only the instructed students are involved in the procedure, because the uninstructed students typically convey frustration instead of information. The procedure entails conducting a classroom discussion or individual interviews to elicit student reactions to the items and test structure. Much can be learned about test quality from a student critique that otherwise would not be disclosed from a quantitative analysis. The feedback can provide valuable insights and directions for improving the test. Specific test weaknesses, such as item ambiguity and cuing, miskeyed answers, inappropriate vocabulary, and unclear item and test directions, can be revealed by asking leading questions pertinent to the item content and structure, test directions, and test format. Such questions may include the following:

1. Did any of the items seem confusing?
2. Did you find any item with no correct answer or with more than one correct answer?
3. Were there any words you did not know or that gave you difficulty?
4. Did you have any difficulty understanding what to do as you progressed through the test?

Since students are commonly not requested to participate or assist in the test improvement process, the novelty of the experience may produce a flood of responses. In many cases, the first question yields more information than may be initially anticipated. As students become attuned to the procedure, however, the quantity of feedback will diminish and the quality of the feedback can be expected to improve.

The five to ten minutes often needed to conduct this analysis coupled with the valuable knowledge it provides the test maker should demonstrate its utility and worth as an attractive adjunct to the statistical measures.

Item difficulty. The difficulty of an item is the percentage of persons who answer the item correctly (percent pass). It is computed using the formula

$$\text{DIFF} = \frac{C}{N} \times 100,$$

where: C = number of students who answer the item correctly
N = total number of students in the group.

The index is equivalent to the mean of the item (the proportion of students who got the item right) multiplied by 100.

Difficulty index values can range from 0 to 100. The higher the index, the easier the item. When all students answer the item correctly, the index equals 100; when all students respond incorrectly, the index is 0.

It is important that estimates of difficulty be obtained for both criterion groups. If difficulty levels are determined only for those students who have received the instruction, there is no way of knowing whether the students would have performed similarly without the instruction, that is, an easy item after instruction may have also been easy prior to instruction.

Item discrimination. The index of item discrimination measures the performance changes (pretest-posttest) or differences (uninstructed-instructed) between the criterion groups. This is consistent with the notion that a criterion-referenced test should maximize discriminations between groups and minimize discriminations among individuals within any one group (Glaser 1963). Differences that do occur between the groups are presumed attributable to the effect of instruction. The interpretation of the index in terms of the instructional program has prompted some proponents of the technique to refer to it as a measure of *instructional sensitivity*.

The vast array of indices found in the literature suggests that there is no single best method for estimating discrimination. Invoking the "law of parsimony" in this context, it is possible to extract four approaches that are conceptually and computationally simple yet statistically sound. These manually calculable indices are evaluated in table 3.3 according to two criteria: (1) *practicability* in terms of the ease with which the statistic could be computed and interpreted and (2) *meaningfulness* in

TABLE 3.3. Evaluation of Item Discrimination Indices

Index	Statistic	Source	Comments
Pretest-posttest difference (DIS$_{PPD}$)	Proportion	Cox and Vargas (1966), Tucker and Vargas (1974), Vargas (1969)	Proportion of students who answered item correctly on posttest minus proportion who answered it correctly on pretest. Range of values is −1.00 to +1.00. *Disadvantage*: Index is not sensitive to individual performance changes, only to total group gain or loss.
Uninstructed-instructed group difference (DIS$_{UIGD}$)	Proportion	Klein and Kosecoff (1976), Levin and Marton (1971), Marton (1973)	Proportion of students in instructed group who answered item correctly minus proportion in uninstructed group who answered it correctly. Range of values is −1.00 to +1.00. Correlates .70 and .12 with DIS$_{PPD}$ (Crehan 1974, Wedman 1973). Relationship with DIS$_{PPD}$ is contingent upon how closely instructed group resembles postinstruction group. *Disadvantage*: Same as DIS$_{PPD}$, but is a function of data base rather than statistic.
Individual gain (DIS$_{IG}$)	Proportion	Roudabush (1973)	Proportion of students who answered item incorrectly on pretest and correctly on posttest. A correction for guessing (Marks & Noll 1967) is optional. Range of values is −1.00 to +1.00 with correction and 0 to +1.00 without correction. *Disadvantage*: Assumptions underlying correction for guessing are questionable.
Net gain (DIS$_{NG}$)	Proportion	Kosecoff and Klein (1974)	Extends DIS$_{IG}$ by considering performance of all students who answered item incorrectly on pretest; DIS$_{IG}$ minus proportion of students who answered item incorrectly on both occasions. Correction for guessing is optional. Range of values is −1.00 to +1.00 with or without correction. Represents net individual gains/losses as a result of instruction. Yields more conservative values than preceding indices. *Disadvantage*: Same as DIS$_{IG}$.

NOTE: All indices were judged manually calculable and easily interpretable.

the context of the test development process. The first two indices are based on the item difficulties expressed as proportions; the last two are based on the item response outcomes of the preinstruction-postinstruction measurements, i.e., incorrect → correct (0 → 1) and incorrect → incorrect (0 → 0). The former are the simplest in that they are computed directly from the difficulty levels for the criterion groups; the latter are the most sensitive to pretest-posttest item score gains.

The choice of which of the four indices to use may be determined initially by the criterion groups available for the analysis. There is only one index for the case of uninstructed-instructed groups. Among the three indices appropriate for preinstruction-postinstruction measurements, DIS_{PPD} appears to be the simplest and DIS_{NG} the most sensitive. DIS_{NG} uses more information and possesses a greater range of possible values than DIS_{IG}. It is also statistically more sensitive than DIS_{PPD}, since it takes into account the individual gains and losses resulting from the instruction rather than just the total group gain or loss. Overall, the DIS_{NG} index yields a more conservative estimate of item discrimination than the two alternatives.

The foregoing measures of item discrimination provide evidence of item validity. In general, the intent of the test items to discriminate between students who have and students who have not been exposed to instruction on a set of objectives is concurrently validated with group performance on the items. The external criterion was informed teacher judgment about the students' success/failure in a well-defined segment of instruction. This served as the basis for selecting the criterion groups. Given the persistent validation problem of obtaining a satisfactory criterion of success, teacher judgment should prove adequate for estimating validity at the classroom level. Certainly a more reliable, comprehensive alternative would be desirable. At present, however, such an alternative does not seem available.

Since the empirical item validation process is inherent in the test item analysis, its interpretation is subject to the conditions under which the item analysis is performed. The fact that each analysis is uniquely related to the set of objectives, students' abilities and attributes, and instructional procedures characteristic of each classroom implies that *test items that are valid for one class may not be valid for other classes.* Teachers should not attempt to generalize the results beyond the context for which the items were originally designed.

Seven other discrimination indices were also identified. They are evaluated in table 3.4, using the same criteria as above. These indices were judged less practical than the previous indices since they could not be computed efficiently without a computer program. Hence, they may be of limited value and utility for teacher-made tests and assessments at the

TABLE 3.4. Evaluation of Item Discrimination Indices

Index	Statistic	Source	Comments
Maximum possible gain	Proportion	Brennan (1974), Brennan and Stolurow (1971)	Extension of DIS_{PPD} index; proportion of maximum possible difference accounted for by obtained difference (DIS_{PPD}). Correlates .92 with DIS_{PPD} (Wedman 1973). *Disadvantages*: Range of values and interpretations are different from most other discrimination indices.
B index	Proportion	Brennan (1972), Hsu (1971)	Criterion level is used to define master and nonmaster groups within one instructed group. *Disadvantages*: Validity of the criterion becomes a necessary condition for the validity of the item statistic. Index cannot be computed when all or none of the students meet the criterion. Interpretation of index values is rather unorthodox, i.e., ideal index is 0.
Internal sensitivity	Proportion	Koscoff and Klein (1974)	Criterion level is used to define master and nonmaster groups for both pretest and posttest. *Disadvantage*: Dependence on criterion.
Combined groups item-total r	Correlation	Haladyna (1974), Helmstadter (1972)	Application of traditional item-total r to sample consisting of both criterion groups. Correlates from .64 to .86 with DIS_{PPD}. Index can be computed with most norm-referenced test item analysis programs, such as ITEMAN (Berk & Griesemer 1976). *Disadvantage*: Index is not sensitive to which students are scoring high and low (uninstructed or instructed) and, therefore, may not measure discrimination between designated criterion groups.
Item-criterion partial r	Correlation	Darlington and Bishop (1966), Millman (1974, pp. 369–70)	Correlation of item scores with criterion group classification (0,1) holding total score constant. Several items per iteration method that takes into account interitem correlations is the recommended item selection procedure. Designed to maximize test validity. *Disadvantages*: Computation and item selection process are more complicated than that of preceding indices. Content and importance of objective being assessed are not considered. Index requires a specialized item analysis program or partial correlation program.

| Change-item r | Correlation | Saupe (1966) | Correlation of item change scores (-1, 0, $+1$) with total change scores from pretest to posttest. Designed originally to maximize reliability of change scores (Stanley 1967, Webster 1957) or validity with a criterion variable (Webster 1956). *Disadvantages*: Most complex correlational approach requiring computation of six different covariances. Variance restriction on pretest or posttest scores will limit index values. Content and importance of objective being assessed are not considered in the item selection process. Index requires a specialized item analysis program such as CHANGE-SCORE (Berk & Griesemer 1977). |
| ... | Multiple regression | Millman (1974, pp. 367–68) | Stepwise regression analysis with items entered as predictor variables and criterion group classification serving as the criterion variable. Analysis incorporates interitem correlations. *Disadvantages*: Analysis requires a relatively large sample size. There is no item discrimination index; selection is based on inclusion in prediction equation. Item regression coefficients are used to weight item scores with no consideration given to the objective the items measure. |

NOTE: Indices are listed in order of increasing overall complexity.

local level. Most of them do not simply measure the extent to which an item differentiates between criterion groups. Additional factors are considered (e.g., interitem correlations) that tend to complicate the computation and interpretation of item discrimination. For this reason the indices are listed in order of increasing overall complexity. The major disadvantages or deficiencies of the indices are noted.

Item homogeneity. Four statistics that relate to item-objective congruence are evaluated in table 3.5. These homogeneity measures are intended to verify statistically that items congruent with an instructional objective behave similarly on a single testing or on repeated testings (pretest-posttest). The assumption that the items should yield identical difficulty indices or change scores is questionable. Such "homogeneity" may be unrealistic and, in fact, undesirable in cases where a variety of skills may define the content of an instructional objective that encompasses several weeks of instruction or longer. The generality-specificity of the objective will probably determine the meaningfulness of the homogeneity statistics.

Item Selection. All of the preceding data gathering and analyses are conducted for one reason—to determine the quality or effectiveness of the test items. The characteristics that have been described are simply indicants of item quality. They must now be used to decide whether the items have functioned consistently with the purposes for which they were constructed. The decision regarding the status of an item may take three forms: (1) *accept* the item for inclusion in the final test; (2) *revise* the item before including it in the final test; or (3) *discard* the item and develop a new item to take its place. Criteria for assigning the items to these mutually exclusive categories have been proposed by Berk (1979*b*). They will be considered next.

The item characteristics that weigh most heavily in the item selection process are item-objective congruence, item difficulty, and item discrimination. They may be considered separately or jointly in arriving at any of the above decisions. Guidelines for selecting items according to the three characteristics are outlined in table 3.6. In general, an item that satisfies the criteria should be accepted. When an item does not meet one or more of the criteria, however, should it be retained, revised, or discarded? The decision depends largely upon the criterion and the degree to which it is not being met. A detailed discussion of the factors that influence each item decision follows.

Item-objective congruence. The role of item-objective congruence in item selection was clearly defined at the beginning of this chapter. It

TABLE 3.5. Evaluation of Item Homogeneity Measures

Statistic	Source	Comments
Chi-square	Pettie and Oosterhof (1976)	Modification of Popham's (1971) chi-square method for the case of one test administration (pretest only). Difficulty index of each item measuring an instructional objective is compared with the median difficulty of the set of items using chi-square. *Disadvantages*: Same as Popham's (1971) measure.
Chi-square	Popham (1971)	Pretest-posttest item frequencies are compared with median (expected) frequencies of a prototypic item using chi-square. Median values are derived from the frequencies of items measuring the same instructional objective. Items that behave differently from the prototype are considered for revision. *Disadvantages*: No critical value has been established for identifying abnormal items. Method is insensitive to the direction of the abnormality (Henrysson & Wedman 1974).
...	Engel and LaDuca (1977), Loevinger (1947)	Modification of Long's (1934) index of item homogeneity. Accounts for the relationship between item and total score. Conceptually similar to traditional index of item discrimination. *Disadvantages*: Interpretation of a zero index is unclear. Sampling distribution of statistic is unknown; therefore, no significance level can be determined. Item-total score phi coefficient has been the preferred approach (White & Saltz 1957).
...	Epstein (1977)	Average squared discrepancy index is designed to identify items that yield inconsistent response patterns. Based on the individual discrepancies of item scores from a student x item matrix. Interpretation of index values seems meaningful for criterion-referenced test items. *Disadvantages*: Computation is more complicated than preceding measures. No critical index value has been established for identifying "bad" items.

NOTE:Indices are listed in order of increasing overall complexity.

TABLE 3.6 Guidelines for Selecting Criterion-Referenced Test Items

Item Characteristic	Criterion	Index Value
Item-objective congruence	Matches objective being assessed	None[a]
Difficulty	Difficult for uninstructed group	0–50
	Easy for instructed group	70–100
Discrimination	Discriminates positively between criterion groups[b]	High positive[b]

[a]There is no index of item-objective congruence for teacher-made tests. An index of agreement among content specialists for tests developed at the district and state levels can be used (Rovinelli & Hambleton 1977). For those applications the index values should be high positive.

[b]The actual value will vary according to the method used to compute discrimination.

cannot be overemphasized that this characteristic is crucial to the effectiveness of the total test and the usefulness of the results. Irrespective of all other characteristics, *an item that is not congruent with its objective should not be included in the test.* It would contribute nothing to the measurement of the objective.

In addition to accounting for the degree of correspondence between an item and an objective, two other factors related to the objective itself need to be considered in the item selection process: (1) the content of the objective and (2) the importance of the objective.

The level of cognition being assessed will frequently dictate the magnitude of the item statistics. Items that measure behavioral objectives requiring simple recall of factual content may exhibit large performance differences between the criterion groups. Such differences or gains should be anticipated. On the other hand, it would also be reasonable to expect that items that measure complex concepts or skills at the upper levels of the cognitive hierarchy may not demonstrate pronounced changes in individual or group performance as a result of the specific instructional treatment. The content of an objective, therefore, is often the primary determinant of the values one might expect for the statistical characteristics.

At this stage in test construction it might seem contradictory to perceive the importance of an objective as a factor. After all, if a teacher wrote the objective as part of the content domain specification, he or she must have deemed it important and worthy of appraisal. It has been recommended, however, that as long as an item reflects an *important attribute* it need not be discarded (Popham & Husek 1969). While strictly following this advice would diminish the importance of the item statistics, there are a few instances where the ultimate selection decision might rest with this factor. It becomes an issue when an item is judged valid in relation to its objective, yet appears to be invalid according to the item statistics. What weight should be attached to the statistical evidence? Ideally the item should be valid in terms of both characteristics. If an item fails to discriminate between the criterion groups, it should be retained when one or both of the following conditions exist: (1) due to the specificity of the behavioral objective no other item could be written to measure it and/or (2) the low or zero discrimination index suggests that the item may validly measure the absence of an instructional effect (Cronbach 1975). Alternatively, the item should be either revised or replaced with a new item.

Item difficulty and discrimination. As item-objective congruence builds into the test the property of content/descriptive validity, item discrimination builds into the test the property of decision validity (see Hambleton, chapter 4). This type of validity is reflected in the *accuracy* with which students are classified as masters and nonmasters of an instructional objective (cf. Berk 1976). Items with high positive discrimination indices improve the accuracy of these decisions. The relationship between the magnitude of the indices and classification decision accuracy is substantiated by the literature on personality test construction (Edwards 1970, Wiggins 1973). It suggests that selecting only the best discriminating items would produce the best test in terms of decision-making. This approach, however, tends to maximize decision validity at the expense of content validity. Items associated with particular behavioral objectives would be systematically discarded if their discrimination indices were low or zero. Given the extent to which the content of an objective governs the values of the statistical characteristics, it would be inappropriate to evaluate item effectiveness purely on statistical grounds. A more comprehensive interpretation of index values should be considered. The interpretation that follows takes into account the objective being measured, the students being tested, and the instructional program that has occurred.

The difficulty and discrimination indices should represent at minimum a logical trend—the difficulty index should be lower for the uninstructed students than for the instructed students, and this should be reflected in a positive discrimination index. The range of values shown in table 3.6 should be viewed from the perspective of *what seems reasonable* relative to the content and importance of the behavioral objective, the abilities and background characteristics of the students, and the actual instruction to which the students were exposed. In each case a teacher/evaluator needs to answer the question *Does this index express the performance on the item that was expected*?

All items judged *acceptable* according to these criteria should be identified first. Those items that remain will require further analyses to determine their status. Pending the outcomes of those analyses the items may be retained, revised, or discarded.

Where *minimum competencies* are being assessed, the preceding guidelines need to be modified. It is implicit in the measurement of minimum skills essential for success in a particular program that the students in the criterion success group perform 100 percent on each item (DIFF = 100). Allowing for some margin of error (e.g., 5 percent) in the estimation of the difficulty index DIFF values between 95 and 100 should be expected to validate adequately the items for this group. Students in the second criterion group chosen on the basis of their inability to demonstrate success on the objectives should perform less than 100 percent on each item (DIFF < 100). These DIFF values might be expected to vary between 0 and 94. Given that possible range, the magnitude of the discrimination indices could also be expected to exhibit wide variability. This suggests that item discrimination may not be as meaningful a statistic in this application as it is in the typical uninstructed-instructed group comparison. Only a positive index is required. A restriction on the magnitude of the index would be inappropriate. In effect, the specific difficulty indices for each group provide sufficient information to judge whether the items function as they were intended.

The simplest analysis for determining acceptable items occur in content domains where *no prior knowledge* on the objectives is possible. No uninstructed group data are gathered. This automatically reduces the interpretation of three indices down to one. Since $DIFF_U$ can be set equal to zero for each item, DIS_{UIGD} is computed only from the instructed group performance. It is, in fact, equivalent to $DIFF_I$. This index is all that a teacher needs to evaluate item quality. It should fall within the range of values specified in table 3.6.

Difficulty and discrimination indices that deviate from the above criteria may be explained in terms of the item, the objective, or the instruction. While the first inclination is to revise or discard an item that does not meet the specifications, the most common explanation for a difficulty index that is higher or lower than expected relates to the objective being measured. Possible explanations for the different index values are presented in table 3.7. The actions that are most appropriate for these conditions involve changes in the objectives and/or the instructional program, not the item. The item would be *retained* until the changes were completed.

If the inconsistency between the expected and the actual index value is not attributable to the objective or instruction, the item itself must be scrutinized. The most conspicuous "flag" of a faulty item is a *negative*

TABLE 3.7. Possible Explanations and Actions for Items with Unexpected Statistical Outcomes

Index	Index Value	Possible Explanation	Suggested Action
$DIFF_{U/PRE}$	Much higher than expected (e.g., expected $= 20$; actual $= 45$)	Objective may have been taught previously	Write a higher level objective/relocate objective earlier in program
$DIFF_{I/POST}$	Much lower than expected (e.g., expected $= 80$; actual $= 50$)	Objective may be too difficult or complex	Write a lower level objective/relocate objective later in program
		Instruction may have been ineffective	Correct deficiencies in the instruction with different emphases, new materials, or other modifications
DIS	Much lower than expected	One or a combination of the above explanations	One or a combination of the above actions

discrimination index. It may indicate ambiguity, two correct answers, or ineffective distractors. An examination of the internal structure of the item coupled with the information obtained from the students' reviews will often reveal the part(s) that should be *revised.* When the item is in mutiple-choice format, a quantitative analysis of each response choice should be considered. This type of analysis is described in the next section.

In the case of an item that possesses no visible flaws yet fails to yield statistical indices that are acceptable, it is recommended that the item be *discarded* and a new item written to replace it. However, this procedure should be viewed as a last resort. It is generally much easier to revise an item than to construct a new one. The new item will also be "untested." It is imperative that an item that must be eliminated be *replaced.* If it is not, the measurement of the respective instructional objective as well as the overall content validity of the test are weakened.

Items with difficulty and discrimination indices that do not conform to the "guidelines" may occur in the development of teacher-made tests due to the tentative nature of the results. The objectives, students, and instructional techniques vary from one classroom to another. In addition, the relatively small number of students commonly available for the item analysis affects the stability of the indices. An analysis conducted on one occasion may yield data quite different from an analysis conducted on another occasion.

In view of these factors it would be not only unrealistic but rather imperceptive to recommend that teachers strive for items with 0 (un-instructed) and 100 (instructed) difficulty levels and $+1.00$ discrimination indices. The sources of variability noted above will generally preclude attainment of these statistical properties. Furthermore, it is incorrect to assume that the students' performances on items measuring objectives at varying levels of complexity should be the same. *The ideal or desired statistical outcomes need not be similar for all items.*

Item Revision. When the informal student feedback and/or statistical analyses suggest that a multiple-choice format item is faulty, an analysis of its internal structure can provide insight into what needs to be revised. The most common types of error in the stem and answer choices are often detected by the students and others who review the items. In order to identify flaws that may not be readily apparent, a more rigorous analysis based on the student performance data is required. This is particularly appropriate for items yielding low positive, zero, or negative discrimination indices.

The analysis involves the visual inspection of the students' responses to each choice. Both criterion groups are employed to determine whether the distractors are functioning properly. The criteria for evaluating a choice response pattern are as follows:

1. Each distractor should be selected by more students in the uninstructed group than in the instructed group.
2. At least a few uninstructed students should choose each distractor.
3. No distractor should receive as many responses by the instructed group as the correct answer.

If any of these patterns is not observed, it is likely that particular distractors are ambiguous or implausible. Within a given item one or more flaws may be identified. Depending upon the nature of the error(s), either revision or replacement of the specific part is generally indicated. A judgment concerning the amount of modification may also dictate that a completely new item be written. As noted previously, this should be considered only as a last resort. Data would then have to be gathered on the new item to assure that it functions properly.

The procedures described above are applicable to most test items expressed in a multiple-choice format. This includes multiple-choice cloze and matching items as well as the traditional three- to five-choice item. The data formats for the analyses presented below can be adapted easily to matching items.

The process of analyzing the choice response patterns of multiple-choice items is illustrated for both preinstruction-postinstruction measurements and uninstructed-instructed groups. Two different sets of data from two items are used.

The pretest and posttest responses of twenty tenth-grade students to one item from a criterion-referenced biology test are displayed in table 3.8. The item has a DIS$_{PPD}$ index of .05. The teacher felt this was inadequate in terms of the objective being measured. Of the twenty students tested, essentially just as many answered the item correctly (B) before instruction as after instruction. An examination of the three distractors (A, C, and D) indicates that the desired response pattern is not occurring consistently. Distractor A appears to be marginally effective, since only one more student selected it prior to instruction than after instruction. More conspicuous is the fact that so many students in each group chose distractor C. This suggests that the instructed students may have misread the question or that C is possibly a second correct answer. The latter would seem most likely. Distractor C should be revised. Distractor D is completely ineffective, since it attracted no one. It reduces the four-choice item to a three-choice item. This distractor should be replaced by one that will be plausible to the preinstruction students.

The response analysis of this test item indicates that the item can be improved by revising distractor C and replacing distractor D.

In the next example, twenty fifth-grade students served as the uninstructed group and fifteen sixth-grade students served as the instructed group. The item has been selected from a vocabulary test. The choice responses are shown in table 3.9. The item has a DIS$_{UIGD}$ index of $-.15$. This is evident from the proportionately greater number of students in the uninstructed group who answered D compared to those in the instructed group. Both distractors B and C appear to be functioning effectively. It is obvious, however, that more students in each group chose C than any other choice, including the correct answer. This response pattern, along with the negative trend characteristic of choices A and D, suggests that the item stem may be ambiguous. Inconsistent responses

TABLE 3.8. Illustrative Preinstruction-Postinstruction Item Data for Choice-Response Analysis

Item	Group	A	B[a]	C	D	Omits	Total
10	Postinstruction	2	10	8	0	0	20
	Preinstruction	3	9	8	0	0	20
	Total	5	19	16	0	0	40

[a]Correct answer

TABLE 3.9. Illustrative Uninstructed-Instructed Groups Item Data for Choice-Response
Analysis

Item	Group	Response Choice				Omits	Total
		A	B	C	D[a]		
14	Instructed	4	2	6	3	0	15
	Uninstructed	1	4	8	7	0	20
	Total	5	6	14	10	0	35

[a]Correct answer

to three of the four choices indicate that a new item should be written
to measure the objective.

Suggestions for Future Research

The preceding review of the item-objective congruence, item statistics,
item selection, and item revision stages of the item analysis process indicates that the technology for assessing the quality/effectiveness/validity
of criterion-referenced test items has been established. This applies to
tests developed at the classroom, district, state, and national levels.
While there is a need for further research on some of the technical issues,
a firm conceptual foundation and substantial evidence exist to support
the use of the various methodologies for current practices.

The specific aspects of item analysis that require additional study are
delineated as follows:

1. *Statistical validation of items for the special case of "no prior knowledge."* One of the most obvious limitations of the criterion groups
   validation model is where no uninstructed group data can be obtained
   due to the nature of the content domain. When a group of students
   cannot be expected to have any prior knowledge related to a particular
   set of objectives, the computation and interpretation of item discrimination loses meaning. The application of item discrimination indices
   and item selection criteria under those circumstances requires clarification.

2. *Relationship between DIS*PPD *and DIS*UIGD. The relationship between
   the item discrimination indices based on the two alternative types of
   criterion group needs to be investigated. The conflicting results of the
   previous studies (Crehan 1974, Wedman 1973) suggest that DIS$_{PPD}$
   and DIS$_{UIGD}$ may be quite different depending upon how closely the
   selected instructed group resembles the postinstruction group.

3. *Relationship between preinstruction-postinstruction discrimination*

indices. The numerous indices based on preinstruction-postinstruction measurements (see tables 3.3 and 3.4) should be compared to determine how they ultimately affect the final selection of items. An empirical evaluation of the simple and complex statistics would also be of value in assessing their relative sensitivity to performance gains and instructional treatments. Some preliminary work in this area has been conducted by Haladyna and Roid (1978).

4. *Relationship between item discrimination and classification accuracy and consistency.* There is no evidence using criterion-referenced item and test data regarding the relationship between item discrimination and the selection and validation of a cut-off score based on the criterion groups model (cf. Berk 1976). A recent study by Smith (1978) examined the effect of item selection on one type of reliability. It is important to appraise how the magnitude of the discrimination indices affects the accuracy and consistency of mastery-nonmastery classification decisions.

5. *Role of item homogeneity indices in item analysis.* The homogeneity of items constructed from domain specifications is often perceived as a highly desirable characteristic. It is, in fact, claimed to be one of the major benefits to result from operationally defining a content domain. Two basic statistical approaches are recommended: (*a*) compute an item statistic from among those listed in table 3.5 and compare performance on one item with performance on the set of items, and (*b*) analyze the performance on the set of items using analysis of variance procedures to determine whether the set is homogeneous (e.g., Hively, Patterson, & Page 1968; Macready & Merwin 1973). The use of the former approach in an item analysis, however, is not clear. The magnitude of the proposed indices tends to fluctuate from item to item as a function of the generality-specificity of the objective from which the items were generated. How should a homogeneity index be incorporated into the item selection process? Should item validity be assessed in terms of three statistics—difficulty, discrimination, and homogeneity? While further insight in an attempt to resolve this confusion might accompany additional research efforts, it is also important to question whether that line of research is productive and meaningful. Perhaps Nitko's (1974) reflections on this point are worth pondering:

The insistence on homogeneity . . . is too sweeping and is poor psychology. It leads to statistical techniques being used to drive the definition of performance domains. There is no logical basis for contending *a priori* that any domain of performance identified as instructionally relevant ought to be homogeneous (cf. Cronbach, 1971). Homogeneity should be viewed as a question for empirical experimentation and item performance theory (cf. Bormuth, 1970) and would probably vary with the target population and the class of behaviors under consideration. (P. 66)

Guidelines for Practitioners

It can be concluded from the review of item analysis procedures that the topic has received considerable attention by psychometricians. Their lack of use, however, suggests that little attention has been devoted to item-objective congruence and item statistics by practitioners. The findings of this paper should be encouraging. From a statistical standpoint, the indices that are relatively complex offer few, if any, advantages over the ones that are manually calculable and easily interpretable. The difficulty index and an appropriate discrimination index selected from table 3.3 should provide sufficient information for estimating item validity in most applications. In addition, there is a strong reliance upon teacher judgment throughout the item analysis process in determining item-objective congruence, selecting the criterion groups, and selecting the final set of items.

The step-by-step procedure by which a teacher or evaluator could conduct a criterion-referenced test item analysis is summarized below:

1. Review the items in relation to their instructional and behavioral objectives to determine whether they are valid measures of these objectives. Item-objective congruence should be evaluated according to three criteria: behavior, content, and hierarchical classification. The greatest emphasis should be placed on the third criterion. The Rovinelli-Hambleton index of agreement among content specialists' judgments should be used for tests developed at the district and state levels. Any discrepancies that occur in the analysis should be corrected.
2. Define the criterion of success for the set of items constructed. A teacher should select one class for preinstruction-postinstruction measurements or one uninstructed and one instructed class. At least three or four classes per group should be employed for district- and state-level analyses to provide reliable estimates of the item statistics.
3. Administer the test to the criterion groups.
4. Immediately following the administration to the instructed group, conduct a class discussion of the items and test structure. Use the student feedback to improve the test.
5. Score the items (0,1) for each student in the two groups and assemble the data into two student × item matrices (see tables 3.1 and 3.2).

6. Compute the difficulty index of each item for both uninstructed and instructed groups.
7. Compute the discrimination index for each item. DIS_{PPD}, DIS_{IG}, or DIS_{NG} can be used for preinstruction-postinstruction measurements; DIS_{UIGD} can be used for uninstructed-instructed groups (see table 3.3).
8. Summarize the three item statistics for each item into three lists. A numerical scheme identifying the behavioral objectives to which the items are coded should also be included. An exemplary format is shown in table 3.10.
9. Evaluate the extent to which the items discriminate between masters and nonmasters of each instructional objective. This assessment of item validity should be based on the "guidelines" presented in table 3.6. Good judgment and common sense are an integral part of the assessment in interpreting the item difficulty and discrimination indices in terms of the objective being measured, the students for whom the test was designed, and the instructional program that has occurred. If the statistical item characteristics seem reasonable in view of these considerations, select the item. Items that are questionable should be subjected to further analysis (see table 3.7). This may result in their retention, revision, or elimination.
10. Conduct a choice response analysis of those questionable items in multiple-choice format that are suspected of having internal flaws. This serves to identify the specific defects and guides the item revision process.
11. Assemble the items into the final test. All improvements and changes undertaken as a result of the item validation should be incorporated into this version.

TABLE 3.10. Exemplary Format for Assembling Item Analysis Results

Objective	Item	DIFF$_I$	DIFF$_U$	DIS$_{UIGD}$
1.1	1	100	58	.42
1.1	2	100	54	.46
1.2	3	91	58	.33
1.2	4	86	33	.53
1.3	5	100	33	.67
1.3	6	96	17	.79
1.3	7	86	21	.65
1.3	8	82	8	.74
2.2	9	100	13	.87
2.2	10	100	8	.92
.	.	.	.	.
.	.	.	.	.

References

Barcikowski, R. S., and Patterson, J. L. 1972. A computer program for randomly selecting test items from an item population. *Educational and Psychological Measurement* 32: 795-98.

Berk, R. A. 1976. Determination of optimal cutting scores in criterion-referenced measurement. *Journal of Experimental Education* 45: 4-9.

_____. 1978. A consumers' guide to criterion-referenced test item statistics. *Measurement in Education* 9: 1-8.

_____. 1979a. A critical review of content domain specification/item generation strategies for criterion-referenced tests. Paper presented at the annual meeting of the American Educational Research Association, April 1979, San Francisco.

_____. 1979b. Selection of criterion-referenced test items based on item statistics. Manuscript, The Johns Hopkins University.

Berk, R. A., and Griesemer, H. A. 1976. ITEMAN: An item analysis program for tests, questionnaires, and scales. *Educational and Psychological Measurement* 36: 189-91.

_____. 1977. Change-score item and reliability analyses program. *Applied Psychological Measurement* 1: 40.

Block, J. H., ed. 1971. *Mastery learning: Theory and practice.* New York: Holt, Rinehart and Winston.

Block, J. H., and Burns, R. B. 1976. Mastery learning. In *Review of Research in Education,* ed. L. S. Shulman. Vol. 4. Itasca, Ill.: F. E. Peacock.

Bormuth, J. R. 1970. *On the theory of achievement test items.* Chicago: University of Chicago Press.

Brennan, R. L. 1972. A generalized upper-lower item discrimination index. *Educational and Psychological Measurement* 32: 289-303.

_____. 1974. *The evaluation of mastery test items.* Final Report, Project no. 2B118. Washington, D.C.: National Center for Educational Research and Development, U.S. Office of Education.

Brennan, R. L., and Stolurow, L. M. 1971. An empirical decision process for formative evaluation. Paper presented at the annual meeting of the American Educational Research Association, February 1971, New York.

Carroll, J. B. 1963. A model of school learning. *Teachers College Record* 64: 723-33.

_____. 1970. Problems of measurement related to the concept of learning for mastery. *Educational Horizons* 48: 71-80.

Cox, R. C., and Vargas, J. S. 1966. A comparison of item selection techniques for norm-referenced and criterion-referenced tests. Paper presented at the annual meeting of the National Council on Measurement in Education, February 1966, Chicago.

Crehan, K. D. 1974. Item analysis for teacher-made mastery tests. *Journal of Educational Measurement* 11: 255-62.

Cronbach, L. J. 1971. Test validation. In *Educational measurement,* ed. R. L. Thorndike. 2nd ed. Washington, D.C.: American Council on Education. Pp. 443-507.

_____. 1975. Comment: Dissent from Carver. *American Psychologist* 30: 602-3.

Cronbach, L. J., and Meehl, P. E. 1955. Construct validity in psychological tests. *Psychological Bulletin* 52: 281-302.

Dahl, T. A. 1971. The measurement of congruence between learning objectives and test items. Ph.D. dissertation, University of California, Los Angeles.

Darlington, R. B., and Bishop, C. H. 1966. Increasing test validity by considering inter-item correlations. *Journal of Applied Psychology* 50: 322-30.

Edwards, A. L. 1970. *The measurement of personality traits by scales and inventories.* New York: Holt, Rinehart and Winston.

Engel, J. D., and LaDuca, A. 1977. Validity issues in the development of criterion-referenced tests. Paper presented at the annual meeting of the National Council on Measurement in Education, April 1977, New York.

Epstein, K. I. 1977. Predictive sample reuse and application for criterion-referenced test item analysis. Paper presented at the annual meeting of the American Educational Research Association, April 1977, New York.

Glaser, R. 1963. Instructional technology and the measurement of learning outcomes: Some questions. *American Psychologist* 18: 519-21.

Gorth, W. P., Allen, D. W., and Grayson, A. 1971. Computer programs for test, objective, and item banking. *Educational and Psychological Measurement* 31: 245-50.

Gorth, W. P., and Grayson, A. 1969. A program to compose and print tests for instructional testing using item sampling. *Educational and Psychological Measurement* 29: 173-74.

Haladyna, T. M. 1974. Effects of different samples on item and test characteristics of criterion-referenced tests. *Journal of Educational Measurement* 11: 93-99.

Haladyna, T. M., and Roid, G. 1978. *The role of instructional sensitivity in the empirical review of criterion-referenced test items.* Monmouth, Ore.: Teaching Research Division, Oregon State System of Higher Education.

Hambleton, R. K., Swaminathan, H., Algina, J., and Coulson, D. B. 1978. Criterion-referenced testing and measurement: A review of technical issues and developments. *Review of Educational Research* 48: 1-47.

Hamer, R., and Young, F. W. 1978. TESTER: A computer program to produce individualized multiple-choice tests. *Behavior Research Methods & Instrumentation* 10: 77.

Helmstadter, G. C. 1972. Comparison of traditional item analysis selection procedures with those recommended for tests designed to measure achievement following performance-oriented instruction. Paper presented at the annual meeting of the American Psychological Association, September 1972, Honolulu.

Hemphill, J., and Westie, C. M. 1950. The measurement of group dimensions. *Journal of Psychology* 29: 325-42.

Henrysson, S., and Wedman, I. 1974. Some problems in construction and evaluation of criterion-referenced tests. *Scandinavian Journal of Educational Research* 18: 1-12.

Hively, W., Patterson, H. L., and Page, S. A. 1968. A "universe-defined" system of arithmetic achievement tests. *Journal of Educational Measurement* 5: 275-90.

Hsu, T. C. 1971. Empirical data on criterion-referenced tests. Paper presented at the annual meeting of the American Educational Research Association, February 1971, New York.

Jackson, R. 1970. *Developing criterion-referenced tests.* TM Reports, no. 1. Princeton, N.J.: Educational Testing Service.

Klein, S. P., and Kosecoff, J. B. 1976. Issues and procedures in the development of criterion-referenced tests. In *Readings in measurement and evaluation in education and psychology,* ed. W. A. Mehrens. New York: Holt, Rinehart, and Winston. Pp. 276-93.

Kosecoff, J. B., and Klein, S. P. 1974. *Instructional sensitivity statistics appropriate for objectives-based test items.* CSE Report no. 91. Los Angeles: Center for the Study of Evaluation, University of California.

Levin, L., and Marton, F. 1971. *Provteori och provkonstruktion.* Stockholm: Almqvist & Wiksell.

Lippey, G., ed. 1974. *Computer-assisted test construction.* Englewood Cliffs, N.J.: Educational Technology Publications.

Loevinger, J. 1947. A systematic approach to the construction and evaluation of tests of ability. *Psychological Monograph* 61, no. 4 (Whole No. 285).

Long, J. A. 1934. Improved overlapping methods for determining the validities of test items. *Journal of Experimental Education* 2: 264-68.

Macready, G. B., and Merwin, J. C. 1973. Homogeneity within item forms in domain-referenced testing. *Educational and Psychological Measurement* 33: 351-60.

Marks, E., and Noll, G. A. 1967. Procedures and criteria for evaluating reading and listening comprehension tests. *Educational and Psychological Measurement* 27: 335-48.

Marton, F. 1973. Evalueringsteori och metodik. In *Universitetsundervisning,* ed. G. Handal, L. G. Holmström, and O. B. Thomson. Malmö: Studentlitteratur.

Menne, J. W. 1977. Computer-assisted test construction. *Interchange* 3: 1-6.

Millman, J. 1974. Criterion-referenced measurement. In *Evaluation in education: Current applications,* ed. W. J. Popham. Berkeley, Calif.: McCutchan. Pp. 311-97.

Millman, J., and Popham, W. J. 1974. The issue of item and test variance for criterion-referenced tests: A clarification. *Journal of Educational Measurement* 11: 137-38.

Nitko, A. J. 1974. Problems in the development of criterion-referenced tests: The IPI Pittsburgh experience. In *Problems in criterion-referenced measurement,* ed. C. W. Harris, M. C. Alkin, and W. J. Popham. CSE Monograph Series in Evaluation, no. 3. Los Angeles: Center for the Study of Evaluation, University of California, Pp. 59-82.

Pettie, A. A., and Oosterhof, A. C. 1976. Indices of item adequacy for individually administered mastery tests. Paper presented at the annual meeting of the National Council on Measurement in Education, April 1976, San Francisco.

Popham, W. J. 1971. Indices of adequacy for criterion-referenced test items. In *Criterion-referenced measurement: An introduction,* ed. W. J. Popham. Englewood Cliffs, N.J.: Educational Technology Publications. Pp. 79-98.

Popham, W. J., and Husek, T. R. 1969. Implications of criterion-referenced measurement. *Journal of Educational Measurement* 6: 1-9.

Roudabush, G. E. 1973. Item selection for criterion-referenced tests. Paper presented at the annual meeting of the American Educational Research Association, February 1973, New Orleans.

Rovinelli, R. J., and Hambleton, R. K. 1977. On the use of content specialists in the assessment of criterion-referenced test item validity. *Dutch Journal of Educational Research* 2: 49-60.

Saupe, J. L. 1966. Selecting items to measure change. *Journal of Educational Measurement* 3: 223-28.

Smith, D. U. 1978. The effects of various item selection methods on the classification accuracy and classification consistency of criterion-referenced instruments. Paper presented at the annual meeting of the American Educational Research Association, March 1978, Toronto.

Stanley, J. C. 1967. General and special formulas for reliability of differences. *Journal of Educational Measurement* 4: 249-52.

Tucker, S. B., and Vargas, J. S. 1974. Item analysis of criterion-referenced tests for a large individualized course. Paper presented at the annual meeting of the National Council on Measurement in Education, April 1974, Chicago.

Vargas, J. S. 1969. Item selection techniques for norm-referenced and criterion-referenced tests. Ph.D. dissertation, University of Pittsburgh.

Webster, H. 1956. Maximizing test validity by item selection. *Psychometrika* 21: 153-64.

————. 1957. Item selection methods for increasing test homogeneity. *Psychometrika* 22: 395-403.

Wedman, I. 1973. Reliability, validity and discrimination measures for criterion-referenced tests. *Educational Reports,* Umea no. 4.

White, B. W., and Saltz, E. 1957. The measurement of reproducibility. *Psychological Bulletin* 54: 81-99.

Wiggins, J. S. 1973. *Personality and prediction: Principles of personality assessment.* Reading, Mass.: Addison-Wesley.

Wood, R., and Skurnik, L. S. 1969. *Item banking.* London: National Foundation for Educational Research in England and Wales.

Woodson, M.I.C.E. 1968. Computer program produces forms with randomly selected and ordered items. *Educational and Psychological Measurement* 28:857-58.

Zieky, M. J., 1973. *Methods of setting standards for criterion-referenced item sets.* Princeton, N.J.: Educational Testing Service.

4

TEST SCORE VALIDITY
AND STANDARD-SETTING METHODS

Ronald K. Hambleton

Introduction

Numerous useful contributions to the criterion-referenced testing
literature have been made since the late 1960s (for reviews, see Hambleton et al. 1978, Millman 1974, Popham 1978*b*), but criterion-referenced test score validity remains an essentially unexplored topic. This is
surprising because of its importance. Only a few researchers have attempted to clarify the scope of the topic, to resolve any of the complex
problems, or to offer practitioners guidelines for validating criterion-referenced test scores (Linn 1979, Messick 1975, Millman 1974, Popham
1975). This state of affairs must be changed, since millions of individuals
at every level of education are administered criterion-referenced tests
every day in diverse settings (for example, schools, businesses, and the
military). Criterion-referenced tests are used to monitor individual progress through objectives-based instructional programs, to diagnose learning deficiencies, to evaluate educational and social action programs,
and to assess competence on certification and licensing examinations.
But the usefulness of these and other applications depends directly on

Originally published as *Laboratory of Psychometric and Evaluative Research Report No.
85* (Amherst, Mass.: School of Education, University of Massachusetts, 1978). The project
reported here was performed persuant to a grant from the National Institute of Education,
Department of Health, Education, and Welfare. However, the opinions expressed in it do
not necessarily reflect the position or policy of the National Institute of Education, and no
official endorsement by the National Institute of Education should be inferred.

the validity of the descriptions, decisions, and interpretations of the test scores.

It would seem that most criterion-referenced test developers have assumed the validity of their test scores rather than establishing it in any formal way. A colleague and I recently completed a review of twelve commercially prepared criterion-referenced tests (Hambleton & Eignor 1978). Not even one of the test manuals we reviewed included a discussion of what we felt was a satisfactory test score validity investigation. In the area of criterion-referenced testing technology (or competency testing, as it is sometimes called), validity considerations arise at three steps: (1) the selection of objectives (or competencies), (2) the measurement of objectives included in a criterion-referenced test, and (3) the uses of test scores. The first area will not be covered in this chapter and the second will be discussed only with respect to objectively scored test items.

The purposes of this chapter are (1) to review several criterion-referenced test score validity issues, (2) to offer methods for conducting validation studies of criterion-referenced test scores, (3) to review methods of standard setting, (4) to offer suggestions for research and development efforts, and (5) to offer several guidelines for conducting validation and standard-setting studies. The purpose of the first section, steps in test development and validation, is to provide a framework for the material that will be considered in the remainder of the chapter.

Steps in Test Development and Validation

A twelve-step model for developing and validating criterion-referenced tests is presented in figure 4.1 (from Hambleton & Eignor 1979a). The importance of each step in the model depends upon the size and scope of the test development and validation project. An agency with the responsibility of producing a statewide criterion-referenced test will proceed through the steps in a rather different way from a small consulting firm or a school district.

In brief, the twelve steps are as follows:

1. Objectives or domain specifications must be prepared or selected before the test development process can begin.
2. Test specifications are needed to clarify the test's purposes, desirable test item formats, number of test items, instructions to item writers, etc.
3. Test items are written to measure the objectives included in a test (or tests, if parallel forms are required).
4. Initial editing of test items is completed by the individuals writing them.

5. A systematic assessment of items prepared in steps 2 and 3 is conducted to determine their match to the objectives they were written to measure and to determine their "representativeness."
6. Based on the data from step 5, additional item editing is done. Also, test items are discarded that do not at least adequately measure the objectives they were written to measure.
7. The test(s) is assembled.
8. A method for setting standards to interpret examinee performance is selected and implemented.
9. The test(s) is administered.
10. Data addressing reliability, validity, and norms are collected and analyzed.
11. A user's manual and technical manual are prepared.
12. A final step is included to reinforce the point that it is necessary, in an on-going way, to be compiling technical data on the test items and tests as they are used in different situations with different examinee populations.

Attention in this chapter is concentrated on steps 5a, 7b, 8, and part of 10 in figure 4.1.

Review of Validity Issues

Many criterion-referenced test developers have argued that to "validate" their tests and test scores it is sufficient to assess their "content validity." This usually means that judgments are made concerning the match between the content of a test and the objectives to be measured by that test. Since the analysis is in terms of test content, the expression "content validity" is used. It is clear that content validity is a characteristic or description of the test. It does not vary in different samples of examinees or over time. However, descriptions of an examinee's level of performance or instructional decisions (assignment of examinees to "mastery states") in several skill or knowledge areas are made from examinee responses to the test items. It is possible that these responses do not adequately reflect or address the skills of interest. For example, consider the case of a criterion-referenced test that is administered, perhaps by mistake, under highly speeded testing conditions. The validity of any descriptions or decisions based on test scores obtained from the test administration will be lower than if the test had been administered with a suitable time limit. The content validity of the test does not depend on the speed of test administrations, but the validity of any use of the scores does. Clearly, content validity evidence is not sufficient to establish "validity of criterion-referenced test score uses."

As obvious and important as the point is about the necessity of val-

1. Preparation and/or selection of objectives
2. Preparation of test specifications (for example, available time, selection of objectives to be measured by the test, number of test items/domain specification, appropriate vocabulary, method of scoring)
3. Writing test items "matched" to objectives
4. Preliminary review of test items
5. Determination of content validity of the test items
   (a) Involvement of content specialists
   (b) Collection and analysis of examinee response data
6. Additional editing of test items
7. Test assembly
   (a) Determination of number of test items/domain specification
   (b) Test item selection
   (c) Preparation of directions and sample questions
   (d) Layout and test booklet preparation
   (e) Preparation of scoring keys
   (f) Preparation of answer sheets
8. Setting standards for interpreting examinee test performance
9. Test administrations
10. Assessment of test score reliability and validity; complilation of test score norms (optional)
11. Preparation of a user's manual and a technical manual
12. Periodic collection of additional technical information

FIGURE 4.1. Steps for Developing Criterion-Referenced Tests and Validating Test Score Uses

idating each criterion-referenced test score use in groups and situations where the test is used, it has been neglected or missed by many criterion-referenced test developers (and I include myself among the misinformed). Cronbach (1971) made the point clearly but his paper was not in the mainstream of the criterion-referenced testing literature and therefore its relevance was not noted. The lesson was most clearly brought to the attention of educators by Messick (1975) and Linn (1979). Messick (1975) wrote:

> The major problem ... is that content validity ... is focused upon test *forms* rather than test *scores,* upon *instruments* rather than *measurements.* Inferences in educational and psychological measurment are made from scores, and scores are a function of subject responses. Any concept of validity of measurement must include reference to empirical consistency. Content coverage is an important consideration in test construction and interpretation, to be sure, but in itself it does not provide validity. Call it "content relevance," if you will, or "content representativeness," but don't call it "content validity," because it doesn't provide evidence for the interpretation of responses or scores. (Pp. 960-61)

Linn (1979) makes a similar point: "Questions of validity are questions for the soundness of the interpretations of a measure.... Thus, it is the interpretation rather than the measure that is validated. Measurement results may have many interpretations which differ in their degree of validity and in the type of evidence required for the validation process" (p. 109).

Both Messick and Linn have argued strongly for the construct validation of criterion-referenced test scores. They have stressed the need for evidence of the validity of the intended interpretation and use of any set of test scores. Fortunately, there is a wide assortment of methods (intratest, intertest, experimental, prediction) that can be used to marshall validity evidence in favor of the intended uses of a set of test scores. Of course, accumulating construct validation evidence is a never-ending process. The amount of time and energy that is expended in the direction of construct validation must be consistent with the importance of the testing program. Criterion-referenced tests that are being used to monitor student progress in a curriculum on a day-to-day basis should demand less of our time, obviously, than tests that will be used to determine whether or not students graduate from high school.

The resolution of the validity question with criterion-referenced tests and test scores would seem to be this: a content validity study is completed at the test development stage, and the content validity of a criterion-referenced test will influence the kinds of test score interpretation that are possible. Also, it is most important to conduct construct validation studies to validate the intended use of the test scores. The nature of those studies will depend on the different uses of the scores.

In spite of its stated importance, it cannot be argued either that the nature of content validation studies with criterion-referenced tests is well understood. Guion (1977), for one, discusses many of the problems surrounding the topic. It is only recently that any progress (i.e., the development and field testing of content validation methods with criterion-referenced tests) has been made (Millman 1974, Popham 1978b, Rovinelli & Hambleton 1977).

In summary, content validation studies will be necessary to address the content relevance of a test (i.e., the match between item content and the objectives the items are written to measure). Also, construct validation studies are required to assess the validity of test scores for accomplishing their intended uses. Finally, if the criterion-referenced test scores are being used to make decisions (i.e., to assign examinees to "mastery states"), the validity of these classifications must also be established. Among other things, the method of establishing a standard must be evaluated, and criterion groups must be defined and their performance on the test in relation to the standard must be studied.

Content Validity. Content validity has proven to be a fuzzy and confusing concept, even for norm-referenced test developers. Guion (1977) prefers the term *content representativeness* to *content validity* because the former expression is more descriptive. *Content* is broadly defined to include material from the cognitive, affective, and psychomotor domains.

Perhaps first it is necessary to define what is meant by a domain specification and to explain how this concept differs from that of a behavioral objective. In recent years, it has been very popular to write instructional objectives in "behavioral" terms. However, while behavioral objectives have some desirable features (for example, they are relatively easy to produce), they often lack sufficient clarity to permit a clear determination of the domain of test items measuring the behaviors intended to be defined by an objective. If the proper domain of test items measuring an objective is not clear, it is impossible to select a representative sample of test items from *that* domain. Representative samples of test items measuring each objective included in a test are necessary to obtain unbiased estimates of examinee performance in the full domain of behaviors measuring each objective.

What is to be done? Certainly, behavioral objectives are better than no objectives at all. On the other hand, more useful than behavioral objectives are "amplified" objectives. According to Millman (1974, p. 335), "An amplified objective is an expanded statement of an educational goal which provides boundary specifications regarding testing situations, response alternatives, and criteria of correctness." The importance of these additional guidelines to a behavioral objective is that they help to define the appropriate domain of test items. There is still some ambiguity in the domain definition, but the situation is considerably improved over using behavioral objectives.

Domain specifications are another new development in the field of criterion-referenced testing introduced by Popham (1975). An excellent example is offered in chapter 1. A domain specification clarifies the intended content spanned by an objective. A domain can be thought of as a collection or set of well-defined skills organized around a broader skill. Of interest is an examinee's level of performance in relation to the domain of skills. There are at least four steps outlined by Popham for the development of a domain specification (see chapter 1). It should be noted that there appear to be several other promising ways for test developers to define the content domain keyed to each objective of interest (see Millman, chapter 2). These include facet theory (Berk 1978), item transformations (Anderson 1972), and algorithms (Scandura 1977).

Perhaps the best examples of domain specifications to date are those prepared by Ebel (1962) and by Hively, Patterson, and Page (1968). Their work is based on two requirements: (*a*) all the items that could be written from the content domain to be tested must be written (or known)

in advance of the final item selection process, and (b) a random or stratified random sampling procedure must be used in the item selection
process. One way to achieve these two requirements is through the process of *item forms analysis*. An item form is actually a process having
the following characteristics: it generates items with a fixed syntactical
structure, it contains one or more variable elements, and it defines a
class of item sentences by specifying the replacement sets for the variable elements. One of the obvious advantages of such a system is that
the workload that would be required in writing the larger number of
items needed to satisfy the conditions for generalizability would be reduced.

The Hively, Patterson, and Page (1968) study is important in that it
demonstrated that it was possible to develop and use item generation
rules to construct a test. This study also underscored one of the major
weaknesses of item generation procedures—the procedures are more
easily employed with highly structured subject matter areas such as
mathematics. Unfortunately, we are unlikely to be able to produce the
clarity of domain specifications offered by Ebel and by Hively and his
colleagues in many of the content areas of interest to educators.

The importance of having well-written domain specifications (or amplified objectives) cannot be overemphasized. Popham (1974) described
the problem clearly. When the domain of items measuring an objective
is unclear (or unspecified, as with objectives-referenced tests), only the
weakest form of a criterion-referenced test score interpretation is possible. Test performance must be interpreted in terms of the *particular*
items included in a test. A generalization of examinee performance to
a larger class of behaviors (a "strong" interpretation) is *not* warranted.
When users of objectives-referenced tests make unwarranted generaliza-
tions, it leads to what Popham has called "cloud-referenced interpretations."

Test items can be written once a domain specification has been prepared. Determination of content validity involves a consideration of
three features of the test items: (1) item validities (i.e., the extent to
which each test item actually measures some aspect of the content included in a domain specification), (2) technical quality, and (3) representativeness. These three features will be considered individually.

Item validity. Generally speaking, the quality of criterion-referenced
test items can be determined by the extent to which they reflect, in terms
of their content, the domains from which they were derived. The problem here is one of item validation; unless one can say with a high degree of confidence that the items in a criterion-referenced test measure
the intended instructional objectives, any use of the test score informa-

tion will be questionable. Thus far, the possible use of *item generation forms, amplified objectives,* and *domain specifications* has been considered. When item generation rules are used, a high degree of confidence in terms of items measuring intended objectives is derived through the direct relationship set up between items and the domain. This might be called an a priori approach to item validity; the approach itself assures that the items are valid, or representative of the domains. When amplified objectives or domain specifications are utilized, the domain definitions are never really precise enough to assume, a priori, that the items are valid. Thus, the quality of the items, in a context independent of the process by which the items were generated, must be determined. This is an a posteriori approach to item validation, and the procedures to be discussed are designed to assess whether or not a direct relationship between an item and a domain or objective exists through analysis of data collected after items are written.

There are two general approaches that may be used to establish the content validity of criterion-referenced test items. The first approach, and the approach I feel holds the most merit, involves the judgments of test items by content specialists. These judgments concern the extent of match between the test items and the domains they are designed to measure. The question asked of content specialists about the content validity of test items is this: Is the format and content of an item appropriate to measure some part of the domain specification?

The second approach is to apply empirical techniques in much the same way as empirical techniques are applied in norm-referenced test development. In fact, along with some recently developed empirical procedures for criterion-referenced tests, several norm-referenced test item statistics can (and should) be used. The problem is to ensure that these statistics are used and interpreted correctly in the context of criterion-referenced test development. There are at least four problems involved with the use of empirical procedures. First, most, if not all, of the procedures are dependent upon the characteristics of the group of examinees and the effects of instruction. Second, they often require sophisticated techniques and/or computer programs that are not available to practitioners. Third, when item statistics derived from empirical analyses of test data are used to select items for a criterion-referenced test, the test developer runs the considerable risk of obtaining a nonrepresentative set of items from the domains measuring the objectives included in the test. Last, empirical methods in many instances require pretest and posttest data on the same items. Pretest data are rarely collected. One reason is that there is a reluctance to administer tests to examinees where there is little chance of moderate or high levels of performance.

It is often argued that item discrimination indices will be low, and therefore they will be of limited usefulness. On the contrary, numerous researchers have reported that there is usually sufficient test score variance to permit variation (and nonzero values) among item discrimination indices. Also, test score variance can be assured by the selection of a proper item pilot study sample. Both "masters" and "nonmasters" of the content under study should be located and included in a pilot sample. However, even though studies can be designed so that all item discrimination indices will not (in general) be low, I am not recommending that considerable effort be expended to design and carry out these types of studies. The fact is that empirical data are not very useful for answering the content validity question introduced earlier, and therefore empirical methods have limited usefulness. On the other hand, when construct validity evidence is being sought, examinee response data is *exactly* what is needed.

Empirical methods do have one important use in the content validation process. According to Rovinelli and Hambleton (1977), "In situations where the test constructor is interested in identifying aberrant items, not for elimination from the item pool but for correction, the use of an empirical approach to item validation should provide important information with regard to the assessment of item validity" (p. 51).

In sum, obtaining content specialists' ratings is the method to use for assessing item validities; empirical procedures should be used for the detection of aberrant items in need of correction. An excellent review of item statistics for use with criterion-referenced tests was prepared by Berk (see chapter 3).

Three techniques for the collection and analysis of the judgments of test items by content specialists will be described next. Additional techniques are offered by Popham (1978b). Rovinelli and Hambleton (1977) demonstrated that content specialists can provide meaningful ratings using the strategies sketched below. They reported one useful procedure for studying item validity. The method for collecting data consists of having content specialists judge each item on each of the objectives by assigning a value of $+1$, 0, or -1. A rating of $+1$ indicates a definite feeling that an item is a measure of the objective; 0 shows that the judge is undecided about whether the item is a measure of the objective; -1 shows a definite feeling that an item is *not* a measure of the objective. The content specialists' task is to make a judgment about whether or not a test item reflects the content defined by a domain specification. If, for example, there are ten objectives and five test items/ domain specifications, each content specialist is required to make 500 judgments.

Rovinelli and Hambleton also developed a statistic for providing a numerical representation of the data. They called this statistic the index of item-objective congruence. The assumptions under which this index was developed are: (1) that perfect item-objective congruence should be represented by a value of $+1$ and will occur when all the specialists assign a $+1$ to the item for the appropriate objective and a -1 to the item for all the other objectives; (2) that the worst value of the index an item can receive should be represented by a value of -1 and will occur when all the specialists assign a -1 to the item for the appropriate objective and a $+1$ to the item for all the other objectives; and (3) that the value of the index should not depend on the number of content specialists or the number of objectives.

The index of item-objective congruence is given by

$$I_{ik} = \frac{(N - 1) \sum\limits_{j=1}^{n} X_{ijk} - \sum\limits_{i=1}^{N} \sum\limits_{j=1}^{n} X_{ijk} + \sum\limits_{j=1}^{n} X_{ijk}}{2(N - 1)n}$$

where: I_{ik} is the index of item-objective congruence for item k on objective i,

N is the number of objectives ($i = 1, 2, \cdots, N$),

n is the number of content specialists ($j = 1, 2, \cdots, n$),

X_{ijk} is the rating (-1, 0, $+1$) of item k as a measure of objective i by content specialist j.

The choice of a cut-off score to separate "valid" from "nonvalid" items with the index should be based on experience with content specialists' ratings and with the index itself. In my work, when I feel it desirable to set a cut-off score, I create the poorest set of content specialists' ratings that I would be willing to accept as evidence that an item was in the domain of interest. The value of the index for this set of minimally acceptable ratings serves as the cut-off score for judging the item-objective match of each of the test items. For example, suppose that there are twenty content specialists and ten objectives. I might desire that at least fifteen of the content specialists match the item to the intended objective and that they indicate that the item is not a measure of the other nine objectives. In this case, the index of item-objective congruence would be .75, and so .75 would serve as the criterion against which I would judge items from the content specialists' ratings. With large-scale and/or important test development projects it would be desirable to involve a group of individuals in the process for setting cut-off scores.

The one major drawback to the approach is that it is very time consuming. Even if content specialists are assigned only a portion of the domain specifications and test items to review, the time required to judge the validity of each set of test items as a measure of each domain specification can be substantial.

A second procedure for assessing item-objective match involves the use of a *rating scale*. Content specialists are given an objective or domain specification and a set of test items. Their task is to judge the quality of test items as measures of the intended objectives or domain specifications. A copy of a judge's rating form is presented in appendix A.

The rating scale data may be analyzed without employing any elaborate statistical procedures. Therefore, the scale can easily be used in practical settings, such as by teachers in the classroom. The information needed is the mean and median rating assigned to the items by a group of content specialists. However, the data also lends itself to more elaborate statistical analysis, if that is desired. An examination of the range of the ratings given each item provides an indication of the extent of agreement among the content specialists.

It is also possible to determine the "closeness" of each judge's ratings to the median responses of the group of judges. When one or more of the judges is far out of line and there is evidence of carelessness on the part of the judge, for example, it may be best to eliminate the response and recalculate the statistics. A summary and analysis of the hypothetical ratings of nine judges on fourteen test items measuring four objectives is shown in table 4.1.

A third procedure that can be used to obtain the judgments of content specialists involves the use of a *matching task*. Content specialists are presented with two lists, one with test items and the other with objectives or domain specifications. The content specialist's task is to indicate which objective he or she thinks each test item measures (if any). A contingency table can then be constructed by calculating the number of content specialists matching each item to each objective in the sets of items and objectives being studied. The chi-square test for independence is commonly used to analyze data that are presented in a contingency table format. Also, a visual analysis of the contingency table will reveal the amount of agreement among the specialists and the type and location of disagreements. An example of a judge's summary sheet for the items/objectives matching task is presented in appendix B. Some hypothetical results are reported in table 4.2.

The "accuracy" of each content specialist can be checked if a specified number of "bad" items (i.e., items not measuring any of the objectives) is introduced into the matching task. A content specialist's effectiveness can be measured by the number of such items detected. However, this method of evaluation would tend to favor the overly critical content specialist. The item ratings of content specialists who do not achieve some minimum level of performance in detecting "bad" test items can be removed from the analysis.

TABLE 4.1. Summary of Judges' Ratings of Fourteen Test Items

Objective	Test Item	Judges' Ratings									Summary Statistics		
		1	2	3	4	5	6	7	8	9	Mean	Median	Range
1	2	4	3	5	5	4	5	5	5	4	4.4	5	3
	7	4	2	5	5	5	5	5	4	5	4.4	5	4
	14	4	5	5	5	4	5	5	5	5	4.8	5	2
2	1	3	5	3	2	1	4	5	2	4	3.2	3	5
	3	3	1	4	4	3	4	4	3	3	3.2	3	4
	8	1	3	1	2	1	1	1	1	1	1.3	1	3
	13	1	3	2	1	1	2	1	2	3	1.8	2	3
3	4	4	5	5	4	5	5	5	5	5	4.8	5	2
	6	4	2	4	4	4	4	4	4	4	3.8	4	3
	12	5	3	5	5	5	5	5	5	5	4.8	5	3
4	5	4	3	5	5	4	5	5	4	5	4.4	5	3
	9	2	2	4	1	4	2	4	4	4	3.0	4	4
	10	1	3	1	2	1	1	1	1	1	1.3	1	3
	11	4	3	4	4	5	5	5	5	5	4.6	5	3
Judges' discrepancies from median responses		9	24	2	10	6	4	4	3	3			

TABLE 4.2. Summary of the Judges' Item/Objective Matching Task

Objective	Test Item	Judges' Matches									Percentage of Matches for Each Test Item
		1	2	3	4	5	6	7	8	9	
1	2	1[a]	0	1	0	1	1	1	1	1	78
	7	1	1	1	0	1	1	1	1	1	89
	14	0	1	1	1	1	1	1	1	1	89
2	1	0	0	1	1	1	1	1	1	1	78
	3	1	1	1	1	1	1	1	1	0	89
	8	1	0	1	0	0	0	0	1	0	33
	13	0	0	1	0	0	0	0	0	0	11
3	4	1	0	1	1	1	1	1	1	1	89
	6	0	0	1	0	1	0	1	1	0	44
	12	1	1	1	1	1	1	1	1	1	100
4	5	1	0	1	1	1	1	1	1	1	89
	9	1	1	1	1	0	0	1	1	1	78
	10	0	0	1	0	0	0	0	0	0	11
	11	1	1	1	1	1	1	1	1	0	89
Percentage of matches for each judge		64	43	100	64	71	64	79	86	57	
"Lemons"	1	0[b]	1	0	0	1	0	0	0	0	
	2	1	1	0	1	0	0	0	0	0	
	3	1	1	0	0	0	0	0	0	0	
Number of "lemons" not identified		2	3	0	1	1	0	0	0	0	

[a] A score of "0" means that the judge did not match the test item to the objective it was developed to measure. A score of "1" means that the judge did make the expected match.

[b] A score of "0" means that the judge did not match the "lemon" item to any of the objectives. A score of "1" means that the judge did match the "lemon" item to one of the objectives.

In summary, data from all of the procedures sketched out in this section are useful for addressing item validity. The data derived from any one of the procedures can be used to answer the important ques-tions, Which items failed to "match" the domain specification they were prepared to measure? How successful were the test item writers? How can the validity data on the test items be used to rewrite domain specifications? and Who were the "best" content specialists in the rating process?

Technical quality of test items. The technical quality of test items can be established at the same time as test items are being reviewed for their "match" to the domain specification they were written to measure. An example of a technical review form for multiple-choice test items is presented in appendix C. It is straightforward to tailor technical review forms for other item formats as well (see, for example, Hambleton & Eignor 1979a). One criticism of the technical review form in appendix C is that it is cumbersome when many test items must be reviewed. The directions and technical review form in appendix D and E, respectively, are substantially more convenient. It has been well received by the school districts in which it has been field tested. (The last question [question 19] concerns item validity, but it was included on the technical review form by the content specialists for convenience.)

Representativeness of the test items. This step cannot be completed until the test items to be included in a test have been selected.

It is usually desirable to have test items in a criterion-referenced test that are representative of the domain of items specified in a domain specification. However, only in some highly special cases has it been possible to specify completely a pool of valid test items. For example, there have been some successes in the areas of reading, mathematics, and spelling. But these examples are far removed from the content worlds of interpretative poetry, creative writing, and finite projective geometry. What, then, is to be done?

For starters, test developers need to work hard to develop domain specifications. If relevant content is described clearly, content specialists can make a judgment about the representativeness of items included in a test. A grid can be developed to describe the content in a domain specification, and test items can be selected either to be representative of the domain or at random, and a judgment can be made by content specialists about the representativeness of the selected test items. When representativeness has not been achieved, new test items must be added and others removed from a test.

Another procedure is to carry out Cronbach's duplication experiment.

This requires two teams of equally competent item writers and reviewers to work independently in developing a criterion-referenced test. Cronbach's (1971) directions are: "They would be aided by the same definition of relevant content, sampling rules, instructions to reviewers, and specifications for tryout and interpretation of the data" (p. 456).

If the domain specification is clear, and if sampling is representative, the two tests should be equivalent. Equivalence of forms can be checked be administering both tests to the same group of examinees and comparing the two sets of examinee test scores. One problem with the approach is that "a common blind spot is almost impossible to detect" (Cronbach 1971, p. 456).

Construct Validity. Criterion-referenced test scores are used frequently to make descriptions of examinee levels of performance in the content areas measured by a test and to make decisions. However, it is essential to establish the validity of the descriptions and decisions. Content validity evidence is not sufficient since it pertains to the content of the test, whereas descriptions and decisions are made based on examinee *responses* to the test items. For example, a set of test items, on the basis of content considerations, may appear to be measuring understanding, whereas they are actually measuring recall of factual information. Clearly, it is essential to establish the content representativeness of a set of test items, but the usefulness of a set of criterion-referenced test scores (or for that matter, scores obtained from any test) must be determined by a carefully designed series of construct validation investigations. Messick (1975) has offered a useful definition of construct validation: "Construct validation is the process of marshaling evidence in the form of theoretically relevant empirical relations to support the inference that an observed response consistency has a particular meaning" (p. 955).

Messick (1975) offered several explanations for why construct validation studies have not been more common in eduational measurement. For one, content validity of criterion-referenced tests was seen as sufficient. Second, criterion-referenced test score distributions are often homogeneous (for example, it often happens that before instruction most individuals do poorly on a test and after instruction most individuals do well). Correlational methods do not work very well with homogeneous distributions of scores because of score range restrictions. But, as Messick (1975) has noted, "construct validation is by no means limited to correlation coefficients, even though it may seem that way from the prevalence of correlation matrices, internal consistency indices, and factor analysis" (p. 958).

Construct validation studies should begin with a definite statement of the proposed use of the test scores. A clearly stated use will provide direction for the kind of evidence that is worth collecting. Cronbach (1971, p. 483) says, "Investigations to be used for construct validation, then, should be purposeful rather than haphazard." Later, when all of the data are collected and analyzed, a final conclusion as to the validity of the intended use (or uses) of the test scores can be offered.

Kirsch and Guthrie (1979) have reported a construct validation investigation of functional literacy test scores. In view of the importance being accorded this type of examination, such investigations are long overdue. Their paper is an outstanding example of what can and should be done to validate the intended uses of criterion-referenced test scores. Kirsch and Guthrie studied the effects of six cognitive processes on test performance and investigated the significance of the effects across groups with different educational backgrounds and family income levels. They concluded their paper with the following comment:

> Understanding the requisite abilities needed for completing tasks relating to personal, social, and occupational reading demands is an important step toward developing functional literacy tests that are valid with respect to psychological processes, as well as content coverages. We suggest that construct, as well as content, validity is required for measurement and program development in functional literacy. (P. 44)

Let us hope that there will be many more studies along the lines of the one by Kirsch and Guthrie, for they have provided an excellent model of what should be done.

Some of the investigations that could be conducted will be reviewed next. Others are reviewed by Cronbach (1971).

Guttman scalogram analysis. It frequently occurs that objectives can be arranged linearly or hierarchically. Guttman scaling is a relevant procedure for the construct validation of criterion-referenced test scores in situations where the objectives can be organized into either a linear or a hierarchical sequence. To use Guttman's scalogram analysis as a technique in a test score validation methodology, one would first need to specify the hierarchical structure of a set of objectives. To the extent that examinee objective scores[1] in the hierarchy are predictable from a knowledge of the hierarchy, one would have evidence to support the construct validity of the objective scores. On the other hand, in situations where examinee objective scores are not predictable, one of three situations has occurred: the hierarchy is incorrectly specified, the objective scores are not valid measures of the intended objectives, or a combination of the two explanations.

---

[1]An examinee objective score is obtained by summing his or her scores on items that measure the particular objective.

More precise specifications for the utilization of Guttman scaling will, of course, be needed before the method can be fully implemented in the validation process for criterion-referenced test scores. By substituting item scores for objective scores, Guttman scaling can also be used to assess item validities.

Factor analysis. While factor analysis is a commonly employed procedure for the dimensional analysis of items in a norm-referenced test, or of scores derived from different norm-referenced tests, it has rarely, if ever, been used in construct validation studies of criterion-referenced test scores. Perhaps one reason for its lack of use is that the usual input for factor analytic studies are correlations, and correlations are often low between items on a criterion-referenced test or between criterion-referenced test scores and other variables because score variability is often not very great. However, the problem can be remedied by choosing a sample of examinees with a wide range of ability, for example, a group of masters and nonmasters. The research problem in the language of factor analysis becomes a problem of determining whether or not the factor pattern matrix has a prescribed form. One would expect to obtain as many factors in a factor solution as there are objectives covered in a test, and with items "loading" on only the factor (or objective) that they were designed to measure. Items deviating from this pattern could be carefully studied for flaws.

Similarly, objective scores from many criterion-referenced tests could be factor analyzed and the resulting structure could be compared to some structure specifying a theoretical relationship among the objectives. Correlational studies among examinee scores on different objectives measured by a criterion-referenced test or among objective scores from other tests can be revealing.

Sources of invalidity. There are many sources of error that reduce the validity of an intended use of a set of criterion-referenced test scores. Suppose, for example, that an examinee was estimated to have an 80 percent level of performance on a test measuring "ability to identify the main idea in paragraphs." Is the test score valid for the intended interpretation? An answer depends on the answers to several other questions:

1. Were the test directions clear to the student?
2. Did the student have a problem using the answer sheet?
3. Was the test administered under speeded testing conditions?
4. Was the student motivated to perform to the best of his or her ability?

5. Was the content of the paragraph interesting to the student?
6. Was the choice of vocabulary suitable?
7. Did test-taking skills play any role in the student's test performance?
8. Was the item format suitable for measuring the desired skill?
9. Was the scheduling of the test at a proper time during the day?

To the extent that any of these and many other factors influence test scores, the usefulness of the test scores is reduced.

Experimental studies of potential sources of error to determine their effect on test scores are an important way to assess the construct validity of a set of test scores. Logical analyses and observations of testing methods and procedures can also be used to detect sources of invalidity in a set of test scores.

Criterion-related validity. Even if scores derived from criterion-referenced tests are descriptive of the objectives they are supposed to reflect, the usefulness of the scores as predictors of, say "job success" or "success in the next unit of instruction" cannot be assured. Criterion-related validity studies of criterion-referenced test scores are no different in procedure from studies conducted with norm-referenced tests. Correlational, group separation, and decision accuracy methods are commonly used (Cronbach 1971).

Experimental methods. Another solution, albeit costly, is to design experiments to assess the construct validity of criterion-referenced test scores. For example, suppose individuals are randomly assigned to one of two groups, one receiving instruction on content contained in a domain specification and the other not. If the treatment is effective, and this could be determined from past experience with the program, higher test scores by the experimental group would support the construct validity hypothesis. Numerous experiments could be conducted, alternating control and experimental groups, so that no single group of examinees would be denied instruction. With more broadly defined competencies, the test performance of individuals assumed to have the competencies could be compared with those that do not.

Decision validity. Criterion-referenced test scores are commonly used to make decisions. In instructional settings, examinees are assumed to be "masters" if their test performance exceeds a minimum level of performance (often referred to as a standard). On the basis of examinee criterion-referenced test performance, decisions concerning high school graduation in many states are being made. These are two of the many examples of decision making with criterion-referenced test scores.

Decision validity, which is simply a particular kind of construct validity, involves (1) the setting of a standard of test performance and (2) the comparison of test performance of two or more criterion groups in relation to the specified standard. Instructional decisions based on classroom criterion-referenced test scores can be validated by comparing the test performance, in relation to a standard of performance of two criterion groups—those who have received instruction and those who have not. Alternatively, two groups might be formed by asking teachers to identify students whom they are certain have an excellent grasp of the skills measured by the test under study and those students who do not. Decision validity on each objective may be assessed by summing the percentage of instructed students who exceed the performance standard and of the uninstructed students who do not. The assumption is that these are the groups who are correctly classified by the testing procedure.

This situation is depicted in figure 4.2. If the standard is set by a group of content specialists at, say, five test items, 74 percent of the students will be "correctly" classified. Of course, the statement is not strictly true, for some of the uninstructed students will have knowledge of the content covered by the test and some of the students in the instructed group will not. The necessity of assuming that all uninstructed students are "nonmasters" and all instructed students are "masters" is one of the limitations of this approach for assessing decision validity.

With high school graduation examinations, it may be possible for teachers to identify two extreme groups—one group consisting of students they are certain have the required competencies to graduate from high school and a second group of students that do not. Borderline students would not be included in a study of this type. Again, the test is administered and the percentage of students who are correctly classified by the testing procedure is calculated and used as an estimate of decision validity.

The advantage of the procedure outlined is that decision validity is reported in a readily interpretable way (percentage of correct decisions). Alternatively, the correlation between two dichotomous variables (group membership and the mastery decision) can be reported and used as an index of decision validity. Other possible statistics are reported by Berk (1976), Hambleton and Eignor (1979a), and Popham (1978b).

Decision validity information is, of course, only reported in those situations where criterion-referenced test scores are being used to make decisions. Still, decision validity evidence is not usually sufficient to establish the construct validity of a set of test scores. Other types of investigation should be carried out as well.

Finally, decision validity will depend on several important factors:

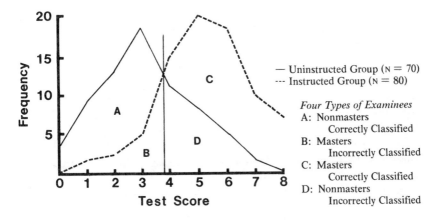

FIGURE 4.2. Frequency polygons of criterion-referenced test scores for two groups (an instructed group and an uninstructed group on the content measured by the test)

(1) the quality of the test under investigation, (2) the appropriateness of the criterion groups, (3) the examinee group, and (4) the minimum level of performance required for mastery (or competence) sometimes called a standard or a cut-off score. Because of the central role of "standards" in using criterion-referenced tests, that topic will be considered in detail in the next section.

Review of Methods for Standard Setting[2]

One of the primary purposes of criterion-referenced testing is to provide data for decision making. Sometimes the decisions are made by classroom teachers concerning the monitoring of student progress through a curriculum. On other occasions, promotion, certification, and/or graduation decisions are made by school, district, and state administrators.

Three topics will be considered in this section: (1) uses of standards, (2) standard-setting methods, and (3) some procedural steps in standard setting.

Uses of Standards. A standard is a point on a test score scale that is used to "sort" examinees into two categories that reflect different levels of proficiency relative to a particular objective (or set of objectives)

[2] The author is grateful to Daniel Eignor and Sally Powell for help in preparing this section of the paper.

measured by a test. It is common to assign labels such as "master" and "nonmaster" to examinees assigned to the two categories.[3] It is not unusual either to assign examinees to more than two categories based on their test performance (i.e., sometimes multiple cut-off scores are used to enable assignment of examinees to one of several levels of proficiency) or to use standards that vary from one objective to another; this may be done when it is felt that certain objectives differ in their importance.

Three types of *standard* are set with criterion-referenced test scores. The following example (Hambleton 1978, pp. 279–80) provides a framework for considering them: "School district A has set the following target—It desires to have 85% or more of its students in the second grade achieve 90% of the reading objectives at a standard of performance equal to or better than 80%." The standards involved in the example are:

1. The 80 percent standard is used to interpret examinee performance on each of the objectives measured by the test.
2. The 90 percent standard is used to interpret examinee performance across all of the objectives measured by the test.
3. The 85 percent standard is applied to the performance of second graders on the set of objectives measured by the test.

Only the first use of standards will be considered further here.

Why are cut-off scores needed? Four questions arise in connection with standards or cut-off scores. An answer to this first question depends on the intended use (or uses) of the test score information. Consider objectives or competency-based programs, since it is with these types of programs that criterion-referenced tests and cut-off scores are most often used. Objectives-based programs, in theory, are designed to improve the quality of instruction by (1) defining the curricula in terms of objectives, (2) relating instruction and assessment closely to the objectives, (3) making it possible for individualization of instruction, and (4) providing for on-going evaluation. Hard evidence of the success of objectives-based programs (or most new programs) is in short supply, but there is some evidence to suggest that when objectives-based programs are implemented fully and properly they are better than more "traditionally oriented" curricula (Klausmeier, Rossmiller, & Saily,

---

[3] Robert Linn stated recently (as a discussant at a symposium on standard setting at the 1979 NCME meeting in San Francisco) that perhaps there would be less resistance to using standards for assigning examinees to mastery states if value-laden terms such as "competent," "masters," and "nonmasters" were avoided when describing examinees. His suggestion is worthy of additional consideration.

1977; Torshen 1977). Individualization of instruction is "keyed" to descriptive information provided by criterion-referenced tests relative to examinee performance on test items measuring objectives in the curriculum. But descriptive information such as "examinee A has correctly answered 85 percent of the test items measuring a particular objective" must be evaluated and decisions made based upon that interpretation. Has a student demonstrated a sufficiently high level of performance on an objective to lead to a prediction that he or she has a good chance of success on the next objective in a sequence? Does a student's performance level indicate that he or she may need some remedial work? Is the student's performance level high enough to meet the target for the objective defined by teachers of the curriculum? In order to answer these and many other questions it is necessary to set *standards*. How else can decisions be made? Comparative statements about students (for example, student A performed better than 60 percent of her classmates) are largely irrelevant. Cut-off scores carefully developed by qualified teams of experts can contribute substantially to the success of an objectives-based program (competency-based program or basic skills program) because cut-off scores provide a basis for effective decision making.

There has been criticism (Glass 1978*a*, 1978*b*) of the use of cut-off scores with "life skills" or "survival skills" tests. These are terms currently popular with state departments of education, school districts, test publishers, and the press. Of course, Glass is correct when he notes that it would be next to impossible to validate the classifications of examinees into "mastery states," that is, those predicted to be "successful" or "unsuccessful" in life. On the other hand, if what is really meant by the term *life skills* is "graduation requirements," then standards of performance for "basic skills" or "high school competency" tests can probably be set by appropriately chosen groups of individuals.

What methods are available for setting standards? Numerous researchers have catalogued most if not all of the available methods (Hambleton & Eignor 1979*b*, Hambleton et al. 1978, Jaeger 1976, Meskauskas 1976, Millman 1973, Shepard 1976). Many of these methods have also been reviewed by Glass (1978*b*). It suffices to say here that there exist methods based on a consideration of (1) item content, (2) guessing and item sampling, (3) empirical data from mastery and nonmastery groups, (4) decision-theoretic procedures, (5) external criterion measures, and (6) educational consequences. Several of the more promising methods will be described later.

It is useful to state at the outset that *all* standard-setting methods involve judgment and are arbitrary. I am not aware of anyone who would dispute that statement. Popham (1978*b*) has given an excellent answer, however, to the concern expressed by some researchers about arbitrary standards:

> Unable to avoid reliance on human judgment as the chief ingredient in standard-setting, some individuals have thrown up their hands in dismay and cast aside all efforts to set performance standards as *arbitrary*, hence unacceptable.
>
> But *Webster's Dictionary* offers us two definitions of arbitrary. The first of these is positive, describing arbitrary as an adjective reflecting choice or discretion, that is, "determinable by a judge or tribunal." The second definition, pejorative in nature, describes arbitrary as an adjective denoting capriciousness, that is, "selected at random and without reason." In my estimate, when people start knocking the standard-setting game as arbitrary, they are clearly employing Webster's second, negatively loaded definition.
>
> But the first definition is more accurately reflective of serious standard-setting efforts. They represent genuine attempts to do a good job in deciding what kinds of standards we ought to employ. That they are judgmental is inescapable. But to malign all judgmental operations as capricious is absurd. (P. 168)

Hambleton (1978) and Popham (1978*a*, 1978*b*) have both stressed that many things that are done in life are arbitrary. Fire standards, health standards, environmental standards, highway safety standards, even standards for the operation of nuclear reactors are set arbitrarily, but in the positive sense of the word. And in educational settings, it is clear that teachers make arbitrary decisions about what to teach in their courses, how to teach the material, and at what pace they should teach. If teachers are deemed qualified to make these other important decisions, they are equally qualified to set standards or cut-off scores for the monitoring of student progress in their courses. But what if a standard is set too high (or too low) or if students are misclassified? Through experience, with high-quality criterion-referenced tests and with careful evaluation work, standards that are not "in line" with others can be identified and revised.

A comment by Ebel (1978) is particularly appropriate:

> Pass-fail decisions on a person's achievement in learning trouble some measurement specialists a great deal. They know about errors of measurement. They know that some who barely pass do so only with the help of errors of measurement. They know that some who fail do so only with the hindrance of errors of measurement. For these, passing or failing does not depend on achievement at all. It depends only on luck. That seems unfair, and indeed it is. But as any measurement specialist can explain, it is also entirely unavoidable. Make a better test and we reduce the number who will be passed or failed by error. But the number can never be reduced to zero. (P. 549)

The consequences of false positive and false negative errors with basic skills assessment or high school certification tests are, however, considerably more serious than errors made on classroom tests, and so more attention must be given to the design of these testing programs.

How should a method be selected? There are many factors to consider in selecting a method for determining standards. These include: (*a*) the importance of the decisions, (*b*) the amount of available time to set a standard, (*c*) the resources available (people and money) to get the job done, (*d*) the capabilities of the judges (some methods require more knowledge of the content and examinees to be tested than others), and (*e*) the appropriateness of the method for the type of test under study.

The most interesting work I have seen to date regarding the selection of a method was offered by Jaeger (1976). He considers several methods for determining cut-off scores, several approaches for assigning examinees to mastery states, and various threats to the validity of assignments. While Jaeger's work is theoretical, it provides an excellent starting point for anyone interested in initiating research on the merits of different methods. One thing seems clear from his work—all of the methods he studied appear to have numerous potential drawbacks, and so the selection of a method in a given situation should be made carefully.

What guidelines are available for applying particular methods successfully? There are relatively few guidelines available for applying any of the methods. Zieky and Livingston (1977) have provided a very helpful set for applying several methods (the popular Nedelsky method and the Angoff method are two of the methods included). A work by Popham (1978*c*) is also very helpful. More materials of this type and quality are needed. Some procedural steps for standard setting with respect to two important uses of tests—daily classroom assessment, and basic skills assessment for yearly promotions and high school certification—are provided later in this chapter.

Standard-Setting Methods. Many of the available standard-setting methods are reported in table 4.3. This table is a slight modification of a figure that appeared in a paper by Hambleton and Eignor (1979*b*). The methods are organized into three categories labeled "judgmental," "empirical," and "combination." All of the judgmental methods require data to be collected from judges for setting standards, or require judgments to be made about the presence of variables (for example, guessing) that influence the setting of a standard. The empirical methods require the collection of examinee test data to aid in the standard-setting process. The combination methods use both judgmental data and empirical data in the standard-setting process.

TABLE 4.3. A Classification of Methods for Setting Standards

Judgmental Methods	Empirical Models[a]	Combination Models
Item Content	Data-Criterion Measure	Judgmental-Empirical
Nedelsky (1954)	Livingston (1975)	Contrasting groups
Angoff (1971)	Livingston (1976)	(Zieky & Livingston 1977)
Modified Angoff	Van der Linden and	Borderline groups
(ETS, 1976)	Mellenbergh (1977)	(Zieky & Livingston 1977)
Ebel (1979)		Criterion groups (Berk 1976)
Jaeger (1978)	Decision-Theoretic[b]	
	Kriewall (1972)	Educational Consequences
Guessing		Block (1972)
Millman (1973)		
		Bayesian Methods
		Hambleton and Novick
		(1973)
		Schoon, Gullion, and Ferrara
		(1978)

SOURCE: Based on material from a paper by Hambleton and Eignor (1979*b*).
[a] Involve the use of examinee response data
[b] In addition, there are a number of decision-theoretic models that deal with test length considerations. These are also applicable to cut-off score determination (see, for example, Millman 1974).

Judgmental methods. In these methods, individual items are inspected, with the level of concern being how the minimally competent person would perform on the test item. Judges are asked to assess how or to what degree an individual who could be described as minimally competent would perform on each item.

In Nedelsky's method, judges are asked to identify distractors in multiple-choice test items that they feel minimally competent students (Nedelsky calls them "D-F students") should be able to eliminate as incorrect. The minimum passing level (MPL) for that item then becomes the reciprocal of the remaining alternatives. It is the "chance score" on the test item for the minimally competent student. Table 4.4 summarizes the MPLs. The judges proceed with each test item in like fashion, and upon completion of the judging process each judge sums the minimum passing levels across the test items to obtain a standard. Individual judges' standards are averaged to obtain a standard for the test.

Nedelsky felt that if one were to compute the standard deviation of individual judges' standards, this distribution would by synonymous with the (hypothesized or theoretical) distribution of the scores of the borderline students. This standard deviation, σ, should then be multiplied by a constant, K, decided upon by the test users, and added to (or subtracted from) the standard to regulate the approximate number of borderline students who will pass or fail.

Ebel (1979) has judges rate test items along two dimensions, relevance and difficulty, using four levels of relevance (essential, important, acceptable, and questionable) and three levels of difficulty (easy, medium, and hard). These levels form a 3×4 grid. Next, the judges are asked to do two things: locate each of the test items in the proper cell, based upon their relevance and difficulty, and assign a percentage to each cell (that percentage being the percentage of items in the cell that the minimally qualified examinee should be able to answer). Then the number of test items in each cell is multiplied by the appropriate percentage (agreed upon by the judges), and the sum of all the cells, when divided by the total number of test items, yields the standard.

When using Angoff's method, judges are asked to assign a probability to each test item directly, thus circumventing the analysis of a grid or the analysis of response alternatives. Angoff (1971) states:

> ask each judge to state the *probability* that the "minimally acceptable person" would answer each item correctly. In effect, the judges would think of a number of minimally acceptable persons instead of only one such person, and would estimate the proportion of minimally acceptable persons who would answer each item correctly. The sum of these probabilities, or proportions, would then represent the minimally acceptable score. (P. 515)

Jaeger (1978) recently offered a method for standard setting on the North Carolina High School Competency Test. His method is iterative, uses judges from a variety of backgrounds, and employs normative data. Further, rather than asking a question involving "minimal competence," a term that is hard to operationalize, Jaeger's questions are instead: "Should every high school graduate be able to answer this item correctly?" "__Yes, __No." and "If a student *does not* answer this item correctly, should he/she be denied a high school diploma?" "__Yes, __No" (P. 10).

After a series of iterative processes involving judges from various areas of expertise, and after the presentation of some normative data, standards determined by all groups of judges of the same type are pooled and a median is computed for each type of judge. The minimum median across all groups is selected as the standard. Jaeger's method appears to have considerable merit for setting standards on very important tests, such as high school graduation examinations.

Empirical methods. Livingston (1975) suggests the use of a set of linear or semilinear utility functions in viewing the effects of decision-making accuracy based upon a particular performance standard or cut-off score. That is, the functions relating the benefit and cost of a decision are related linearly to the cut-off score in question.

TABLE 4.4. Probability of Correct Responses As a Function of Remaining Answer Choices

Number of Choices Remaining	Minimum Passing Level
5	.20
4	.25
3	.33
2	.50
1	1.00

Livingston bases his procedure upon any suitable criterion measure (not just instructed versus uninstructed), and also specifies the relationship between utility (benefit or loss) and cut-off scores as linear. The relationship does not have to be linear; however, using a linear relationship simplifies matters somewhat. In such a situation the cost of a bad decision is proportional to the size of the errors made and the benefit of a good decision is proportional to the size of the errors avoided.

Combination methods. Berk (1976), Zieky and Livingston (1977), and, more recently, Popham (1978c) have suggested three methods that are based upon a combination of judgmental and empirical data. In addition, they have included an in-depth discussion of how to implement the techniques, something that has been lacking with many other methods. The two methods presented by Zieky and Livingston, the Borderline-Group and Contrasting-Group methods, are procedurally similar. They differ in the sample of students on which performance data are collected. Further, while judgments are required, they are about students, not items, as with many of the other judgmental methods (Nedelsky, Angoff, Ebel, etc.). Zieky and Livingston make the case that judging individuals is likely to be a more familiar task than judging items. Teachers are the logical choice as judges, and for them the assessment of individuals is commonplace. Berk's method is similar to the Contrasting-Groups method. The differences are that Berk uses instructed and uninstructed groups and offers several statistics to interpret the results.

The Borderline-Group method requires that judges first define what they would envision as minimally acceptable performance on the content area being assessed. The judges are then asked to submit a list of students whose performances are so close to the borderline between acceptable and unacceptable that they can't be classified into either group. The test is administered to this group, and the median test score for the group may be taken as the standard. Alternatively, a decision can be made to pass some other percentage of minimally competent students.

In the Contrasting-Groups method, once judges have defined minimally acceptable performance for the subject area being assessed, they are asked to identify those students they are certain are either definite masters or nonmasters of the skills measured by the test. Stable statistical results will be obtained if the groups of students are not too small. The test score distributions for the two groups are then plotted and the point of intersection is taken as the initial standard. (For an example, refer to figure 4.2.) Zieky and Livingston suggest adjusting the standard up or down to reduce "false masters" (students identified as masters by the test but who have not adequately mastered the objectives) or "false nonmasters" (students identified as nonmasters by the test but who have adequately mastered the objectives). The direction to move the cut-off score will depend on the relative seriousness of the two types of error.

Berk (1976) presented a method that is very similar to the Contrasting-Groups method. It involves a consideration of test responses of instructed and uninstructed groups of students. Various standards are set and the effect of the value of the standard on the percentage of false positive and false negative errors is studied. Berk offers a number of statistics to use in conjunction with the available data. For example, he selects a standard to minimize the sum of false positive and false negative errors. In another, errors are weighted to reflect their importance, and a standard is set to minimize a weighted sum of false positive and false negative errors. His procedures hold considerable promise in classroom instructional settings. The problem involved with using his method for setting standards on minimum competency tests is that there is no simple way of establishing groups who were either instructed or uninstructed on the competencies included in the test.

Berk also mentions that the optimal cutting point for a criterion-referenced test can be located by observing the frequency distributions for the instructed and uninstructed groups: "The instructed and uninstructed group score distributions are the primary determinants of the extent to which a test can accurately classify students as true masters and true nonmasters of an objective. The degree of accuracy is, for the most part, a function of the amount of overlap between the distributions" (p. 5).

If the test distributions overlap completely, no decisions can be made. The ideal situation would be one in which the two distributions have no overlap at all. In figure 4.2, the distributions of test scores for two groups of examinees (one instructed group and one uninstructed group) are shown.

Some Procedural Steps in Standard Setting.[4] In earlier parts of this section, issues and several methods for standard setting were discussed. In this part, procedures will be outlined for setting standards on criterion-referenced tests used for two different purposes, classroom testing and basic skills testing for yearly promotion and high school graduation. Classroom testing is emphasized, since classroom teachers have fewer technical resources available to them than do the larger testing programs.

Certain things are assumed. First, in each case a set of objectives or competencies has been agreed upon, and they are described using domain specifications or some other equally appropriate method. Second, it is assumed that no fixed selection ratio exists (in effect, one might be fixed by having resources to provide only a certain number of students with remedial work), since if it does, there is no reason to set standards.

Preliminary considerations. Before any standard setting is undertaken for any purpose, an analysis of the decision-making context and the resources available for the project should be done. The results of this analysis will determine how extensive and sophisticated the standard-setting procedure should be. Analysis of the decision-making context involves judging the importance of the decisions that are to be made using the test, the probable consequences of those decisions, and the costs of errors. Others have discussed using these same considerations in adjusting the final standard, but they may also be helpful in choosing a standard-setting method. Formal procedures for using this information are probably not necessary; a discussion of the issues by those directing the project should suffice. Some issues to consider would include the number of people directly and indirectly affected by the decisions to be based on the test; possible educational, psychological, financial, social, and other consequences of the decisions; and the duration of the consequences.

The next step should be a consideration of the resources available for the standard setting. Resources include money, materials, clock time, personnel time, and expertise. How much of the total amount of available resources will be dedicated to the standard setting will depend upon the results of the prior discussion of decision context. The final decision as to the resources to be invested will determine how large and technically sophisticated the standard-setting enterprise may be.

A great deal of information needs to be collected on the actual expenditures of various resources that have been required to carry out standard setting by different methods in different contexts. Actual time

---

[4]The material in this section is from a paper by Hambleton and Powell (in preparation).

and money data would be invaluable to practitioners in choosing a method for their own situation. In the following discussion, procedural steps in increasing order of expense and complexity will be offered but real data on these factors are lacking and that data constitute a pressing need.

Classroom testing. The classroom teacher is most likely to use criterion-referenced tests for diagnostic purposes, that is, for determining whether a student has mastered an area or needs further work in it. This would seem to be the most common situation calling for the setting of standards. Here the teacher must decide what level of test performance constitutes "mastery." In the same testing context he or she may set additional performance standards, above and/or below the minimal level, for the awarding of grades on the material.

Typically the classroom teacher works alone, or at most with one or more teachers of the same grade. It is also quite often the case that a classroom exam is used only once. In these situations, methods based only on judgment of test content may be the only ones practicable. The methods developed by Ebel, Nedelsky, and Angoff would be appropriate.

When available resources permit involving more people in the standard setting, parents and other community members might be enlisted, or a group of teachers of one grade from an entire school district might collaborate in setting standards. Again, if resources permit, data on group performance on individual items may be tabulated and considered in setting the standards on subsequent tests or, if tests are retained from year to year, the performance data from the previous year might be used. Of course, this can also be done by teachers working alone. The following is a list of steps for involving parents of students in a particular class in setting standards for classroom tests over units of instruction; some of these may be omitted if resources are limited. The method borrows heavily from Jaeger (1978). (It is assumed that the objectives have been identified and the teacher[s] has prepared domain specifications.)

1. At the beginning of the school year, a letter is sent to parents explaining the project and inviting them to a meeting where more information will be given.
2. At the meeting parents are given copies of domain specifications for the first test, along with sample items. They are asked to indicate for each objective a percentage of items that, answered correctly, would demonstrate that the student had mastered the material *adequately.* At this meeting they should be encouraged to discuss the task and to ask any questions they might have about it.

Instructions accompanying the standard-setting task should indicate to the parents how their judgments will be employed (for example, averaged with the percentages indicated by every other parent, and the resulting standard applied to every child in that class or grade). I have suggested for reasons of test security that the parents base their judgments on domain specifications rather than on actual test items; if test forms from previous years are available and thought to be parallel to the new exam, it may be easier for parents to make their judgments as a percentage correct of items on the parallel test.

3. The teacher constructs the criterion-referenced test from the domain specifications *before* looking at the parents' standards.
4. Class performance data are tabulated after the test is administered.
5. Parental judgment for the second test (or set of tests) is solicited by mail. The mailing packet includes instructions, domain specifications (duplicating those given at the earlier meeting) and performance data from the first test (number of students achieving each set standard). Instructions would also stress that judgments were to be based primarily on domain specifications and only secondarily on performance data.
6. Step 5 is repeated during the year whenever a competency-type test is to be given. (Alternatively, this procedure might be reserved for those instructional units judged to cover basic, required objectives for that grade; parents' instructions would then identify the tested materials as such.)
7. The teacher keeps files for each test, including the domain specifications, parental judgment forms, the actual exam, and performance data.
8. Periodic meetings can be held to review the instructions and to discuss the procedure and its results.

Other variants on this procedure can include appointing a small committee of parents, possibly working with several teachers, instead of an open parents group. A parent-objective matrix sampling strategy could be employed to reduce the number of judgments required of each parent.

Basic skills testing for annual promotion and high school graduation. These are clearly areas where greater importance is attached to the consequences of testing and, hence, more resources will be allocated than for classroom testing.

Jaeger (1978) has provided an excellent guide to implementing a procedure involving representative groups affected by standards set for high school graduation. The method was discussed earlier, but a brief review at this point seems useful. In general terms, it is an iterative procedure for soliciting item-by-item judgments from groups of judges. Information fed back to the judges at each iteration includes (*a*) group performance on each test item in a pilot administration; (*b*) the percentage of students who would have passed, given several different standards; and (*c*) a distribution of the standards suggested by the judges in the group. The median passing score for each type of judge is computed, and the lowest of the medians is taken as the standard.

The principal attraction of plans such as Jaeger's is their political viability. By involving a broad cross section of constituents in the setting of the standard, one increases the acceptability of that standard. However, no actual control or very significant influence over the educational process is transferred to the constituency; the objectives and the test, after all, are presented to them as givens, and their contribution in setting the standard is really quite limited. Moreover, the consensus method, while probably not harmful, may not produce results that make any pedagogical sense. Where obtaining popular support is not a critical problem, educators may prefer to rely upon the judgments of subject matter and measurement "experts" to set standards. This may produce a more coherent, if less universally accepted, result. Such a procedure could be implemented as follows (the steps would be executed for *each* subject matter area by content experts working with measurement experts):

1. Categorize the educational objectives or competencies as being of the knowledge/information type or of the rule-learning type. (This distinction corresponds to Meskauskas's [1976] continuum versus state mastery models.) In the first case it makes sense to speak of a domain score, and to sample randomly from the domain to estimate that score. In the second, since learning is presumed to be all or nothing, sampling considerations are not relevant, but construction of a few test items that accurately reflect the ability is critically important.
2. For objectives or competencies of the first type, construct tests with the aid of domain specifications, items matched to the domain specifications, and a suitable item sampling plan.
3. Ebel's standard-setting method (or one of the other content-focused methods) may then be used to set the standard for these parts of the test. To use Ebel's method the items from all of the knowledge/information (or continuum) domains would be considered together.
4. Pooling the judgments of all the experts may present a problem. Simply averaging the ratings given to each item (on relevance and

difficulty) and/or the standards assigned to each category will probably not give a very meaningful result. Ideally, the experts will go through a series of iterations in which they compare their independent judgments (first of the item categorization and next of the standards they assigned to each category), note discrepancies, discuss the rationale for each judgment, possibly decide upon revisions in the test (this will direct the procedure back to step 2, to ensure that any revisions do not distort the test's domain representativeness), and/or persuade each other to change their judgments. Unanimity might be required in order to proceed from this step.

5. For those objectives or competencies classified as being of the "state" variety, smaller sets of items are required since the domains are more homogeneous, but item construction must be, if anything, more painstaking. Ideally, experimental evidence would be garnered to show that item performance truly reflected the competencies of interest.

6. Standards on these state-type objectives can be adjusted back from 100 percent if the probabilities of false positive and false negative classification errors can be estimated. Similarly, domain scores can be adjusted by a Bayesian procedure (e.g., Hambleton & Novick 1973) to compensate for relative losses associated with the classification errors.

When the tests are used for yearly promotions, students' performance in the next grade can be used as a criterion in order to estimate the possibilities of classification errors.

Suggestions for Future Research

Several suggestions for future research and development are divided according to the two topics considered here.

Validity of Criterion-Referenced Test Scores. Researchers could make use of the content and technical review forms in appendixes A, B, C, D, and E (and variations on them) and evaluate and report the results of their efforts. Questions such as How many judges are required? How should judges be selected? On what basis can the ratings of a judge(s) be discarded? and Can nonmeasurement specialists be trained to conduct technical reviews of test items? require satisfactory answers for successful implementation of content validation investigations.

Another problem involves the development of a system for the integrative use of content specialists' ratings and empirical methods in establishing item validities. While an integration of approaches could be accomplished through logical analysis, perhaps a better way to proceed would be actually to employ the different techniques in a variety of situations and through practical experience evolve a system for the combined use of content specialists' ratings and empirical methods. The work of Cronbach (1971) may help to provide a conceptual framework for this integration, since his treatment of test validity is the most comprehensive to date.

Standard-Setting Methods. Although many standard-setting methods exist in the literature, they need to be described accurately and their advantages and disadvantages noted. This information will aid practitioners in selecting standard-setting methods.

Implementation strategies for the more promising standard-setting methods need to be developed, validated, and made ready for wide use. There are only a few guidelines or procedural steps available for applying any of the standard-setting methods. (An exception is some work by Popham [1978a, 1978c] and by Zieky and Livingston [1977].)

Prior to developing guidelines for applying particular standard-setting methods, questions such as the following need to be answered: (a) How do directions to judges about their task influence their ratings? (b) How does one decide about the types of people who should be involved in a standard-setting project? (c) When multiple groups (teachers, curriculum specialists, parents, community leaders, etc.) independently set standards, how should the data from each group be combined to arrive at a single standard? Should the data from some groups be given more weight? (d) Which factors should be considered in arriving at a decision about the standard-setting method to use in particular testing situations? (e) In situations where tests must remain secure, can reliable and valid standards be set from only domain specifications or general test descriptions (sometimes called a "table of specifications" or a "test blueprint")?

Guidelines for Practitioners

Papers by Cronbach (1971), Messick (1975), and Linn (1979) have had considerable influence on my understanding and views of criterion-referenced test score validity. Perhaps I can now be absolved of my sin, in 1973, of saying, "Above all else, a criterion-referenced test must have content validity" (Hambleton & Novick 1973, p. 168). Certainly, any good criterion-referenced test must have content validity, but content validity evidence will *not* be sufficient to insure the validity of the many different uses of criterion-referenced test scores.

I would like to offer a few guidelines for improving the development, validation, and uses of criterion-referenced tests:

1. Prepare domain specifications. Domain specifications provide clear statements about the desired content and behaviors to be measured by a criterion-referenced test. Domain specifications are like a good road map: if you get lost in the test development jungle, you can always refer back to them and find your way.
2. Follow the criterion-referenced test development steps offered in figure 4.1. Each step is an integral part of the test development process. Technically sound tests can be produced if the steps are followed carefully. Popham (1978b), Hambleton and Eignor (1979a, 1979b), and the other chapters in this volume provide implementation strategies for the steps.
3. All of the steps in figure 4.1 are important. Steps 5, 8, and 10 were emphasized in this chapter. The size and importance of the test development project will influence the scope and depth of the content and construct validation investigations (steps 5 and 10). *All* criterion-referenced tests must have content validity, which is assessed by a consideration of item validities, technical quality of the test items, and item representativeness. The validity of criterion-referenced test score uses is carried out within the framework of construct validation methodology. Spend the required time and resources in this area to insure that an appropriate amount of evidence is available on test score validity.
4. No matter how technically sound a test is, or how much content validity a test has, all efforts will have been in vain if considerable care and attention is not given to the standard-setting process. The best set of tests is sabotaged by an inappropriate standard. Therefore,
   a. Select a standard-setting method carefully. It should be one that can be efficiently handled by judges.
   b. Be sure that all interested groups have an opportunity to participate in the standard-setting process.
   c. Spend time training judges so that they understand their task.
   d. Be sure that the judges understand the purpose of the testing program, have a description of the group of examinees to be assessed, and share a common definition of what it means to be a "master" and a "nonmaster" of test content.
   e. Tests should be pilot tested and decision-validity information reported for several standards of test performance. With both examinee test results and independently derived standards from judges available, a revised standard can be set and used.
   f. It is necessary to review standards occasionally. Curriculum prior-

ities change and so do instructional methods and students. These shifts should be reflected in the standards that are used.

The purposes of criterion-referenced testing programs can only be accomplished if technically sound criterion-referenced tests are constructed and if scores derived from the tests are interpreted and used correctly. I hope this chapter will contribute to the accomplishment of both objectives.

Appendix A

An Example of a Judge's Item Rating Form

Item Content Review Form

Reviewer: _____ Date: _____ Content Area: _____

First, read carefully through the lists of domain specifications and test items. Next, please indicate how well you feel each item reflects the domain specification it was written to measure. Judge a test item solely on the basis of the match between its content and the content defined by the domain specification that the test item was prepared to measure. Please use the five-point rating scale shown below:

Poor	Fair	Good	Very Good	Excellent
1	2	3	4	5

Circle the number corresponding to your rating beside the test item number.

Objective	Test Item	Item Rating					Comments
1	2	1	2	3	4	5	
	7	1	2	3	4	5	
	14	1	2	3	4	5	
2	1	1	2	3	4	5	
	3	1	2	3	4	5	
	8	1	2	3	4	5	
	13	1	2	3	4	5	
3	4	1	2	3	4	5	
	6	1	2	3	4	5	
	12	1	2	3	4	5	
4	5	1	2	3	4	5	
	9	1	2	3	4	5	
	10	1	2	3	4	5	
	11	1	2	3	4	5	

Appendix B

An Example of a Judge's Summary Sheet for the Items/Objectives Matching Task

---

| Items/Objectives Matching Task |

Reviewer: _____ Date: _____ Content Area: _____

First, read carefully through the lists of domain specifications and test items. Your task is to indicate whether or not you feel each test item is a measure of *one* of the domain specifications. It is, if you feel examinee performance on the test item would provide an indication of an examinee's level of performance in a pool of test items measuring the domain specification. Beside each objective, write in the test item numbers corresponding to the test items that you feel measure the objective. In some instances, you may feel that items do not measure any of the available domain specifications. Write these test item numbers in the space provided at the bottom of the rating form.

Objective	Matching Test Items
1	
2	
3	
4	
No Matches	

Appendix C

An Example of a Technical Review Form for Multiple-Choice Test Items

| Item Review Form
(Multiple-Choice) | .

Objective (Domain Specification) Number: _____ Test Item Number: _____
Reviewer: _____ Date: _____

Objective:

Test Item:

Section I.   Technical Quality

Place a "✓" under the column corresponding to your rating of the test item for the questions in this section and the next one.

	Yes	Questionable	No
1. Is the item stem clearly written for the intended group of examinees?	___	___	___
2. Is the item stem free of irrelevant material?	___	___	___
3. Is a problem clearly defined in the item stem?	___	___	___
4. Are the choices clearly written for the intended group of examinees?	___	___	___
5. Are the choices free of irrelevant material?	___	___	___
6. Is there a correct answer or a *clearly* best answer?	___	___	___
7. Have words like "always," "none," or "all" been removed?	___	___	___
8. Are likely examinee mistakes used to prepare incorrect answers?	___	___	___
9. Is "all of the above" avoided as a choice?	___	___	___
10. Are the choices arranged in a logical sequence (if one exists)?	___	___	___
11. Was the correct answer randomly positioned among the available choices?	___	___	___
12. Are all repetitious words or expressions removed from the choices and included in the item stem?	___	___	___
13. Are all of the choices of approximately the same length?	___	___	___
14. Do the item stem and choices follow standard rules of punctuation and grammar?	___	___	___
15. Are all negatives underlined?	___	___	___
16. Are grammatical cues between the item stem and the choices, which might give the correct answer away, removed?	___	___	___
17. Is the item format appropriate for measuring the intended objective?	___	___	___

Suggested Revisions:

Final Rating (Check One):

☐   ☐   ☐

Accept   Accept (with revisions—see above)   Reject

Appendix D

Instructions for Using the Item Technical Review Form

---

1. Obtain a copy of a domain specification and the test items written to measure it.
2. Place the domain specification number, your name, and today's date in the space provided at the top of the Item Review Form.
3. Place the numbers corresponding to the test items you will evaluate in the spaces provided near the top of the Item Review Form. The numbers should be in ascending order as you read from left to right. (This must be done if processing of your data along with data from many other reviewers is to be done quickly and with a minimum number of errors.)
4. Read the domain specification carefully.
5. Read the first test item carefully and answer the first 18 questions. Mark " ✓ " for "yes"; mark "X" for "No"; and mark "?" if you are "unsure."
   The last question requires you to provide an overall evaluation of the test item as an indicator of the domain specification it was written to measure.
   There are five possible ratings:

5- Excellent
4 - Very Good
3 - Good
2 - Fair
1 - Poor

6. Write any comments or suggested wording changes on or beside the test item.
7. Repeat the rating task for each of the available test items.
8. Staple your Item Review Form, domain specification, and copy of the test items together.

Appendix E

An Example of an Item Technical Review Form

```
┌─────────────────────────────────┐
│   Item Technical Review Form    │
│         Multiple Choice         │
└─────────────────────────────────┘
```

Domain Specification No. _____   Reviewer: _____   Date: _____

Test Item Characteristics (Mark "✓" for Yes, "X" for No, and "?" for Unsure)

Test Item Numbers

1. Is the item stem clearly written for the intended group of students?											
2. Is the item stem free of irrelevant material?											
3. Is a single problem clearly defined in the item stem?											
4. Are the answer choices clearly written for the intended group of students?											
5. Are the answer choices free of irrelevant material?											
6. Is there a correct answer or a *clearly* best answer?											
7. Have words like "always," "none," or "all" been removed?											
8. Are likely student mistakes used to prepare incorrect answers?											
9. Is "all of the above" avoided as an answer choice?											
10. Are the answer choices arranged in a logical sequence (if one exists)?											

Appendix E *Continued*

11. Was the correct answer randomly positioned among the available answer choices?									
12. Are all repetitious words or expressions removed from the answer choices and included in the item stem?									
13. Are all of the answer choices of approximately the same length?									
14. Do the item stem and answer choices follow standard rules of punctuation and grammar?									
15. Are all negatives underlined?									
16. Are grammatical cues between the item stem and the answer choices, which might give the correct answer away, removed?									
17. Are letters used in front of the possible answer choices to identify them?									
18. Have expressions like "which of the following is *not*" been avoided?									
19. Disregarding any technical flaws that may exist in the test item (addressed by the first 18 questions), how well do you think the content of the test item matches with some part of the content defined by the domain specification? (Remember the possible ratings: 1 = poor, 2 = fair, 3 = good, 4 = very good, 5 = excellent).									

References

Anderson, R. C. 1972. How to construct achievement tests to assess comprehension. *Review of Educational Research* 42: 145-70.

Angoff, W. H. 1971. Scales, norms, and equivalent scores. In *Educational measurement,* ed. R. L. Thorndike. 2nd ed. Washington, D.C.: American Council on Education. Pp. 508-600.

Berk, R. A. 1976. Determination of optimal cutting scores in criterion-referenced measurement. *Journal of Experimental Education* 45: 4-9.

_____. 1978. The application of structural facet theory to achievement test construction. *Educational Research Quarterly* 3: 62-72.

Block, J. H. 1972. Student learning and the setting of mastery performance standards. *Educational Horizons* 50: 183-90.

Cronbach, L. J. 1971. Test validation. In *Educational measurement,* ed. R. L. Thorndike. 2nd ed. Washington, D.C.: American Council on Education. Pp. 443-507.

Ebel, R. L. 1962. Content standard test scores. *Educational and Psychological Measurement* 22: 15-25.

_____. 1978. A case for minimum competency testing. *Phi Delta Kappan* 59: 546-49.

_____. 1979. *Essentials of educational measurement.* Englewood Cliffs, N.J.: Prentice-Hall.

Educational Testing Service. 1976. *Report on a study of the use of the National Teachers' Examination by the state of South Carolina.* Princeton, N.J.: Educational Testing Service.

Glass, G. V. 1978a. Minimum competence and incompetence in Florida. *Phi Delta Kappan* 59: 602-5.

_____. 1978b. Standards and criteria. *Journal of Educational Measurement* 15: 237-61.

Guion, R. M. 1977. Content validity: The source of my discontent. *Applied Psychological Measurement* 1: 1-10.

Hambleton, R. K. 1978. On the use of cut-off scores with criterion-referenced tests in instructional settings. *Journal of Educational Measurement* 15: 277-90.

Hambleton, R. K., and Eignor, D. R. 1978. Guidelines for evaluating criterion-referenced tests and test manuals. *Journal of Educational Measurement* 15: 321-27.

_____. 1979a. *A practitioner's guide to criterion-referenced test development, validation, and test score usage.* Laboratory of Psychometric and Evaluative Research Report no. 70. Amherst, Mass.: School of Education. University of Massachusetts.

_____. 1979b. Competency test development, validation, and standard-setting. In *Minimum competency achievement testing,* ed. R. M. Jaeger and C. K. Tittle. Berkeley, Calif.: McCutchan.

Hambleton, R. K., and Novick, M. R. 1973. Toward an integration of theory and method for criterion-referenced tests. *Journal of Educational Measurement* 10: 159-70.

Hambleton, R. K.; Swaminathan, H.; Algina, J.; and Coulson, D. B. 1978. Criterion-referenced testing and measurement: A review of technical issues and developments. *Review of Educational Research* 48: 1-47.

Hively, W.; Patterson, H. L.; and Page, S. A. 1968. A "universe-defined" system of arithmetic achievement tests. *Journal of Educational Measurement* 5: 275-90.

Jaeger, R. M. 1976. Measurement consequences of selected standard-setting models. *Florida Journal of Educational Research* 18: 22-27.

————. 1978. A proposal for setting a standard on the North Carolina High School Competency Test. Paper presented at the annual meeting of the North Carolina Association for Research in Education, Chapel Hill.

Kirsch, I., and Guthrie, J. T. 1979. *Toward a construct validity of functional reading tasks.* Newark, Del.: International Reading Association.

Klausmeier, H. J.; Rossmiller, R. A.; and Saily, M. 1977. *Individually guided elementary education.* New York: Academic Press.

Kriewall, T. E. 1972. Aspects and applications of criterion-referenced tests. Paper presented at the annual meeting of the American Educational Research Association, February 1972, Chicago.

Linn, R. L. 1979. Issues of validity in measurement for competency-based programs. In *Practices and problems in competency-based measurement,* ed. M. A. Bunda and J. R. Sanders. Washington, D.C.: National Council on Measurement in Education. Pp. 108-23.

Livingston, S. A. 1975. *A utility-based approach to the evaluation of pass/fail testing decision procedures.* Report no. COPA-75-01. Princeton, N.J.: Center for Occupational and Professional Assessment, Educational Testing Service.

————. 1976. *Choosing minimum passing scores by stochastic approximation techniques.* Report no. COPA-76-02. Princeton, N.J.: Center for Occupational and Professional Assessment, Educational Testing Service.

Meskauskas, J. A. 1976. Evaluation models for criterion-referenced testing: Views regarding mastery and standard-setting. *Review of Educational Research* 46: 133-58.

Messick, S. A. 1975. The standard problem: Meaning and values in measurement and evaluation. *American Psychologist* 30: 955-66.

Millman, J. 1973. Passing scores and test lengths for domain-referenced measures. *Review of Educational Research* 43: 205-16.

————. 1974. Criterion-referenced measurement. In *Evaluation in education: Current applications,* ed. W. J. Popham. Berkeley, Calif.: McCutchan. Pp. 311-97.

Nedelsky, L. 1954. Absolute grading standards for objective tests. *Educational and Psychological Measurement* 14: 3-19.

Popham, W. J. 1974. Selecting objectives and generating test items for objectives-based tests. In *Problems in criterion-referenced measurement,* ed. C. W. Harris, M. C. Alkin, and W. J. Popham. CSE Monograph Series in Evaluation, no. 3. Los Angeles: Center for the Study of Evaluation, University of California. Pp. 13-25.

————. 1975. *Educational evaluation.* Englewood Cliffs, N.J.: Prentice-Hall.

_____. 1978a. As always, provocative. *Journal of Educational Measurement* 15: 297–300

_____. 1978b. *Criterion-referenced measurement.* Englewood Cliffs, N.J.: Prentice-Hall.

_____. 1978c. *Setting performance standards.* Los Angeles: Instructional Objectives Exchange.

Rovinelli, R. J., and Hambleton, R. K. 1977. On the use of content specialists in the assessment of criterion-referenced test item validity. *Dutch Journal of Educational Research* 2: 49–60.

Scandura, J. M. 1977. *Problem-solving: A structural/process approach with educational implications.* New York: Academic Press.

Schoon, C. G.; Gullion, C. M.; and Ferrara, P. 1978. Credentialing examinations, Bayesian statistics, and the determination of passing points. Paper presented at the annual meeting of the American Psychological Association, September 1978, Toronto.

Shepard, L. A. 1976. Setting standards and living with them. *Florida Journal of Educational Research,* 18: 23–32.

Torshen, K. P. 1977. *The mastery approach to competency-based education.* New York: Academic Press.

Van der Linden, W. J., and Mellenbergh, G. J. 1977. Optimal cutting scores using a linear loss function. *Applied Psychological Measurement* 1: 593–99.

Zieky, M. J., and Livingston, S. A. 1977. *Manual for setting standards on the Basic Skills Assessment Tests.* Princeton, N.J.: Educational Testing Service.

PART THREE

RELIABILITY

THERE ARE AT LEAST three major conceptualizations of criterion-referenced test reliability: (1) consistency of mastery-nonmastery decision making across repeated measures with one test form or parallel test forms, (2) consistency of squared deviations of individual scores from the cut-off score across parallel or randomly parallel test forms, and (3) consistency of individual scores across parallel or randomly parallel test forms. The first two types of reliability are described in chapters 5 and 6, respectively: they pertain to criterion-referenced tests where mastery-nonmastery classification decisions are made on the basis of a cut-off score. This is the most common decision framework for teachers and evaluators. The third type of reliability, also treated to some extent in chapter 6, is concerned with estimating each student's domain score or proportion correct without reference to a cut-off score or mastery-nonmastery decisions. For a comprehensive review of procedures related to this estimation, the reader is referred to the article by Hambleton, Swaminathan, Algina, and Coulson (1978, pp. 17–20).

In chapter 5, Professor Michael J. Subkoviak critically surveys five methods of determining decision-consistency reliability. The first method, proposed by Carver (1970), is not sensitive to the classification consistency component of reliability, and consequently emphasis is placed on the four other methods. Those four methods actually involve only two statistics: P_0, the proportion of individuals consistently classified as masters and nonmasters across parallel test forms, and κ, the proportion of individuals consistently classified beyond that expected by chance. A step-by-step computation of each method is provided using an illustrative data set. The methods are briefly summarized as follows: (1) estimates of P_0 and κ based on two administrations of one test form or two parallel test forms (Swaminathan, Hambleton, & Algina 1974), (2) and (3) two different estimates of P_0 and κ based on one test administration (Huynh 1976, Subkoviak 1976), and (4) one estimate of P_0 based on one test administration (Marshall & Haertel 1976). Professor Subkoviak's theoretical, empirical, and practical comparisons suggest that Huynh's single-administration, conservative estimates of P_0 and κ are reasonably accurate but computationally tedious and Swaminathan's two-administration, unbiased estimates of P_0 and κ are relatively less accurate but computationally simple. Finally, he clarifies the distinction between P_0 and κ in terms of the types of consistency (overall consistency versus test consistency alone) a practitioner should consider in selecting a specific measure.

127

The generalizability theory approach reviewed in chapter 6 by Dr. Robert L. Brennan extends the principles originally documented by Cronbach, Gleser, Nanda, and Rajaratnam (1972) to the properties and uses of criterion-referenced tests. A random-effects linear model serves as the basic scheme for analyzing the variance components of a persons $\times$ items design. Given this model, which assumes that both persons and items are random samples from their respective domains, and a particular definition of error, Dr. Brennan develops two indices of reliability (or dependability) for criterion-referenced tests: $\Phi(\lambda)$ and Φ, where λ represents the cut-off score. The index $\Phi(\lambda)$ provides an estimate of the dependability of mastery-nonmastery decisions based on the testing procedure, and the index Φ is a "general purpose" index that is independent of a cut-off score and that can be used to estimate individual domain scores. Other interpretations of these indices are described in terms of signal/noise concepts and agreement coefficients. Relationships among the two indices and Kuder-Richardson coefficients 20 and 21 and Livingston's (1972) reliability coefficient are also demonstrated. Dr. Brennan stresses the importance of reporting the variance components of a generalizability study in addition to the magnitudes of $\Phi(\lambda)$ and Φ. The computational examples in the chapter follow that approach.

Both authors evaluate the merits of the decision-consistency and generalizability theory conceptualizations. The discussions focus on the practical implications of applying a threshold loss function (chapter 5) as compared to a squared-error loss function (chapter 6). The threshold loss or agreement function implies that only mastery-nonmastery misclassifications constitute errors and assumes the losses associated with such misclassifications are equally serious. When this assumption is upheld in practice and distinctions among different levels of mastery and nonmastery are unimportant, one of the estimates of P_0 or κ is recommended. Alternatively, the squared-error loss function is sensitive to the magnitude of all errors of measurement, including those that do not lead to misclassification. When degrees of mastery and nonmastery are important and the assumption of the threshold loss function is violated, the indices $\Phi(\lambda)$ and/or Φ are recommended.

5

DECISION-CONSISTENCY APPROACHES

Michael J. Subkoviak

Introduction

In a recent, excellent review of the literature, Hambleton, Swaminathan, Algina, and Coulson (1978, pp. 15-23) distinguished among three different concepts of reliability that arise in the context of criterion-referenced testing: (a) "reliability of mastery classification decisions," (b) "reliability of criterion-referenced test scores," and (c) "reliability of domain score estimates." This chapter focuses on the first of these types of reliability. Specifically, it is concerned with approaches to criterion-referenced reliability that emphasize the *consistency of mastery and nonmastery decisions* over repeated testing of the same group (cf. Huynh 1976; Marshall & Haertel 1976; Subkoviak 1976; Swaminathan, Hambleton, & Algina 1974).

For example, table 5.1 shows the total scores of thirty students on two ten-item tests; both the students and the items were drawn from larger pools described elsewhere (Subkoviak 1978). Let us assume that a student in table 5.1 must answer correctly eight or more items on the test to be considered a master, otherwise he or she is classified as a nonmaster. The "reliability of mastery classification decisions," the topic of the present chapter, refers to the consistency (or lack thereof) with which individuals are designated as masters or nonmasters across both forms 1 and 2 in table 5.1. Student 2, for instance, is consistently classified as a master on both forms when the cut-off score is set at eight out of ten items correct, while students 3 to 30 are consistently classi-

TABLE 5.1. Performance of Thirty
Students on Parallel Ten-Item Tests

Student	Total Score	
	Form 1	Form 2
1	9	7
2	8	8
3	7	7
4	7	4
5	7	3
6	6	7
7	6	7
8	6	5
9	6	4
10	5	6
11	5	4
12	5	2
13	5	2
14	4	7
15	4	7
16	4	7
17	4	6
18	4	4
19	4	4
20	4	4
21	4	3
22	4	2
23	3	6
24	3	4
25	3	4
26	3	4
27	3	2
28	3	2
29	2	4
30	1	1

NOTE: Mastery cut-off score $= 8$

fied as nonmasters on both forms. Thus, twenty-nine of the students, or a proportion of $29/30 = .97$, are consistently classified; student 1, who is a master on form 1 but a nonmaster on form 2, is the only exception.

The "reliability of criterion-referenced test scores," concept (b) above, is the topic of Brennan's chapter. Discussions are also found in Brennan and Kane (1977a, 1977b) and in Livingston (1972a, 1972b, 1972c). Basically, this type of reliability is concerned with the deviations of students scores about the cut-off score of 8 in table 5.1 and the consistency of these deviations across forms 1 and 2.

Finally, the "reliability of domain score estimates," concept (c) above, is concerned with the consistency of an individual student's scores across forms 1 and 2, without reference to a cut-off score. Hambleton, Swaminathan, Algina, and Coulson (1978, pp. 17–20) reviewed a number of coefficients that can be used to measure this type of reliability; one such index is the familiar standard error of measurement.

Review of Decision-Consistency Approaches

At least five separate approaches for assessing the consistency of mastery classification decisions can be found in the literature: (1) Carver (1970); (2) Swaminathan, Hambleton, and Algina (1974); (3) Huynh (1976); (4) Subkoviak (1976); and (5) Marshall and Haertel (1976). In the review that follows, each of these will be illustrated, discussed, and evaluated. By the way of introduction, it is noted that Carver's method is not generally recommended for reasons outlined below.

Carver Method.   The first formal proposal for assessing classification consistency seems to be due to Carver (1970), who suggested two possible procedures. One involved the administration of two parallel tests to the same group, followed by a comparison of the percentages of students on each test that were classified as masters. If the two percentages were the same or nearly the same, then the tests were considered reliable. Note, however, that two tests can be quite unreliable and still produce equal percentages of masters. For example, half of the group could be classified as masters on one test, while the other half of the group could be classified as masters on the second test. In each case the percentage is 50 percent, but the mastery group is totally different. Carver's second procedure involved administration of the same test to two comparable groups, with subsequent comparison of the percentage of masters in each group, but it suffers from the same limitation. As illustrated, the basic problem with Carver's procedures is that they are not sensitive to the consistency of *individual* classifications, and this method will not be discussed further. However, the methods that follow are sensitive to this key ingredient of reliability, and thus they will be considered in greater detail.

Swaminathan-Hambleton-Algina Method. Subsequent to Carver's proposal, Hambleton and Novick (1973, p. 168) suggested that the proportion of individuals consistently classified as master/master and nonmaster/nonmaster on two tests be used as an index of reliability. Swaminathan, Hambleton, and Algina (1974) later expanded upon this notion.

For example, if the criterion is 8 in table 5.1, the mastery-nonmastery outcomes on forms 1 and 2 can be summarized as in table 5.2. For instance, student 2 is the only testee classified as master/master on forms 1 and 2, respectively, so 1 is the entry in the first cell of table 5.2. Students 3 to 30 are classified nonmaster/nonmaster, so 28 is the entry in the fourth cell; the 1 in the off-diagonal cell of table 5.2 corresponds to the inconsistent mastery/nonmastery outcome for student 1. Thus, the proportion of individuals in table 5.2 consistently classified on the two tests is

$$\hat{p}_o = \frac{1}{30} + \frac{28}{30}$$

$$= \frac{29}{30}$$

$$= .97,$$

as previously noted. More generally, the proportion of individuals consistently classified into m mastery states (e.g., high, medium, and low with $m = 3$) is given by

$$\hat{p}_o = \sum_{k=1}^{m} p_{kk}, \tag{1}$$

where $\hat{p}_{kk}$ is the proportion of individuals consistently classified in the kth category on both tests.

TABLE 5.2. Mastery-Nonmastery Outcomes on Forms 1 and 2 of Table 5.1

	Form 2		
Form 1	Mastery	Nonmastery	Total
Mastery	1	1	2
Nonmastery	0	28	28
Total	1	29	

NOTE: Mastery cut-off score = 8

The upper limit of $\hat{p}_o$ is, of course, 1.00, which occurs only if all individuals are consistently classified. For two equivalent tests, the lower limit of $\hat{p}_o$ is the proportion of consistent classifications on two tests expected by chance alone (although values of $\hat{p}_o$ less than chance are possible in practice for unusual data sets). In table 5.2, the proportion of consistent classifications expected by chance is obtained from the product of corresponding row and column totals:

$$\hat{p}_c = \frac{2}{30} \times \frac{1}{30} + \frac{28}{30} \times \frac{29}{30}$$

$$= \frac{2}{900} + \frac{812}{900}$$

$$= .90,$$

which is the proportion of consistent outcomes expected for this particular group if the classifications on forms 1 and 2 were statistically independent of one another. In other words, $\hat{p}_c$ can be thought of as the proportion of consistent outcomes expected in two flips of a biased coin whose sides are weighted or "loaded" according to the relative numbers of masters and nonmasters in the group. More generally, the proportion of individuals consistently classified into m categories by chance is

$$\hat{p}_c = \sum_{k=1}^{m} \hat{p}_{k.} \, \hat{p}_{.k}, \tag{2}$$

where $\hat{p}_{k.}$ and $\hat{p}_{.k}$ are the proportions of testees assigned to category k on forms 1 and 2, respectively; for example, in table 5.2, $\hat{p}_{1.} = 2/30$ $\hat{p}_{.1} = 1/30$, $\hat{p}_{2.} = 28/30$, and $\hat{p}_{.2} = 29/30$.

Swaminathan, Hambleton, and Algina (1974) suggested that the proportion of consistent decisions expected by chance, $\hat{p}_c = .90$, be deleted from the proportion actually observed, $\hat{p}_o = .97$, in formulating an index of reliability for table 5.2. Accordingly, they recommended the use of Cohen's (1960) kappa coefficient:

$$\hat{\kappa} = \frac{\hat{p}_o - \hat{p}_c}{1 - \hat{p}_c}$$

$$= \frac{.97 - .90}{1 - .90} \tag{3}$$

$$= .70.$$

$\hat{\kappa}$ can be interpreted as the proportion of consistent classifications beyond that expected by "chance" or, more precisely, beyond that attributable to the particular proportions ($\hat{p}_{k\cdot}$ and $\hat{p}_{\cdot k}$ in Equation 2) of masters and nonmasters in the group tested. The upper limit of $\hat{\kappa}$ is again 1.00, indicating perfect reliability. In the present context, values of $\hat{\kappa}$ less than zero are unlikely, except for unusual data sets, and near-zero values indicate a condition where most of the observed consistency is attributable to the proportions of masters and nonmasters in the group.

The properties of $\hat{\kappa}$ have been widely discussed (Cohen 1960, 1968; Fleiss, Cohen & Everitt 1969; Hubert 1977). In fact, in many instances kappa differs little from the familiar Pearson correlation for dichotomous data, i.e., the phi coefficient (Reid & Roberts 1978). For the present, it should simply be noted that the two coefficients $\hat{p}_o$ and $\hat{\kappa}$ defined above are sensitive to different aspects of classification consistency, have different lower limits, and, subsequently, require different interpretations. More will be said about the properties of $\hat{p}_o$ and $\hat{\kappa}$ after the various methods for estimating these coefficients have been introduced.

The three reliability methods discussed next have the advantage of requiring only *one* test administration (Huynh 1976, Marshall & Haertel 1976, Subkoviak 1976), whereas the Swaminathan-Hambleton-Algina method of table 5.2 requires two administrations. However, these one-test procedures are computationally much more difficult than the Swaminathan-Hambleton-Algina approach, although computer programs are available for performing the required computations for each method.

Huynh Method. The reader will recall that the coefficients $\hat{p}_o$ and $\hat{\kappa}$ were based on table 5.2, which, in turn, was obtained from the joint distribution of scores on forms 1 and 2 in table 5.1. But suppose form 2 does not exist, so that only the scores on form 1 are available. Keats and Lord (1962) showed that given only the scores on form 1 and granted certain assumptions, scores on the nonexistent form 2 could be simulated. The steps involved in this simulation are as follows (Huynh 1976, pp. 254–258).

1. Compute the mean ($\hat{\mu}$), variance ($\hat{\sigma}^2$), and Kuder-Richardson 21 coefficient ($\hat{\alpha}_{21}$) of the scores (x) on form 1 of table 5.1. In the formulas below, N represents the number of students and n represents the number of test items. Specifically, $N = 30$ and $n = 10$ for table 5.1.

$$\hat{\mu} = \frac{\Sigma x}{N} = \frac{139}{30} = 4.63$$

$$\hat{\sigma}^2 = \frac{\Sigma x^2}{N-1} - \frac{(\Sigma x)^2}{N(N-1)} = \frac{739}{30-1} - \frac{(139)^2}{30(30-1)} = 3.27$$

$$\hat{\alpha}_{21} = \frac{n}{n-1}\left[1 - \frac{\hat{\mu}(n-\hat{\mu})}{n\hat{\sigma}^2}\right] = \frac{10}{10-1}\left[1 - \frac{(4.63)(10-4.63)}{(10)(3.27)}\right] = .27$$

2. Compute parameters $\hat{\alpha}$ and $\hat{\beta}$, which, together with the number of test items (n), determine the particular shape of the joint distribution of scores on forms 1 and 2.

$$\hat{\alpha} = \left(-1 + \frac{1}{\hat{\alpha}_{21}}\right)\hat{\mu} = \left(-1 + \frac{1}{.27}\right)(4.63) = 12.52$$

$$\hat{\beta} = -\alpha + \frac{n}{\hat{\alpha}_{21}} - n = \left(-12.52 + \frac{10}{.27} - 10\right) = 14.52$$

3. Using the values of $\hat{\alpha}$, $\hat{\beta}$, and n above, determine the joint distribution of scores on forms 1 and 2, as shown in table 5.3. This distribution is symbolized $\hat{f}(x,y)$, which represents the proportion (probability) of persons scoring x on form 1 and y on form 2. For example, given $\hat{\alpha} = 12.52$, $\hat{\beta} = 14.52$, and $n = 10$, the value of $\hat{f}(x,y)$ for the scores $x = 0$ and $y = 0$ is obtained as follows:

$$\hat{f}(0,0) = \prod_{i=1}^{2n} \frac{2n + \hat{\beta} - i}{2n + \hat{\alpha} + \hat{\beta} - i}$$

$$= \frac{20 + 14.52 - 1}{20 + 12.52 + 14.52 - 1} \times \frac{20 + 14.52 - 2}{20 + 12.52 + 14.52 - 2} \times \cdots$$

$$\times \frac{20 + 14.52 - 20}{20 + 12.52 + 14.52 - 20}$$

$$= .0002 \text{ (approximately)}.$$

Then given $\hat{f}(0,0) = .0002$, values of $\hat{f}(x,y)$ for other x and y pairs, like $x = 1$ and $y = 0$, are obtained as follows:

$$\hat{f}(x+1,y) = \hat{f}(x,y) \cdot \frac{(n-x)(\hat{\alpha} + x + y)}{(x+1)(2n + \hat{\beta} - x - y - 1)}$$

$$\hat{f}(0+1,0) = \hat{f}(0,0) \cdot \frac{(10-0)(12.52 + 0 + 0)}{(0+1)(20 + 14.52 - 0 - 0 - 1)}$$

$$= .0006 \text{ (approximately)}.$$

Also, $\hat{f}(x,y)$ is symmetric in the sense that $\hat{f}(x,y) = \hat{f}(y,x)$. Thus, for example, $\hat{f}(0,1) = \hat{f}(1,0) = .0006$. Huynh (1976, pp. 254-58) also

TABLE 5.3. Joint Distribution of Scores on Test Forms 1 and 2

Form 1 (x)	Form 2 (y)										
	0	1	2	3	4	5	6	7	8	9	10
0	0002	0006	0011	0013	0012	0008	0004	0002	0000	0000	0000
1	0006	0024	0050	0069	0068	0050	0028	0012	0004	0001	0000
2	0011	0050	0116	0174	0188	0152	0093	0043	0014	0003	0000
3	0013	0069	0174	0286	0338	0299	0201	0101	0036	0008	0001
4	0012	0068	0188	0338	0436	0421	0308	0169	0066	0017	0002
5	0008	0050	0152	0299	0421	0444	0354	0211	0090	0025	0003
6	0004	0028	0093	0201	0308	0354	0308	0200	0093	0028	0004
7	0002	0012	0043	0101	0169	0211	0200	0142	0072	0024	0004
8	0000	0004	0014	0036	0066	0090	0093	0072	0040	0014	0003
9	0000	0001	0003	0008	0017	0025	0028	0024	0014	0006	0001
10	0000	0000	0000	0001	0002	0003	0004	0004	0003	0001	0000

NOTE: Each entry in the body of this table represents the proportion of examinees that would obtain score x on form 1 and y on form 2. Decimal points are omitted.

provides formulas that are somewhat more manageable than those above for values of x and y near n. In either case, after much computation, the joint distribution of scores on forms 1 and 2 is obtained, as shown in table 5.3. Each entry of the table represents the proportion of examinees that would obtain score x on form 1 and score y on form 2. Note that decimal points have been omitted from the table for the sake of readability.

4. Coefficient $\hat{p}_0$, the proportion of consistent classifications, is obtained by summing appropriate entries in table 5.3. For example, if the mastery cut-off is again set at 8, the proportion of persons consistently classified as masters on both tests is the sum of the nine entries in the lower right-hand corner of table 5.3.

$$.0040 + .0014 + .0003 + .0014 + .0006 + .0001 + .0003 +$$
$$.0001 + .0000 = .0082.$$

Similarly, the proportion of persons consistently classified as nonmasters on both tests is the sum of the sixty-four entries in the upper left-hand corner of the table, or .8928. Thus, the total proportion of consistent decisions in table 5.3, derived solely from form 1, is:

$$\hat{p}_0 = .0082 + .8928$$
$$= .90.$$

The previous two-form estimate of this quantity, derived from table 5.2, was $\hat{p}_0 = .97$. The actual value in the population from which the thirty students in the example were drawn is $\hat{p}_0 = .88$ (Subkoviak 1978). More will be said later about the accuracy and comparability of one- versus two-form estimates of $\hat{p}_0$.

5. Coefficient $\hat{\kappa} = (\hat{p}_o - \hat{p}_c)/(1 - \hat{p}_c)$, the proportion of consistent decisions beyond that expected by chance, can also be obtained from table 5.3 as follows. Proportion $\hat{p}_0 = .90$ is given above. The proportion of consistent decisions due to chance, $\hat{p}_c$, is a function of the marginal proportions of masters and nonmasters in table 5.3. Specifically, the proportion of masters on form 1 (or form 2) is the sum of the last three rows (columns) of the table, or .0577; the proportion of nonmasters is $1 - .0577 = .9423$. Thus, the proportion of consistent decisions expected by chance is

$$\hat{p}_c = .0577 \times .0577 + .9423 \times .9423$$
$$= .89.$$

The previous two-form estimate of this quantity in table 5.2 was similarly $\hat{p}_c = .90$.

Finally, the proportion of consistent decisions beyond that expected by chance is

$$\hat{\kappa} = \frac{\hat{p}_o - \hat{p}_c}{1 - \hat{p}_c}$$

$$= \frac{.90 - .89}{1 - .89}$$

$$= .09$$

The previous two-form estimate of kappa based on table 5.2 was quite different, $\hat{\kappa} = .70$. Again, more will be said about the accuracy of one- versus two-form estimates of $\hat{\kappa}$ later.

As noted earlier, certain assumptions are implicit in the Huynh procedure outlined above (see Keats & Lord 1962, Huynh 1976). Basically, two conditions must be met. The first is that students' true scores on the test must be distributed as a beta distribution. Beta distributions can take a variety of different forms—skewed or symmetric, peaked or flat—corresponding to different values of $\hat{\alpha}$, $\hat{\beta}$, and n in step 2 above. Some examples are bell, rectangular, J, and U shapes (see LaValle 1970, for more illustrations). Many real data sets meet or closely approximate this first condition (see Keats & Lord 1962); exceptions would be multi-humped distributions, which are uncommon if not rare.

The second condition is as follows. If n-item tests were repeatedly administered to a fixed individual, the resulting distribution of test scores is assumed to be binomial in form. This assumption is most tenable if (a) the test items (or "trials") are scored 0 or 1, (b) the items are statistically independent so that the outcome on one does not determine or affect the outcome on others, and (c) the items are equally difficult. Requirement (a) above does not represent a significant limitation, since most objective items are scored as either right (1) or wrong (0). Similarly, condition (b) can be approximated by insuring, for instance, that incorrect computations on one item do not automatically lead to incorrect computations on others, by including rest periods to minimize fatigue effects on the latter items of a long test, and so forth. However, at first glance, condition (c) appears to be problematic, since in practice test items do vary in difficulty. Yet, this aspect of the Keats-Lord model appears to be quite robust with respect to the violations of item homogeneity that occur on actual tests. Specifically, violations of condition (c) seem to result in slightly conservative estimates of reliability, $\hat{p}_0$ or $\hat{\kappa}$ (Subkoviak 1978, Huynh & Saunders 1979). Wilcox (1978) has also noted in another context that the simple binomial model used here compares favorably to a more complex compound binomial model, which provides explicitly for items of varying difficulty.

Lord (1965, 1969) has extended the earlier work of Keats and Lord (1962) by replacing the beta and binomial assumptions used above with somewhat less simplistic conditions that more closely approximate actual test data. Consequently, reliability procedures like Huynh's (1976) could be based on these latter, more sophisticated models (for example, see Livingston 1978). However, an advantage of the Huynh procedure is that it involves the estimation of only two paramters, $\hat{\alpha}$ and $\hat{\beta}$ in step 2, which can be accomplished with relatively small subject samples (e.g., $N > 40$ for very short tests or $N > 2n$ for longer tests [Huynh 1978, personal communication]); whereas the latter models involve more parameters and require much larger subject samples (e.g., $N > 1,000$).

The computations involved in steps 1 to 5 obviously become quite tedious, if not prohibitive, unless performed by a computer. However, Huynh (1976, p. 258) has also proposed an approximation method that involves much less computation and still requires only one test administration. The method assumes that if both forms 1 and 2 were administered (again, only one form need actually be administered), the joint distribution of scores on the two forms would be approximately normal or bell shaped. Huynh suggests that this may be reasonable if $n > 8$ and if $\hat{\mu}/n$ is between .15 and .85 (see Novick, Lewis, & Jackson 1973); of course, the shape of the observed score distribution should also shed light on the reasonableness of this normal assumption. Using the scores on form 1 of table 5.1 as an example, the steps involved in the approximation are as follows.

1. Compute the mean ($\hat{\mu}$), standard deviation ($\hat{\sigma}$), Kuder-Richardson 21 coefficient ($\hat{\alpha}_{21}$), and alpha parameter ($\hat{\alpha}$), and specify the cut-off score (c), as before.

$$\hat{\mu} = \frac{\Sigma x}{N} = \frac{139}{30} = 4.63$$

$$\hat{\sigma} = \sqrt{\frac{\Sigma x^2}{N-1} - \frac{(\Sigma x)^2}{N(N-1)}} = \sqrt{\frac{739}{30-1} - \frac{(139)^2}{30(30-1)}} = 1.81$$

$$\hat{\alpha}_{21} = \frac{n}{n-1}\left[1 - \frac{\hat{\mu}(n - \hat{\mu})}{n\hat{\sigma}^2}\right] =$$
$$\frac{10}{10-1}\left[1 - \frac{(4.63)(10 - 4.63)}{10(3.27)}\right] = .27$$

$$\hat{\alpha} = \left(-1 + \frac{1}{\hat{\alpha}_{21}}\right)\hat{\mu} = \left(-1 + \frac{1}{.27}\right)(4.63) = 12.52$$

2. Next, compute the following quantities.

$$\hat{\mu}' = \sin^{-1}\sqrt{\hat{\mu}/n} = \sin^{-1}\sqrt{4.63/10} = .75$$

$$\hat{\sigma}' = \sqrt{(\hat{\alpha}_{21} + 1)/(\hat{\alpha} + n)} = \sqrt{(.27 + 1)/(12.52 + 10)} = .24$$

$$\hat{\rho} = \hat{\alpha}_{21}\sqrt{(n - 1)/(n + \hat{\alpha}_{21})} =$$
$$(.27)\sqrt{(10 - 1)/(10 + .27)} = .25$$

$$c' = \sin^{-1}\sqrt{(c - .5)/n} = \sin^{-1}\sqrt{(8 - .5)/10} = 1.05$$

These values correspond respectively to the mean, standard deviation, reliability, and cut-off score after an arcain transformation of the test scores. The intended purpose of the transformation is to "normalize" the data, as required. However, a study by Peng (1979) seems to suggest that, in many cases, as good or better results are achieved without this transformation.

3. Compute the normal deviate corresponding to the cut-off score.

$$z = (c' - \hat{\mu}')/\hat{\sigma}' = (1.05 - .75)/.24 = 1.25$$

4. Using tables found in most statistical texts, obtain the probability $(\hat{p}_z)$ that a standard normal variable is less than $z = 1.25$: $\hat{p}_z = .89$.

5. Using *Tables of the Bivariate Normal Distribution Function and Related Functions* (1959) or an equivalent (Gupta 1963), obtain the probability $(\hat{p}_{zz})$ that two standardized normal variables with correlation $\hat{\rho} = .25$ are less than $z = 1.25$: $\hat{p}_{zz} = .81$.

6. Finally, compute $\hat{p}_0$ or $\hat{\kappa}$.

$$\hat{p}_0 = 1 - 2(\hat{p}_z - \hat{p}_{zz}) = 1 - 2(.89 - .81) = .84$$

$$\hat{\kappa} = \frac{\hat{p}_{zz} - \hat{p}_z^2}{\hat{p}_z - \hat{p}_z^2} = \frac{.81 - (.89)^2}{.89 - (.89)^2} = .18$$

To reduce even further the amount of computation involved, Huynh (1978) has also tabled values of the proportion of consistent classifications $(\hat{p}_0)$ and kappa $(\hat{\kappa})$ for short tests containing between five and ten items. A complete set of these tables is presented in the appendix. By way of example, suppose the reliability is desired for a five-item test with a mastery cut-off of 3. Then the page of the appendix corresponding to $n = 5$ and $c = 3$ contains the relevant values. Suppose further that the test mean is 1.5 and the Kuder-Richardson 21 coefficient is .400 for the scores of $M = 100$ students (see step 1 above for the appropriate computing formulas). Corresponding to these values, the appendix provides four figures: (a) $\hat{p}_o = 0.755$ (the proportion of consistent classifications); (b) $\sqrt{M}\ \hat{\sigma}_{\hat{p}_o} = 0.267$ (the square root of M, or the number of students, times the standard error, or standard deviation of $\hat{p}_o$ estimates over repeated samples of size M); (c) $\hat{\kappa} = 0.268$ (kappa); and (d) $\sqrt{M}\ \hat{\sigma}_{\hat{\kappa}} = 0.784$ (the square root of M times the standard error of $\hat{\kappa}$ estimates).

Generally, $\hat{p}_o = 0.755$ and $\hat{\kappa} = 0.268$ are the values of primary interest; however, $\sqrt{M}\ \hat{\sigma}_{\hat{p}_o} = 0.267$ and $\sqrt{M}\ \hat{\sigma}_{\hat{\kappa}} = 0.784$ also provide useful information about the *accuracy* of the $\hat{p}_o$ and $\hat{\kappa}$ estimates, respectively. Specifically, if $\hat{p}_o$ estimates are computed repeatedly for independent samples of $M = 100$ students, the standard error or standard deviation of these $\hat{p}_o$ estimates (about the true population value of p_o) is given by $\hat{\sigma}_{\hat{p}_o} = 0.267/\sqrt{M} = 0.267/\sqrt{100} = 0.0267$, which means that $\hat{p}_o$ estimates tend to deviate from the true population value by about 0.0267 on the average. Similarly, the standard error of the $\hat{\kappa}$ estimates is given by $\hat{\sigma}_{\hat{\kappa}} = 0.784/\sqrt{M} = 0.784/\sqrt{100} = 0.0784$.

Now consider test form 1 of table 5.1—a ten-item test with a mastery cut-off score of 8. The page of the appendix corresponding to $n = 10$ and $c = 8$ contains the appropriate reliability information. However, the scores of the thirty students on form 1 have a mean of 4.63, which falls between the values 4.0 and 5.0 in the left margin of the page; and the KR-21 coefficient of form 1 is .27, which falls between the values .200 and .300 at the top of the page. Thus, *interpolation* must be used to obtain exact values of $\hat{p}_o$, $\sqrt{M}\ \hat{\sigma}_{\hat{p}_o}$, and $\hat{\kappa}$, and $\sqrt{M}\ \hat{\sigma}_{\hat{\kappa}}$ for form 1. Incidentally, interpolation is not recommended, in general, unless the values of $\hat{\alpha}_{21} = .27$, $\hat{\mu}/n = 4.63/10 = .463$, and $c/n = 8/10 = .80$ are all between .20 and .80, in which case the tabled values of the appendix increase or decrease consistently within both rows and columns, making interpolation possible.

Interpolation will now be used to obtain the appropriate value of $\hat{p}_o$ for form 1. On the page of the appendix corresponding to $n = 10$ and $c = 8$, let $u_1 = .200$ and $u_2 = .300$ be the two tabled values of KR-21 closest to $u = .27$, the $\hat{\alpha}_{21}$ value for form 1. Similarly, let $v_1 = 4.0$ and $v_2 = 5.0$ to be tabled mean values closest to $v = 4.63$, the mean ($\hat{\mu}$) of form 1. Next, compute $p = (u - u_1)/(u_2 - u_1) = (.27 - .200)/(.300 - .200) = .70$ and $q = (v - v_1)/(v_2 - v_1) = (4.63 - 4.0)/(5.0 - 4.0) = .63$. Then the interpolated value of $\hat{p}_o$ for form 1 is given by the following expression, in which $f(\ ,\ )$ represents the *tabled* value of $\hat{p}_o$, corresponding to the quantities in parenthesis:

$$\hat{p}_o = (1 - p)(1 - q)f(u_1,v_1) + p(1 - q)f(u_2,v_1) + \\ q(1 - p)f(u_1,v_2) + pqf(u_2,v_2)$$

$$= (1 - .70)(1 - .63)f(.200,4.0) + (.70)(1 - .63)f(.300,4.0) + \\ (.63)(1 - .70)f(.200,5.0) + (.70)(.63)f(.300,5.0)$$

$$= (.30)(.37)(.958) + (.70)(.37)(.947) + (.63)(.30)(.869) + \\ (.70)(.63)(.856)$$

$$= .89$$

Interpolated values of $\sqrt{M}\,\hat{\sigma}_{\hat{p}_o}$, $\hat{\kappa}$, and $\sqrt{M}\,\hat{\sigma}_{\hat{\kappa}}$ for form 1 are similarly obtained:

$$\sqrt{M}\,\hat{\sigma}_{\hat{p}_o} = (1 - .70)(1 - .63)(.160) + (.70)(1 - .63)(.176) + \\ (.63)(1 - .70)(.271) + (.70)(.63)(.258) = .23$$

$$\hat{\kappa} = (1 - .70)(1 - .63)(.039) + (.70)(1 - .63)(.079) + (.63) \\ (1 - .70)(.071) + (.70)(.63)(.124) = .09$$

$$\sqrt{M}\,\hat{\sigma}_{\hat{\kappa}} = (1 - .70)(1 - .63)(.389) + (.70)(1 - .63)(.512) + \\ (.63)(1 - .70)(.564) + (.70)(.63)(.623) = .56$$

It should also be noted, for example, that for a five-item test, tables are only provided for cut-off scores of 3, 4, and 5. To obtain tabled values for a cut-off of 2 on a five-item test with a mean of 1.5 and a KR-21 of .500, simply enter the table for a five-item test with a cut-off of $n - c + 1 = 5 - 2 + 1 = 4$, a mean of $n - \hat{\mu} = 5 - 1.5 = 3.5$, and the same KR-21 of .500. Thus, the appropriate tabled values on the page corresponding to $n = 5$ and $c = 4$ for the example would be 0.691, (0.345), 0.374, and (0.678).

In summary, Huynh's method represents a mathematically sophisticated procedure for estimating classification consistency from a single administration of a mastery test. The next method to be considered is mathematically less elegant than the former, but in practice the two procedures generally provide similar results (Subkoviak 1978). This is not totally unexpected, since the assumptions involved in the two methods are basically equivalent despite outward appearances.

Subkoviak Method. Again, suppose that only the scores on form 1 of table 5.1 are available and that one wishes to estimate either the proportion of consistent classifications $(\hat{p}_o)$ or coefficient kappa $(\hat{\kappa})$. The steps involved in Subkoviak's (1975, 1976) procedure are illustrated in table 5.4.

1. The first two columns of the table contain the scores (x) and the frequency of each score (N_x) in the sample of thirty students. The mean and Kuder-Richardson 20 coefficient of the scores are, respectively, $\hat{\mu} = 4.63$ and $\hat{\alpha}_{20} = .47$. These two quantities are used in the next step.

2. The ten-item test in the example can be thought of as a sample of items from an actual or hypothetical universe of such items. The third column of table 5.4 contains an estimate of the proportion of items in that universe $\hat{p}_x$ that a person with test score x would be expected to answer correctly. Thus, $\hat{p}_x$ can be thought of as the probability of a correct item response. The $\hat{p}_x$ values in table 5.4 are obtained from the following equation:

$$\hat{p}_x = \hat{\alpha}_{20}(x/n) + (1 - \hat{\alpha}_{20})(\hat{\mu}/n)$$
$$= .47(x/10) + (1 - .47)(4.63/10)$$

For example, if $x = 9$, then $\hat{p}_x = .47(9/10) + (1 - .47)(4.63/10) = .67$. Hambleton, Swaminathan, Algina, and Coulson (1978, pp. 5–10) also review other methods for estimating $\hat{p}_x$; in fact, the simple estimate $\hat{p}_x = x/n$ provides reasonably accurate results if n is large, e.g., $n > 40$.

TABLE 5.4. An Illustration of Subkoviak's Estimation Procedure

x	N_x	$\hat{p}_x$	$\hat{P}_x$	$1 - 2(\hat{P}_x - \hat{P}_x^2)$	$N_x[1 - 2(\hat{P}_x - \hat{P}_x^2)]$	$N_x P_x$
9	1	.67	.3070	.5745	.5745	.3070
8	1	.62	.2013	.6784	.6784	.2013
7	3	.57	.1236	.7834	2.3502	.3708
6	4	.53	.0791	.8543	3.4172	.3164
5	4	.48	.0420	.9195	3.6780	.1680
4	9	.43	.0202	.9604	8.6436	.1818
3	6	.39	.0103	.9796	5.8776	.0618
2	1	.34	.0039	.9922	.9922	.0039
1	1	.29	.0012	.9976	.9976	.0012
Total	30				27.2093	1.6122

3. If a student's probability of a correct response to a single item is $\hat{p}_x = .67$, what is the probability that the student will correctly answer eight or more items on the ten-item test, and thus be classified as a master? If the items can be considered as trials in a binomial process, the probability of eight or more successes in ten trials is $\hat{p}_x = .3070$ for such a student, as indicated in the fourth column of table 5.4 (see *Tables of the Binomial Probability Distribution,* 1949). The other values in column four were similarly obtained.

4. The probability that the above student will be consistently classified as a master on two independent testings is $\hat{P}_x{}^2$; conversely, the probability that this student will be consistently classified as a nonmaster is $(1 - \hat{P}_x)^2$. Thus, the probability of consistent classification for this individual is $\hat{P}_x{}^2 + (1 - \hat{P}_x)^2 = 1 - 2(\hat{P}_x - \hat{P}_x{}^2) = .5745$, as indicated in the fifth column of the table. The other values in column five were obtained in the same way.

5. The probability of consistent classification across the entire group, $\hat{p}_o$, is obtained from the total of column six (27.2093).

$$\hat{p}_o = \frac{\Sigma N_x[1 - 2(\hat{P}_x - \hat{P}_x{}^2)]}{N}$$

$$= \frac{27.2093}{30}$$

$$= .91$$

6. Finally, the chance probability of consistent classification $\hat{p}_c$ is obtained from the total of column seven (1.6122), and subsequently coefficient kappa ($\hat{\kappa}$) can be computed.

$$\hat{p}_c = 1 - 2\left[\frac{\Sigma N_x P_x}{N} - \left(\frac{\Sigma N_x P_x}{N}\right)^2\right]$$

$$= 1 - 2\left[\frac{1.6122}{30} - \left(\frac{1.6122}{30}\right)^2\right]$$

$$= .90$$

$$\hat{\kappa} = \frac{\hat{p}_o - \hat{p}_c}{1 - \hat{p}_c}$$

$$= \frac{.91 - .90}{1 - .90}$$

$$= .10$$

In short, the estimates of $\hat{p}_o$, $\hat{p}_c$, and $\hat{\kappa}$ derived from tables 5.3 (Huynh) and 5.4 (Subkoviak) are similar. As previously noted, this is not un-expected, since the two methods involve certain common assumptions. For instance, both posit a binomial distribution of observed scores over repeated testing of an individual. The Marshall-Haertel method, to be discussed next, likewise involves this same assumption. However, the three methods are not identical; all are conceptually distinct, and all lead to somewhat different numerical results.

Marshall-Haertel Method. Like the Huynh and Subkoviak procedures, the Marshall-Haertel (1976) method requires only a single test administration and involves the assumption that if an individual were repeatedly tested, his or her distribution of observed scores would be binomial in form.

Given the scores on an n-item test, like form 1 of table 5.1, and granted the binomial assumption, Marshall and Haertel estimate the group's scores on a *hypothetical* $2n$-item test. Theoretically, this test could be split into half-tests of n items each; and the proportion of consistent classification on the two half-tests could be estimated as in table 5.2. Moreover, such an estimate could be obtained for each of the many possible ways that a $2n$-item test can be partitioned into half-tests. Marshall and Haertel take the average of the various split-half estimates as their final estimate of $\hat{p}_o$, the proportion of consistent classifications on two tests. As illustrated below, Marshall and Haertel obtained this average via a computing formula.

Given the frequency (N_x) of scores (x) on form 1 of table 5.1, Marshall and Haertel obtain the frequency (N_w) of scores (w) on a test twice as long as form 1:

$$N_w = \sum_{x=0}^{n} N_x \binom{2n}{w} \left(\frac{x}{n}\right)^w \left(1 - \frac{x}{n}\right)^{2n-w} \tag{4}$$

For example, the number of students in the example who would receive the score $w = 13$ on a test twice as long as form 1 is estimated to be

$$N_{13} = \sum_{x=0}^{10} N_x \binom{20}{13} \left(\frac{x}{10}\right)^{13} \left(1 - \frac{x}{10}\right)^{20-13}$$

$$= (0)\binom{20}{13}\left(\frac{0}{10}\right)^{13}\left(1 - \frac{0}{10}\right)^{7} + (1)\binom{20}{13}\left(\frac{1}{10}\right)^{13}\left(1 - \frac{10}{10}\right)^{7} + \ldots +$$

$$(1)\binom{20}{13}\left(\frac{9}{10}\right)^{13}\left(1 - \frac{9}{10}\right)^{7} + (0)\binom{20}{13}\left(\frac{10}{10}\right)^{13}\left(1 - \frac{10}{10}\right)^{7}$$

$$= 1.65.$$

Frequencies of the other possible scores on a $2n$-item test (N_0, N_1, ..., N_{20}) are similarly estimated.

Next, the probability of consistent classification on two half-tests for a person with score w on the double-length test is computed. This quantity is symbolized $\Phi_w(a,b)$ and is obtained as follows:

$$\Phi_w(a, b) = \sum_{j=a}^{b} \frac{\binom{w}{j}\binom{2n - w}{n - j}}{\binom{2n}{n}}. \tag{5}$$

In equation 5, values a and b are determined by the particular value of w and the cut-off score (c) on an n-item test. For example, if $w = 13$ and $c = 8$, then $a = w - [c - 1] = 6$ and $b = c - 1 = 7$, and the probability of consistent classification is:

$$\Phi_{13}(6,7) = \sum_{j=6}^{7} \frac{\binom{13}{j}\binom{20 - 13}{10 - j}}{\binom{20}{10}}$$

$$= \frac{\binom{13}{6}\binom{7}{4}}{\binom{20}{10}} + \frac{\binom{13}{7}\binom{7}{3}}{\binom{20}{10}}$$

$$= \frac{(1,716)(35)}{184,756} + \frac{(1,716)(35)}{184,756}$$

$$= .65$$

For certain values of w, the probability of consistent classification is either 0 or 1, and need not be calculated via equation 5.

The computational formula for the Marshall-Haertel estimate combines the quantities obtained by equations 4 and 5 as follows:

$$\hat{p}_o = \frac{1}{N}\left[\sum_{w=0}^{c-1} N_w + \sum_{w=c}^{2c-2} N_w \cdot \Phi_w(w - [c - 1], c - 1) + \sum_{w=2c}^{n+c-1} N_w \cdot \Phi_w(c, w - c) + \sum_{w=n+c}^{2n} N_w\right], \quad (6)$$

where N = number of examinees

n = number of items

c = cut-off score of an n-item test

N_w = frequency of score w given by equation 4

$\Phi_w(a, b)$ = probability of consistent classification given by equation 5.

Thus, the Marshall-Haertel estimate for form 1 of table 5.1 with $c = 8$ is

$$\hat{p}_o = \frac{1}{30}\left[\sum_{w=0}^{8-1} N_w + \sum_{w=8}^{16-2} N_w \cdot \Phi_w(w - [8 - 1], 8 - 1) + \sum_{w=16}^{10+8-1} N_w \cdot \Phi_w(8, w - 8) + \sum_{w=18}^{20} N_w\right]$$

$$= .87 .[1]$$

Finally, although Marshall and Haertel do not specifically consider the computation of coefficient kappa ($\hat{\kappa}$), it appears possible to estimate a kappa-like coefficient within the framework of their procedure.

Comparison of Four Approaches. A recent empirical study provides some insight into the various strengths and weaknesses of the four procedures outlined above (Subkoviak, 1977a, 1978). The study involved 1,586 students, each of whom took parallel forms of ten, thirty, and fifty items. On each test, four different mastery criteria were considered: 50 percent, 60 percent, 70 percent, and 80 percent of the items correct.

As indicated in the third column of table 5.5, the proportion of the students consistently classified as master/master or nonmaster/nonmaster on the two forms was computed for each criterion score and

---

[1]Computations provided by Laird Marshall.

test length, for a total of twelve distinct values of p_o, referred to as parameter values.

Next, fifty classroom-size samples of thirty students each were randomly drawn with replacement from the population of 1,586; for example, table 5.1 contains scores for the first such sample on parallel ten-item tests. For each of the fifty samples, the Swaminathan, Huynh, Subkoviak, and Marshall methods were applied, as previously illustrated, to esti-mate each parameter value. Thus, fifty estimates of each parameter value were obtained by each method. The mean and standard error of these fifty estimates were then calculated, as shown in the last four columns of table 5.5. For example, when the parameter value is .67 in table 5.5, the mean of fifty Swaminathan estimates is .68 and their standard error is .08, that is, the estimates deviate .08 units on the average from the parameter value of .67.

The same procedure was also repeated using fifty samples of 300 per-sons, and the resulting means and standard errors are shown in paren-theses in table 5.5. For example, when the parameter is .67, the mean of fifty Swaminathan estimates based on samples of 300 is .67 and the standard error is .02, which is much smaller than the previous standard error due to the larger sample size.

A number of points regarding the relative strengths and limitations of the various methods can be gleaned from table 5.5. The advantages and disadvantages of the methods are discussed below and are also summarized in table 5.6.

The advantages of the Swaminathan method are that it is computa-tionally simple (see table 5.2) and produces unbiased estimates. The latter point can be inferred from the fact that Swaminathan means equal corresponding parameter values in almost all cases in table 5.5. The disadvantages of the Swaminathan method are that it requires two test administrations and that the errors of estimation tend to be relatively large for classroom-size samples. Of course, the first disadvantage might rather be viewed as an advantage if one were interested in studying the effects of nonequivalent test forms or different test occasions on classi-fication consistency. The second disadvantage can be inferred from the comparatively large standard errors observed for the Swaminathan method in table 5.5 for samples of size thirty.

The advantages and disadvantages of the Huynh, Subkoviak, and Marshall methods are generally similar. All three methods have the advantages of requiring only one test administration and of producing estimates having relatively small standard errors for classroom-size samples, which can again be verified in table 5.5. The disadvantages are that the three methods are computationally tedious and produce biased estimates for short tests. Regarding the latter problem, each

TABLE 5.5. Means and Standard Errors of Four Reliability Methods

Test Length (n)	Mastery Criterion (c)	Parameter Value (p₀)	Swaminathan		Huynh		Subkoviak		Marshall	
			Mean	St. Error	Mean	St. Error	Mean	St. Error	Mean	St. Error
10	50%	.67	.68 (.67)	.08 (.02)	.66 (.65)	.06 (.03)	.66 (.64)	.06 (.04)	.74 (.73)	.08 (.06)
	60%	.72	.72 (.72)	.07 (.02)	.67 (.66)	.06 (.06)	.69 (.66)	.06 (.06)	.75 (.74)	.05 (.03)
	70%	.80	.79 (.80)	.08 (.02)	.76 (.74)	.06 (.06)	.79 (.77)	.05 (.03)	.79 (.79)	.03 (.01)
	80%	.88	.87 (.88)	.06 (.02)	.86 (.86)	.05 (.02)	.90 (.90)	.05 (.03)	.85 (.85)	.04 (.03)
30	50%	.79	.79 (.79)	.07 (.02)	.80 (.79)	.03 (.01)	.81 (.79)	.04 (.01)	.82 (.81)	.04 (.02)
	60%	.84	.83 (.84)	.06 (.02)	.82 (.81)	.03 (.03)	.84 (.83)	.04 (.02)	.84 (.84)	.03 (.01)
	70%	.88	.88 (.88)	.06 (.02)	.88 (.88)	.03 (.01)	.89 (.90)	.04 (.02)	.88 (.89)	.03 (.01)
	80%	.94	.93 (.94)	.05 (.01)	.94 (.94)	.02 (.01)	.95 (.96)	.03 (.02)	.93 (.94)	.03 (.01)
50	50%	.83	.84 (.83)	.06 (.02)	.83 (.82)	.02 (.01)	.84 (.83)	.03 (.01)	.84 (.83)	.03 (.01)
	60%	.87	.87 (.87)	.06 (.02)	.86 (.85)	.02 (.01)	.88 (.87)	.03 (.01)	.87 (.87)	.03 (.01)
	70%	.91	.91 (.91)	.05 (.01)	.91 (.91)	.02 (.01)	.93 (.93)	.03 (.01)	.91 (.92)	.03 (.01)
	80%	.96	.96 (.96)	.08 (.01)	.96 (.97)	.02 (.01)	.97 (.97)	.02 (.01)	.96 (.96)	.02 (.01)

NOTE: Means and standard errors based on 50 samples of 30 persons/(300 persons)

TABLE 5.6. Relative Advantages and Disadvantages of Various Reliability Methods

Methods	Advantages	Disadvantages
Swaminathan	computationally simple; unbiased estimates	requires two testings; large errors of estimate for small groups
Huynh	requires one testing; small errors of estimate	computationally tedious (except for approximation); biased (but conservative) estimates for short tests
Subkoviak	requires one testing; small errors of estimate	computationally tedious; biased estimates for short tests
Marshall	requires one testing; small errors of estimate	computationally tedious; biased estimates for short tests

method is characterized by a different type of bias that is most pronounced in the ten-item test of table 5.5. Specifically, the Huynh procedure tends to produce underestimates for all criterion levels on the ten-item test; and Huynh and Saunders (1979) have shown that this tendency also extends to estimates of kappa. If there must be bias, such conservative estimation may be the most tolerable. On the other hand, for short tests the Subkoviak procedure seems to produce slight underestimates for criterion levels, like 50 percent, near the center of the test score distribution and overestimates for criterion levels, like 80 percent, in the tails. This pattern was also detected by Algina and Noe (1978) in a simulated-data study of the Subkoviak method. Conversely, the Marshall method produces overestimates for criterion levels in the center of the distribution and underestimates for criterion levels in the tails. In the Algina and Noe study, the latter type of pattern was related to the use of the observed proportion correct (x/n) as an estimate of the bionomial probability of success, which is the estimate employed in equation 4 of the Marshall procedure.

All things considered, the Huynh procedure seems worthy of recommendation for standard data sets of the type considered above. It requires only one test administration, tends to produce slightly conservative estimates, has an associated normal approximation method, and is based on the mathematically elegant Keats-Lord model. (On the other hand, the Subkoviak and Marshall methods seem also to produce reasonably accurate estimates in practice, and, of course, Swaminathan appears to be the only totally unbiased method.)

Suggestions for Future Research

Hambleton, Swaminathan, Algina, and Coulson (1978, pp. 39–42) identified some eight to ten general areas for future research in criterion-referenced testing. The present section will attempt to offer some specific suggestions for research in the area of test reliability. In this regard, at least five recommendations come to mind immediately.

First, more work is needed to facilitate the computation of criterion-referenced reliability coefficients, particularly for teachers and other practitioners who do not have direct access to computer facilities. Huynh's tables in the appendix are a definite step in the right direction, but at present, these tables include tests of between five and ten items only. Extensions to longer and, perhaps, shorter tests are in order. In the same vein, further study of approximation methods that minimize the computational labor involved in obtaining reliability estimates also seems necessary (cf. Huynh 1976, p. 258; Peng 1979).

Second, there is a need for additional studies, such as Huynh and Saunders (1979), Marshall and Serlin (1979), and Subkoviak (1978), comparing the characteristics and properties of the various methods reviewed here. Further discussion of the relative merits of $\hat{p}_o$, $\hat{\kappa}$, and other consistency coefficients for various purposes would also appear to be worthwhile.

Third, a number of authors have recently demonstrated an interest in deriving coefficients that measure the extent to which observed outcomes on mastery tests agree with the outcomes that would occur if students' true scores were known (Livingston 1978; Subkoviak & Wilcox 1978; Wilcox 1977). For example, Subkoviak and Wilcox (1978) propose a procedure for estimating the proportion of students in a group that is *correctly* classified in the sense that the test classification agrees with the true mastery or nonmastery level of the student. Their approach is based upon the 1962 Keats and Lord model discussed earlier. Livingston's (1978) method is similar in intent but is based on the 1969 Lord model, also alluded to earlier. In practice it may be more relevant and useful to know the extent to which a test leads to correct outcomes than the extent to which it leads to consistent, but possibly incorrect, outcomes. In any event, this line of research warrants further consideration.

Fourth, there is a need for a comprehensive test analysis computer package for criterion-referenced test users who have access to data-processing equipment. Ideally, such a package would include routines for test scoring and for computing item statistics, reliability coefficients, validity coefficients, and the like, for evaluating and improving criterion-referenced tests of various kinds. Presently, a number of iso-

lated programs exist for particular purposes, such as computing the
type of reliability coefficients discussed here, but I am unaware of any
panoramic packages specifically designed for criterion-referenced test
analysis. Certainly, an obvious reason for the apparent nonexistence of
such an inclusive system is the lack of total agreement regarding which
procedures and statistics should be used and the existence of problems
for which practical solutions have yet to be proposed. However, theoretical and practical developments may soon be sufficient to support such
an undertaking.

Finally, there is a need for further study of the relative merits of
the "reliability of mastery classification decisions" reviewed here and
the "reliability of criterion-referenced test scores" reviewed by Brennan
in chapter 6. The final section of this chapter seeks to introduce some
of the relevant distinctions between these two approaches. The interested reader is referred to Kane and Brennan (in press) and Mellenbergh and van der Linden (1978) for more on this topic.

Guidelines for Practitioners

Coefficient $\hat{p}_o$ Versus $\hat{\kappa}$. Having selected a particular reliability method
(Huynh, Marshall, Subkoviak, or Swaminathan), the user is next faced
with the question of which reliability coefficient to report, $\hat{p}_o$ or $\hat{\kappa}$. The
fact that $\hat{p}_o$ and $\hat{\kappa}$ are sensitive to different types of consistency is clearly
illustrated in figure 5.1, which was obtained by computing $\hat{p}_o$ and $\hat{\kappa}$ (a
la Subkoviak) at the points $c = 2,4,6,8$ for form 1 of table 5.1. Also
shown at the bottom of the figure is the distribution of test scores (x)
for the example. The most obvious conclusion to be drawn from figure
5.1 is that coefficients $\hat{p}_o$ and $\hat{\kappa}$ do not measure exactly the same thing.
In fact, $\hat{p}_o$ assumes its largest values in the tails of the score (*) distribution and smallest values in the center, while $\hat{\kappa}$ does just the opposite.

This converse relationship between $\hat{p}_o$ and $\hat{\kappa}$ depicted in figure 5.1
occurs because these two coefficients are sensitive to different types of
consistency, and *the primary reason for choosing one index over the
other should be the desire to measure the type of consistency particular
to that coefficient* (see Subkoviak 1977*b*). To be specific, coefficient
$\hat{p}_o$ represents the total proportion of consistent classification that occurs
for whatever reason on two tests. For example, two of the factors that
contribute to overall consistency as measured by $\hat{p}_o$ are the relative
numbers of masters and nonmasters in the group tested and the precision or accuracy of the test. The latter point needs no explanation;
however, an example may help to clarify the former. If a group is composed entirely or almost entirely of high-ability students, that fact alone

tends to assure a large proportion of consistent mastery/mastery outcomes, just as a heavily biased coin tends to produce consistent results on two independent flips.

If one were primarily interested in the test's contribution to the overall proportion $(\hat{p}_o)$ of consistent classifications, it might be desirable to extract from $\hat{p}_o$ that portion of consistency expected from or attributable to the particular mastery-nonmastery composition of the group tested. Coefficient kappa does just that. In the expression for kappa, $\hat{\kappa} = (\hat{p}_o - \hat{p}_c)/(1 - \hat{p}_c)$, the quantity $\hat{p}_c$ represents the portion of consistency due to the mastery-nonmastery composition of the group, which is subtracted from the overall proportion $\hat{p}_o$; the difference is then divided by $(1 - \hat{p}_c)$, which simply puts kappa on a scale from $+1$ to -1.

The use of $\hat{p}_o$ or $\hat{\kappa}$ should stem primarily from the desire to measure overall consistency or solely test consistency, respectively. Having made that conscious choice, certain other properties of the coefficients become matters for consideration. For example, the standard errors re-

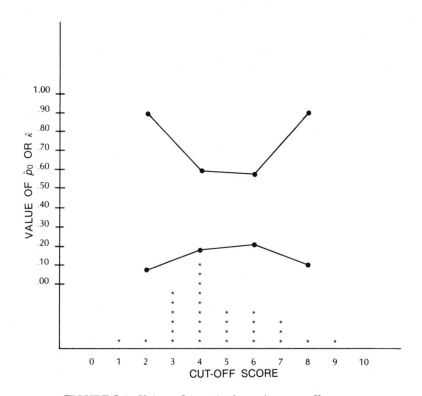

FIGURE 5.1. Values of $\hat{p}_o$ and $\hat{\kappa}$ for various cut-off scores

ported in table 5.5 for estimates of $\hat{p}_o$ are somewhat smaller than would be observed if estimates of $\hat{\kappa}$ and their standard errors had been computed instead (Huynh 1977*a*, Huynh & Saunders 1979, Subkoviak 1977*b*). In other words, for a fixed sample size, like thirty students, $\hat{p}_o$ can generally be estimated with greater precision than $\hat{\kappa}$.

In point of fact, $\hat{p}_o$ and $\hat{\kappa}$ are not the only options open to the user. Huynh (1977*b*) has recently proposed the use of the kappamax coefficient, which is simply the largest value that kappa attains within the range of cut-off scores, and Goodman and Kruskal (1954) discuss a number of others. To date, none of these coefficients has gained universal acceptance. However, as previously indicated, this does not imply that the choice of a coefficient should be made indiscriminately. Rather, a particular coefficient should be selected because of what it measures.

Decision-Consistency Approach versus Generalizability Theory Approach. At the beginning of this chapter, a distinction was drawn between (*a*) the reliability of mastery classification decisions and (*b*) the reliability of criterion-referenced test scores (see chapter 6). In the example of table 5.1 type (*a*) refers to the consistency of mastery/mastery and nonmastery/nonmastery decisions across forms 1 and 2 when the cut-off score is set at 8, while type (*b*) refers to the consistency of deviations from the cut-off across forms 1 and 2. In other words, types (*a*) and (*b*) are respectively concerned with the reliability of *categories* of mastery and *degrees* of mastery, over repeated testing. Thus, a choice must be made between the type (*a*) coefficients discussed here and the type (*b*) coefficients proposed by Livingston (1972*a*,1972*b*,1972*c*) and Brennan and Kane (1977*a*,1977*b*).

Opposition to type (*b*) reliability and support for type (*a*) has been advanced by Hambleton and Novick (1973), who argue that the deviation of an examinee's score from the criterion is not as important as whether or not the examinee is consistently assigned to the same side of the criterion on two tests (also see Hambleton 1974). However, this conjecture awaits confirmation. In a similar vein, Harris's (1972) and Shavelson, Block, and Ravitch's (1972) criticisms of type (*b*) reliability would appear to be primarily matters of "form rather than substance," as Brennan and Kane phrased it (1977*a*, p. 286).

However, one relevant point worth noting is that type (*b*) reliability is sensitive to all errors of measurement that occur on a test, including errors that do not lead to inconsistent mastery-nonmastery classifications (see Brennan & Kane 1977*a*, pp. 286–87). In table 5.1, for example, type (*b*) reliability is reduced by the fact that student 4's score deviations of -1 and -4 from the cut-off of 8 differ from form 1 to form

2, even though the student is consistently classified as a nonmaster on both forms. On the other hand, type (a) reliability is limited in the sense that all inconsistent classifications are regarded as equally serious. Yet the implications in table 5.1 of misclassifying student 1, whose true ability is close to the cut-off score of 8, may be less serious than the implications of misclassifying a student whose true ability is far below (or above) the cut-off. In other words, neither type (a) nor type (b) is optimal for all applications (Brennan & Kane 1977a, p. 287). For the present, perhaps the simplest recommendation would be to use type (b) if *degree* of mastery or nonmastery is an important consideration and to use type (a) if such distinctions among different levels of mastery or different levels of nonmastery are not important. For a more detailed and technical comparison of reliability types (a) and (b), the reader is referred to a paper by Kane and Brennan (in press) that discusses these coefficients within a common mathematical framework.

Appendix

Tables of the Raw Agreement Index and Its Standard Error $\times \sqrt{M}$ and the Kappa Index and Its Standard Error $\times \sqrt{M}$ in the Beta-Binomial Model

Input data to the tables are the number of test items (N), the mastery score (C), the test mean, and the KR-21 reliability ($\hat{\alpha}_{21}$). M is the number of subjects. This notation differs slightly from that used in the text.

For each entry (N, C, $\hat{\mu}$, $\hat{\alpha}_{21}$), four values may be read out: $\hat{p}_o$, $\hat{\sigma}_{\hat{p}_o}$, $\hat{\kappa}$, and $\hat{\sigma}_{\hat{\kappa}}$, respectively. Both $\hat{\sigma}_{\hat{p}_o}$ and $\hat{\sigma}_{\hat{\kappa}}$ are enclosed in parentheses.

Example: Let N $=$ 5, C $=$ 3, $\hat{\mu} = 1.5$, and $\hat{\alpha}_{21} = .400$. The page of the table corresponding to N $=$ 5 and C $=$ 3 provides the values $\hat{p}_o = .755$, $\sqrt{M}\,\hat{\sigma}_{\hat{p}_o} = .267$, $\hat{\kappa} = .268$, and $\sqrt{M}\,\hat{\sigma}_{\hat{\kappa}} = .784$. With $M = 100$, the estimated standard errors are $\hat{\sigma}_{\hat{p}_o} = .0267$ and $\hat{\sigma}_{\hat{\kappa}} = .0784$.

From H. Huynh, *Computation and Inference for Two Reliability Indices in Mastery Testing Based on the Beta-Binomial Model,* Publication Series in Mastery Testing, Research Memorandum 78-1 (Columbia, S.C.: College of Education, University of South Carolina, 1978). Reprinted with permission.

Table of the Raw Agreement Index and its
S.E.*SQRT(M), the Kappa Index and its
S.E.*SQRT(M) in the Beta-binomial Model
M = Number of subjects
Number of items N = 5
Mastery score C = 3

```
-------------------------------------------------------------------
Test  KR21=
Mean   .100    .200    .300    .400    .500    .600    .700    .800    .900
-------------------------------------------------------------------
0.5    0.975   0.966   0.957   0.949   0.942   0.939   0.940   0.948   0.966
      (0.157) (0.172) (0.177) (0.172) (0.157) (0.138) (0.118) (0.105) (0.089)
       0.022   0.062   0.122   0.198   0.288   0.392   0.510   0.643   0.798
      (0.477) (0.734) (0.928) (1.048) (1.091) (1.063) (0.969) (0.808) (0.570)

1.0    0.879   0.869   0.862   0.858   0.858   0.864   0.877   0.901   0.938
      (0.297) (0.276) (0.252) (0.226) (0.202) (0.180) (0.162) (0.146) (0.119)
       0.042   0.096   0.162   0.239   0.325   0.421   0.529   0.652   0.800
      (0.706) (0.808) (0.858) (0.863) (0.831) (0.769) (0.680) (0.563) (0.405)

1.5    0.729   0.734   0.743   0.755   0.772   0.795   0.824   0.864   0.918
      (0.338) (0.313) (0.289) (0.267) (0.245) (0.223) (0.201) (0.175) (0.137)
       0.057   0.122   0.192   0.268   0.351   0.441   0.542   0.659   0.801
      (0.874) (0.865) (0.833) (0.784) (0.720) (0.646) (0.561) (0.463) (0.339)

2.0    0.591   0.617   0.645   0.675   0.709   0.746   0.789   0.840   0.906
      (0.431) (0.397) (0.365) (0.332) (0.299) (0.266) (0.232) (0.195) (0.147)
       0.067   0.137   0.209   0.285   0.365   0.453   0.550   0.662   0.802
      (0.973) (0.898) (0.821) (0.744) (0.666) (0.587) (0.505) (0.417) (0.309)

2.5    0.535   0.571   0.607   0.645   0.685   0.728   0.776   0.832   0.901
      (0.503) (0.454) (0.409) (0.366) (0.325) (0.284) (0.244) (0.201) (0.150)
       0.070   0.142   0.215   0.290   0.370   0.457   0.552   0.664   0.803
      (1.006) (0.909) (0.818) (0.732) (0.649) (0.569) (0.488) (0.403) (0.300)

3.0    0.591   0.617   0.645   0.675   0.709   0.746   0.789   0.840   0.906
      (0.431) (0.397) (0.365) (0.332) (0.299) (0.266) (0.232) (0.195) (0.147)
       0.067   0.137   0.209   0.285   0.365   0.453   0.550   0.662   0.802
      (0.973) (0.898) (0.821) (0.744) (0.666) (0.587) (0.505) (0.417) (0.309)

3.5    0.729   0.734   0.743   0.755   0.772   0.795   0.824   0.864   0.918
      (0.338) (0.313) (0.289) (0.267) (0.245) (0.223) (0.201) (0.175) (0.137)
       0.057   0.122   0.192   0.268   0.351   0.441   0.542   0.659   0.801
      (0.874) (0.865) (0.833) (0.784) (0.720) (0.646) (0.561) (0.463) (0.339)

4.0    0.879   0.869   0.862   0.858   0.858   0.864   0.877   0.901   0.938
      (0.297) (0.276) (0.252) (0.226) (0.202) (0.180) (0.162) (0.146) (0.119)
       0.042   0.096   0.162   0.239   0.325   0.421   0.529   0.652   0.800
      (0.706) (0.808) (0.858) (0.863) (0.831) (0.769) (0.680) (0.563) (0.405)

4.5    0.975   0.966   0.957   0.949   0.942   0.939   0.940   0.948   0.966
      (0.157) (0.172) (0.177) (0.172) (0.157) (0.138) (0.118) (0.105) (0.089)
       0.022   0.062   0.122   0.198   0.288   0.392   0.510   0.643   0.798
      (0.477) (0.734) (0.928) (1.048) (1.091) (1.063) (0.969) (0.808) (0.570)
-------------------------------------------------------------------
```

Table of the Raw Agreement Index and its
S.E.*SQRT(M), the Kappa Index and its
S.E.*SQRT(M) in the Beta-binomial Model
M = Number of subjects
Number of items N = 5
Mastery score C = 4

Test Mean	KR21= .100	.200	.300	.400	.500	.600	.700	.800	.900
0.5	0.998	0.996	0.992	0.987	0.981	0.974	0.968	0.964	0.971
	(0.028)	(0.045)	(0.064)	(0.084)	(0.101)	(0.108)	(0.102)	(0.083)	(0.068)
	0.005	0.021	0.055	0.111	0.192	0.297	0.427	0.583	0.768
	(0.142)	(0.355)	(0.611)	(0.855)	(1.041)	(1.136)	(1.118)	(0.971)	(0.682)
1.0	0.980	0.973	0.963	0.953	0.942	0.932	0.925	0.926	0.945
	(0.120)	(0.140)	(0.157)	(0.167)	(0.167)	(0.156)	(0.133)	(0.108)	(0.094)
	0.014	0.042	0.088	0.152	0.235	0.338	0.459	0.603	0.775
	(0.300)	(0.491)	(0.661)	(0.787)	(0.854)	(0.857)	(0.796)	(0.670)	(0.473)
1.5	0.928	0.916	0.903	0.891	0.882	0.876	0.876	0.889	0.923
	(0.242)	(0.243)	(0.237)	(0.223)	(0.202)	(0.175)	(0.148)	(0.127)	(0.114)
	0.027	0.067	0.123	0.192	0.276	0.374	0.487	0.620	0.782
	(0.483)	(0.620)	(0.715)	(0.764)	(0.767)	(0.727)	(0.650)	(0.537)	(0.384)
2.0	0.830	0.820	0.813	0.808	0.809	0.815	0.830	0.858	0.907
	(0.316)	(0.292)	(0.266)	(0.238)	(0.211)	(0.186)	(0.166)	(0.150)	(0.131)
	0.041	0.093	0.155	0.228	0.311	0.404	0.511	0.635	0.787
	(0.666)	(0.729)	(0.755)	(0.747)	(0.710)	(0.648)	(0.565)	(0.464)	(0.337)
2.5	0.697	0.701	0.709	0.721	0.738	0.761	0.793	0.836	0.899
	(0.323)	(0.299)	(0.277)	(0.256)	(0.237)	(0.218)	(0.199)	(0.178)	(0.146)
	0.055	0.116	0.184	0.258	0.339	0.429	0.530	0.647	0.792
	(0.827)	(0.817)	(0.785)	(0.737)	(0.674)	(0.600)	(0.517)	(0.424)	(0.313)
3.0	0.576	0.601	0.628	0.658	0.692	0.730	0.775	0.829	0.898
	(0.401)	(0.377)	(0.352)	(0.325)	(0.298)	(0.269)	(0.238)	(0.203)	(0.156)
	0.065	0.134	0.205	0.280	0.361	0.448	0.545	0.657	0.796
	(0.952)	(0.884)	(0.812)	(0.737)	(0.660)	(0.581)	(0.499)	(0.412)	(0.308)
3.5	0.538	0.574	0.612	0.650	0.691	0.735	0.784	0.839	0.908
	(0.521)	(0.473)	(0.429)	(0.386)	(0.345)	(0.304)	(0.262)	(0.216)	(0.159)
	0.071	0.144	0.217	0.293	0.374	0.460	0.555	0.664	0.800
	(1.027)	(0.932)	(0.844)	(0.760)	(0.678)	(0.598)	(0.516)	(0.429)	(0.323)
4.0	0.636	0.662	0.689	0.718	0.750	0.785	0.825	0.871	0.927
	(0.464)	(0.428)	(0.392)	(0.358)	(0.324)	(0.289)	(0.252)	(0.208)	(0.150)
	0.070	0.142	0.217	0.294	0.376	0.464	0.560	0.669	0.803
	(1.035)	(0.969)	(0.900)	(0.829)	(0.754)	(0.675)	(0.590)	(0.492)	(0.370)
4.5	0.845	0.844	0.847	0.853	0.864	0.879	0.899	0.925	0.958
	(0.317)	(0.291)	(0.267)	(0.247)	(0.231)	(0.214)	(0.195)	(0.167)	(0.121)
	0.057	0.124	0.198	0.279	0.365	0.458	0.559	0.671	0.805
	(0.952)	(1.028)	(1.052)	(1.036)	(0.988)	(0.913)	(0.810)	(0.677)	(0.502)

For the Mastery score = 2 enter N-xbar in the test mean column

157

Table of the Raw Agreement Index and its
S.E.*SQRT(M), the Kappa Index and its
S.E.*SQRT(M) in the Beta-binomial Model
M = Number of subjects
Number of items N = 5
Mastery score C = 5

Test Mean	KR21= .100	.200	.300	.400	.500	.600	.700	.800	.900
0.5	1.000	1.000	0.999	0.998	0.996	0.993	0.988	0.980	0.975
	(0.002)	(0.005)	(0.010)	(0.019)	(0.032)	(0.051)	(0.072)	(0.081)	(0.062)
	0.000	0.004	0.015	0.040	0.088	0.168	0.288	0.458	0.687
	(0.019)	(0.089)	(0.231)	(0.443)	(0.699)	(0.949)	(1.125)	(1.139)	(0.893)
1.0	0.999	0.997	0.995	0.992	0.986	0.978	0.966	0.954	0.950
	(0.015)	(0.024)	(0.037)	(0.055)	(0.077)	(0.100)	(0.116)	(0.111)	(0.080)
	0.002	0.010	0.028	0.062	0.119	0.205	0.326	0.488	0.702
	(0.059)	(0.158)	(0.303)	(0.476)	(0.649)	(0.787)	(0.853)	(0.807)	(0.613)
1.5	0.992	0.988	0.983	0.975	0.964	0.951	0.935	0.922	0.925
	(0.053)	(0.070)	(0.091)	(0.112)	(0.133)	(0.148)	(0.149)	(0.125)	(0.092)
	0.006	0.019	0.046	0.089	0.154	0.244	0.363	0.517	0.716
	(0.130)	(0.252)	(0.393)	(0.534)	(0.651)	(0.723)	(0.729)	(0.655)	(0.488)
2.0	0.973	0.965	0.954	0.942	0.927	0.911	0.895	0.887	0.904
	(0.127)	(0.147)	(0.165)	(0.180)	(0.188)	(0.184)	(0.164)	(0.127)	(0.105)
	0.012	0.034	0.070	0.122	0.192	0.284	0.400	0.545	0.729
	(0.236)	(0.364)	(0.487)	(0.591)	(0.660)	(0.682)	(0.651)	(0.562)	(0.416)
2.5	0.928	0.915	0.901	0.886	0.870	0.857	0.849	0.853	0.888
	(0.228)	(0.236)	(0.239)	(0.235)	(0.221)	(0.196)	(0.161)	(0.128)	(0.125)
	0.021	0.053	0.098	0.158	0.233	0.325	0.437	0.572	0.741
	(0.376)	(0.483)	(0.579)	(0.641)	(0.667)	(0.652)	(0.595)	(0.500)	(0.371)
3.0	0.843	0.830	0.817	0.806	0.799	0.796	0.803	0.826	0.880
	(0.311)	(0.296)	(0.275)	(0.248)	(0.218)	(0.185)	(0.158)	(0.148)	(0.151)
	0.033	0.076	0.131	0.197	0.275	0.366	0.472	0.597	0.753
	(0.544)	(0.620)	(0.668)	(0.686)	(0.673)	(0.629)	(0.557)	(0.461)	(0.347)
3.5	0.714	0.711	0.711	0.715	0.725	0.742	0.770	0.813	0.883
	(0.314)	(0.285)	(0.257)	(0.234)	(0.216)	(0.205)	(0.201)	(0.197)	(0.178)
	0.047	0.102	0.166	0.237	0.316	0.405	0.505	0.621	0.764
	(0.734)	(0.758)	(0.757)	(0.732)	(0.686)	(0.621)	(0.539)	(0.445)	(0.342)
4.0	0.576	0.597	0.621	0.649	0.683	0.722	0.769	0.827	0.901
	(0.349)	(0.346)	(0.343)	(0.337)	(0.328)	(0.313)	(0.291)	(0.256)	(0.196)
	0.063	0.130	0.201	0.277	0.357	0.443	0.537	0.643	0.775
	(0.945)	(0.910)	(0.861)	(0.799)	(0.727)	(0.646)	(0.558)	(0.464)	(0.366)
4.5	0.560	0.603	0.647	0.691	0.737	0.783	0.832	0.883	0.938
	(0.672)	(0.632)	(0.587)	(0.537)	(0.482)	(0.422)	(0.354)	(0.277)	(0.183)
	0.080	0.158	0.237	0.316	0.396	0.479	0.567	0.664	0.785
	(1.202)	(1.127)	(1.046)	(0.960)	(0.870)	(0.776)	(0.677)	(0.574)	(0.464)

For the Mastery score = 1 enter N-xbar in the test mean column

Table of the Raw Agreement Index and its
S.E.*SQRT(M), the Kappa Index and its
S.E.*SQRT(M) in the Beta-binomial Model
M = Number of subjects
Number of items N = 6
Mastery score C = 3

Test Mean	KR21= .100	.200	.300	.400	.500	.600	.700	.800	.900
0.6	0.959	0.948	0.938	0.930	0.925	0.924	0.928	0.939	0.961
	(0.202)	(0.207)	(0.201)	(0.188)	(0.169)	(0.147)	(0.128)	(0.114)	(0.093)
	0.028	0.074	0.137	0.214	0.304	0.404	0.517	0.643	0.792
	(0.553)	(0.771)	(0.918)	(0.995)	(1.008)	(0.964)	(0.869)	(0.724)	(0.517)
1.2	0.815	0.811	0.811	0.814	0.822	0.836	0.857	0.887	0.931
	(0.320)	(0.293)	(0.267)	(0.242)	(0.220)	(0.199)	(0.179)	(0.157)	(0.123)
	0.051	0.111	0.180	0.256	0.340	0.431	0.533	0.650	0.793
	(0.793)	(0.837)	(0.842)	(0.816)	(0.766)	(0.697)	(0.611)	(0.506)	(0.368)
1.8	0.637	0.657	0.679	0.704	0.732	0.764	0.803	0.849	0.910
	(0.395)	(0.366)	(0.337)	(0.309)	(0.279)	(0.250)	(0.218)	(0.183)	(0.137)
	0.065	0.133	0.204	0.279	0.359	0.446	0.542	0.654	0.793
	(0.930)	(0.873)	(0.810)	(0.741)	(0.668)	(0.592)	(0.510)	(0.421)	(0.311)
2.4	0.538	0.573	0.609	0.646	0.685	0.727	0.774	0.829	0.898
	(0.487)	(0.440)	(0.396)	(0.354)	(0.314)	(0.274)	(0.235)	(0.193)	(0.143)
	0.069	0.140	0.212	0.286	0.365	0.450	0.544	0.654	0.792
	(0.973)	(0.880)	(0.793)	(0.710)	(0.629)	(0.550)	(0.470)	(0.387)	(0.287)
3.0	0.574	0.601	0.629	0.660	0.694	0.732	0.775	0.828	0.896
	(0.416)	(0.384)	(0.353)	(0.321)	(0.289)	(0.257)	(0.222)	(0.185)	(0.140)
	0.066	0.134	0.205	0.279	0.358	0.444	0.539	0.650	0.791
	(0.933)	(0.858)	(0.783)	(0.706)	(0.629)	(0.550)	(0.470)	(0.385)	(0.285)
3.6	0.708	0.713	0.721	0.734	0.750	0.773	0.803	0.844	0.903
	(0.328)	(0.304)	(0.281)	(0.258)	(0.236)	(0.214)	(0.191)	(0.166)	(0.132)
	0.055	0.117	0.185	0.259	0.340	0.428	0.528	0.643	0.788
	(0.820)	(0.807)	(0.774)	(0.724)	(0.660)	(0.586)	(0.503)	(0.411)	(0.300)
4.2	0.857	0.846	0.838	0.833	0.832	0.837	0.849	0.874	0.918
	(0.305)	(0.284)	(0.260)	(0.234)	(0.208)	(0.182)	(0.160)	(0.141)	(0.118)
	0.040	0.091	0.154	0.227	0.311	0.404	0.510	0.633	0.785
	(0.645)	(0.724)	(0.760)	(0.757)	(0.721)	(0.659)	(0.575)	(0.470)	(0.337)
4.8	0.957	0.946	0.934	0.923	0.913	0.906	0.905	0.913	0.940
	(0.192)	(0.203)	(0.206)	(0.200)	(0.185)	(0.163)	(0.137)	(0.115)	(0.099)
	0.022	0.061	0.115	0.185	0.271	0.371	0.486	0.619	0.780
	(0.429)	(0.603)	(0.731)	(0.804)	(0.822)	(0.788)	(0.708)	(0.585)	(0.413)
5.4	0.995	0.991	0.986	0.979	0.971	0.964	0.958	0.957	0.968
	(0.052)	(0.074)	(0.095)	(0.113)	(0.123)	(0.121)	(0.107)	(0.086)	(0.072)
	0.008	0.030	0.073	0.137	0.223	0.329	0.455	0.602	0.775
	(0.210)	(0.448)	(0.694)	(0.896)	(1.024)	(1.062)	(1.006)	(0.853)	(0.595)

For the Mastery score = 4 enter N-xbar in the test mean column

```
                Table of the Raw Agreement Index and its
                S.E.*SQRT(M), the Kappa Index and its
                S.E.*SQRT(M) in the Beta-binomial Model
                         M = Number of subjects
                         Number of items N = 6
                           Mastery score C = 4
-----------------------------------------------------------------------
Test KR21=
Mean   .100    .200    .300    .400    .500    .600    .700    .800    .900
-----------------------------------------------------------------------
0.6    0.995   0.991   0.986   0.979   0.971   0.964   0.958   0.957   0.968
      (0.052) (0.074) (0.095) (0.113) (0.123) (0.121) (0.107) (0.086) (0.072)
       0.008   0.030   0.073   0.137   0.223   0.329   0.455   0.602   0.775
      (0.210) (0.448) (0.694) (0.896) (1.024) (1.062) (1.006) (0.853) (0.595)

1.2    0.957   0.946   0.934   0.923   0.913   0.906   0.905   0.913   0.940
      (0.192) (0.203) (0.206) (0.200) (0.185) (0.163) (0.137) (0.115) (0.099)
       0.022   0.061   0.115   0.185   0.271   0.371   0.486   0.619   0.780
      (0.429) (0.603) (0.731) (0.804) (0.822) (0.788) (0.708) (0.585) (0.413)

1.8    0.857   0.846   0.838   0.833   0.832   0.837   0.849   0.874   0.918
      (0.305) (0.284) (0.260) (0.234) (0.208) (0.182) (0.160) (0.141) (0.118)
       0.040   0.091   0.154   0.227   0.311   0.404   0.510   0.633   0.785
      (0.645) (0.724) (0.760) (0.757) (0.721) (0.659) (0.575) (0.470) (0.337)

2.4    0.708   0.713   0.721   0.734   0.750   0.773   0.803   0.844   0.903
      (0.328) (0.304) (0.281) (0.258) (0.236) (0.214) (0.191) (0.166) (0.132)
       0.055   0.117   0.185   0.259   0.340   0.428   0.528   0.643   0.788
      (0.820) (0.807) (0.774) (0.724) (0.660) (0.586) (0.503) (0.411) (0.300)

3.0    0.574   0.601   0.629   0.660   0.694   0.732   0.775   0.828   0.896
      (0.416) (0.384) (0.353) (0.321) (0.289) (0.257) (0.222) (0.185) (0.140)
       0.066   0.134   0.205   0.279   0.358   0.444   0.539   0.650   0.791
      (0.933) (0.858) (0.783) (0.706) (0.629) (0.550) (0.470) (0.385) (0.285)

3.6    0.538   0.573   0.609   0.646   0.685   0.727   0.774   0.829   0.898
      (0.487) (0.440) (0.396) (0.354) (0.314) (0.274) (0.235) (0.193) (0.143)
       0.069   0.140   0.212   0.286   0.365   0.450   0.544   0.654   0.792
      (0.973) (0.880) (0.793) (0.710) (0.629) (0.550) (0.470) (0.387) (0.287)

4.2    0.637   0.657   0.679   0.704   0.732   0.764   0.803   0.849   0.910
      (0.395) (0.366) (0.337) (0.309) (0.279) (0.250) (0.218) (0.183) (0.137)
       0.065   0.133   0.204   0.279   0.359   0.446   0.542   0.654   0.793
      (0.930) (0.873) (0.810) (0.741) (0.668) (0.592) (0.510) (0.421) (0.311)

4.8    0.815   0.811   0.811   0.814   0.822   0.836   0.857   0.887   0.931
      (0.320) (0.293) (0.267) (0.242) (0.220) (0.199) (0.179) (0.157) (0.123)
       0.051   0.111   0.180   0.256   0.340   0.431   0.533   0.650   0.793
      (0.793) (0.837) (0.842) (0.816) (0.766) (0.697) (0.611) (0.506) (0.368)

5.4    0.959   0.948   0.938   0.930   0.925   0.924   0.928   0.939   0.961
      (0.202) (0.207) (0.201) (0.188) (0.169) (0.147) (0.128) (0.114) (0.093)
       0.028   0.074   0.137   0.214   0.304   0.404   0.517   0.643   0.792
      (0.553) (0.771) (0.918) (0.995) (1.008) (0.964) (0.869) (0.724) (0.517)
-----------------------------------------------------------------------
For the Mastery score =  3  enter N-xbar in the test mean column
```

Table of the Raw Agreement Index and its
S.E.*SQRT(M), the Kappa Index and its
S.E.*SQRT(M) in the Beta-binomial Model
M = Number of subjects
Number of items N = 6
Mastery score C = 5

Test Mean	KR21= .100	.200	.300	.400	.500	.600	.700	.800	.900
0.6	1.000	0.999	0.998	0.996	0.992	0.986	0.979	0.972	0.973
	(0.006)	(0.013)	(0.024)	(0.039)	(0.058)	(0.077)	(0.088)	(0.081)	(0.059)
	0.001	0.009	0.029	0.069	0.137	0.235	0.366	0.532	0.737
	(0.048)	(0.175)	(0.381)	(0.631)	(0.871)	(1.045)	(1.101)	(1.001)	(0.714)
1.2	0.994	0.991	0.985	0.978	0.969	0.958	0.946	0.939	0.946
	(0.047)	(0.065)	(0.086)	(0.107)	(0.125)	(0.135)	(0.129)	(0.105)	(0.080)
	0.006	0.022	0.054	0.106	0.181	0.280	0.406	0.559	0.748
	(0.143)	(0.302)	(0.482)	(0.650)	(0.773)	(0.829)	(0.804)	(0.693)	(0.488)
1.8	0.971	0.962	0.951	0.938	0.925	0.912	0.902	0.902	0.923
	(0.142)	(0.161)	(0.176)	(0.185)	(0.184)	(0.172)	(0.147)	(0.116)	(0.097)
	0.015	0.042	0.086	0.147	0.226	0.324	0.442	0.583	0.757
	(0.291)	(0.446)	(0.582)	(0.681)	(0.730)	(0.724)	(0.663)	(0.552)	(0.389)
2.4	0.909	0.895	0.882	0.869	0.859	0.852	0.853	0.866	0.905
	(0.261)	(0.258)	(0.249)	(0.233)	(0.211)	(0.182)	(0.152)	(0.128)	(0.114)
	0.028	0.068	0.121	0.188	0.269	0.364	0.474	0.604	0.766
	(0.472)	(0.584)	(0.661)	(0.698)	(0.694)	(0.651)	(0.575)	(0.469)	(0.335)
3.0	0.795	0.787	0.781	0.779	0.781	0.789	0.807	0.838	0.893
	(0.320)	(0.293)	(0.266)	(0.239)	(0.212)	(0.188)	(0.167)	(0.150)	(0.131)
	0.042	0.095	0.156	0.227	0.307	0.398	0.502	0.623	0.773
	(0.661)	(0.706)	(0.719)	(0.704)	(0.662)	(0.599)	(0.517)	(0.420)	(0.305)
3.6	0.649	0.659	0.673	0.690	0.712	0.739	0.775	0.823	0.890
	(0.321)	(0.301)	(0.282)	(0.264)	(0.246)	(0.227)	(0.206)	(0.181)	(0.146)
	0.057	0.119	0.187	0.260	0.339	0.426	0.524	0.638	0.780
	(0.831)	(0.805)	(0.763)	(0.708)	(0.642)	(0.568)	(0.486)	(0.397)	(0.294)
4.2	0.543	0.575	0.608	0.643	0.681	0.723	0.771	0.827	0.898
	(0.447)	(0.415)	(0.383)	(0.351)	(0.318)	(0.284)	(0.248)	(0.207)	(0.155)
	0.068	0.137	0.208	0.283	0.362	0.447	0.541	0.650	0.786
	(0.959)	(0.880)	(0.802)	(0.724)	(0.647)	(0.569)	(0.488)	(0.403)	(0.303)
4.8	0.581	0.614	0.647	0.683	0.720	0.761	0.805	0.856	0.918
	(0.509)	(0.463)	(0.420)	(0.379)	(0.339)	(0.300)	(0.258)	(0.212)	(0.152)
	0.071	0.144	0.217	0.293	0.373	0.458	0.551	0.658	0.791
	(1.017)	(0.935)	(0.855)	(0.778)	(0.702)	(0.625)	(0.544)	(0.454)	(0.343)
5.4	0.798	0.803	0.811	0.823	0.839	0.859	0.883	0.914	0.952
	(0.344)	(0.318)	(0.295)	(0.274)	(0.255)	(0.234)	(0.210)	(0.177)	(0.126)
	0.062	0.130	0.204	0.283	0.367	0.457	0.554	0.663	0.795
	(0.967)	(0.996)	(0.990)	(0.957)	(0.903)	(0.829)	(0.736)	(0.617)	(0.462)

For the Mastery score = 2 enter N-xbar in the test mean column

Table of the Raw Agreement Index and its
S.E.*SQRT(M), the Kappa Index and its
S.E.*SQRT(M) in the Beta-binomial Model
M = Number of subjects
Number of items N = 6
Mastery score C = 6

Test Mean	KR21= .100	.200	.300	.400	.500	.600	.700	.800	.900
0.6	1.000	1.000	1.000	0.999	0.999	0.997	0.993	0.986	0.978
	(0.000)	(0.001)	(0.003)	(0.007)	(0.014)	(0.028)	(0.049)	(0.070)	(0.063)
	0.000	0.001	0.007	0.022	0.056	0.121	0.231	0.399	0.644
	(0.005)	(0.035)	(0.119)	(0.275)	(0.503)	(0.771)	(1.010)	(1.109)	(0.918)
1.2	1.000	0.999	0.998	0.997	0.994	0.988	0.979	0.965	0.953
	(0.004)	(0.008)	(0.015)	(0.026)	(0.042)	(0.065)	(0.091)	(0.105)	(0.081)
	0.001	0.004	0.014	0.038	0.082	0.156	0.270	0.434	0.663
	(0.022)	(0.078)	(0.182)	(0.332)	(0.509)	(0.680)	(0.797)	(0.801)	(0.628)
1.8	0.997	0.996	0.993	0.988	0.981	0.970	0.955	0.937	0.929
	(0.022)	(0.032)	(0.047)	(0.066)	(0.089)	(0.113)	(0.131)	(0.127)	(0.088)
	0.002	0.010	0.027	0.060	0.113	0.195	0.311	0.469	0.681
	(0.063)	(0.148)	(0.268)	(0.409)	(0.548)	(0.656)	(0.703)	(0.658)	(0.496)
2.4	0.988	0.983	0.976	0.967	0.954	0.939	0.920	0.903	0.905
	(0.068)	(0.086)	(0.106)	(0.128)	(0.148)	(0.162)	(0.161)	(0.135)	(0.094)
	0.006	0.021	0.047	0.089	0.151	0.238	0.353	0.503	0.698
	(0.137)	(0.245)	(0.368)	(0.488)	(0.586)	(0.643)	(0.641)	(0.567)	(0.418)
3.0	0.961	0.951	0.939	0.925	0.908	0.890	0.874	0.866	0.885
	(0.154)	(0.172)	(0.188)	(0.200)	(0.203)	(0.195)	(0.171)	(0.129)	(0.106)
	0.014	0.037	0.073	0.125	0.194	0.283	0.395	0.535	0.715
	(0.253)	(0.366)	(0.474)	(0.561)	(0.616)	(0.628)	(0.591)	(0.503)	(0.368)
3.6	0.898	0.884	0.869	0.854	0.839	0.827	0.822	0.831	0.873
	(0.263)	(0.265)	(0.260)	(0.248)	(0.227)	(0.196)	(0.159)	(0.130)	(0.131)
	0.024	0.059	0.106	0.166	0.240	0.330	0.437	0.567	0.730
	(0.410)	(0.505)	(0.579)	(0.625)	(0.637)	(0.613)	(0.552)	(0.458)	(0.338)
4.2	0.781	0.770	0.762	0.756	0.755	0.760	0.776	0.809	0.872
	(0.323)	(0.297)	(0.269)	(0.239)	(0.209)	(0.184)	(0.169)	(0.166)	(0.163)
	0.039	0.087	0.144	0.211	0.288	0.377	0.478	0.597	0.745
	(0.606)	(0.658)	(0.684)	(0.683)	(0.656)	(0.604)	(0.528)	(0.433)	(0.327)
4.8	0.620	0.630	0.644	0.662	0.687	0.718	0.759	0.814	0.889
	(0.297)	(0.285)	(0.277)	(0.272)	(0.268)	(0.264)	(0.254)	(0.235)	(0.190)
	0.056	0.118	0.185	0.258	0.337	0.423	0.517	0.625	0.758
	(0.836)	(0.825)	(0.797)	(0.751)	(0.691)	(0.618)	(0.534)	(0.441)	(0.343)
5.4	0.542	0.583	0.625	0.668	0.714	0.761	0.812	0.867	0.928
	(0.596)	(0.570)	(0.538)	(0.500)	(0.457)	(0.408)	(0.349)	(0.279)	(0.188)
	0.076	0.151	0.228	0.305	0.385	0.467	0.554	0.651	0.771
	(1.114)	(1.047)	(0.974)	(0.895)	(0.812)	(0.724)	(0.631)	(0.532)	(0.428)

For the Mastery score = 1 enter N-xbar in the test mean column

Table of the Raw Agreement Index and its
S.E.*SQRT(M), the Kappa Index and its
S.E.*SQRT(M) in the Beta-binomial Model
M = Number of subjects
Number of items N = 7
Mastery score C = 4

Test Mean	KR21= .100	.200	.300	.400	.500	.600	.700	.800	.900
0.7	0.990	0.985	0.978	0.970	0.961	0.953	0.949	0.951	0.964
	(0.081)	(0.104)	(0.123)	(0.136)	(0.139)	(0.131)	(0.113)	(0.091)	(0.076)
	0.011	0.039	0.087	0.156	0.244	0.349	0.471	0.610	0.775
	(0.274)	(0.516)	(0.738)	(0.901)	(0.986)	(0.992)	(0.919)	(0.772)	(0.541)
1.4	0.923	0.911	0.900	0.890	0.883	0.881	0.886	0.901	0.934
	(0.251)	(0.247)	(0.235)	(0.217)	(0.195)	(0.169)	(0.145)	(0.124)	(0.103)
	0.031	0.077	0.136	0.209	0.294	0.391	0.500	0.626	0.779
	(0.537)	(0.675)	(0.760)	(0.793)	(0.780)	(0.728)	(0.644)	(0.529)	(0.376)
2.1	0.775	0.772	0.774	0.779	0.788	0.804	0.826	0.860	0.911
	(0.323)	(0.296)	(0.270)	(0.245)	(0.221)	(0.199)	(0.176)	(0.152)	(0.121)
	0.050	0.109	0.176	0.250	0.331	0.420	0.521	0.637	0.782
	(0.758)	(0.779)	(0.768)	(0.733)	(0.678)	(0.607)	(0.524)	(0.428)	(0.309)
2.8	0.608	0.630	0.654	0.680	0.710	0.744	0.784	0.832	0.897
	(0.387)	(0.359)	(0.331)	(0.302)	(0.272)	(0.241)	(0.209)	(0.174)	(0.131)
	0.064	0.130	0.200	0.274	0.353	0.438	0.533	0.643	0.784
	(0.897)	(0.835)	(0.768)	(0.697)	(0.623)	(0.546)	(0.466)	(0.379)	(0.278)
3.5	0.534	0.569	0.604	0.641	0.680	0.722	0.768	0.823	0.892
	(0.472)	(0.426)	(0.383)	(0.342)	(0.303)	(0.263)	(0.224)	(0.182)	(0.134)
	0.068	0.138	0.209	0.282	0.360	0.443	0.537	0.645	0.784
	(0.945)	(0.853)	(0.767)	(0.685)	(0.605)	(0.527)	(0.448)	(0.365)	(0.269)
4.2	0.608	0.630	0.654	0.680	0.710	0.744	0.784	0.832	0.897
	(0.387)	(0.359)	(0.331)	(0.302)	(0.272)	(0.241)	(0.209)	(0.174)	(0.131)
	0.064	0.130	0.200	0.274	0.353	0.438	0.533	0.643	0.784
	(0.897)	(0.835)	(0.768)	(0.697)	(0.623)	(0.546)	(0.466)	(0.379)	(0.278)
4.9	0.775	0.772	0.774	0.779	0.788	0.804	0.826	0.860	0.911
	(0.323)	(0.296)	(0.270)	(0.245)	(0.221)	(0.199)	(0.176)	(0.152)	(0.121)
	0.050	0.109	0.176	0.250	0.331	0.420	0.521	0.637	0.782
	(0.758)	(0.779)	(0.768)	(0.733)	(0.678)	(0.607)	(0.524)	(0.428)	(0.309)
5.6	0.923	0.911	0.900	0.890	0.883	0.881	0.886	0.901	0.934
	(0.251)	(0.247)	(0.235)	(0.217)	(0.195)	(0.169)	(0.145)	(0.124)	(0.103)
	0.031	0.077	0.136	0.209	0.294	0.391	0.500	0.626	0.779
	(0.537)	(0.675)	(0.760)	(0.793)	(0.780)	(0.728)	(0.644)	(0.529)	(0.376)
6.3	0.990	0.985	0.978	0.970	0.961	0.953	0.949	0.951	0.964
	(0.081)	(0.104)	(0.123)	(0.136)	(0.139)	(0.131)	(0.113)	(0.091)	(0.076)
	0.011	0.039	0.087	0.156	0.244	0.349	0.471	0.610	0.775
	(0.274)	(0.516)	(0.738)	(0.901)	(0.986)	(0.992)	(0.919)	(0.772)	(0.541)

163

Table of the Raw Agreement Index and its
S.E.*SQRT(M), the Kappa Index and its
S.E.*SQRT(M) in the Beta-binomial Model
M = Number of subjects
Number of items N = 7
Mastery score C = 5

```
--------------------------------------------------------------------
Test KR21=
Mean   .100    .200    .300    .400    .500    .600    .700    .800    .900
--------------------------------------------------------------------
0.7    0.999   0.998   0.996   0.992   0.987   0.980   0.972   0.966   0.970
      (0.014) (0.025) (0.041) (0.060) (0.080) (0.095) (0.098) (0.083) (0.062)
       0.003   0.014   0.041   0.092   0.168   0.272   0.403   0.561   0.751
      (0.082) (0.249) (0.479) (0.721) (0.918) (1.028) (1.025) (0.895) (0.625)

1.4    0.986   0.979   0.971   0.961   0.949   0.938   0.929   0.926   0.942
      (0.093) (0.115) (0.135) (0.150) (0.156) (0.152) (0.133) (0.105) (0.084)
       0.011   0.035   0.077   0.138   0.220   0.321   0.443   0.586   0.760
      (0.237) (0.417) (0.588) (0.719) (0.791) (0.796) (0.736) (0.613) (0.427)

2.1    0.932   0.920   0.907   0.894   0.884   0.876   0.875   0.886   0.918
      (0.230) (0.234) (0.231) (0.220) (0.201) (0.176) (0.147) (0.121) (0.102)
       0.025   0.064   0.118   0.186   0.268   0.365   0.476   0.607   0.767
      (0.443) (0.577) (0.672) (0.719) (0.719) (0.677) (0.597) (0.486) (0.342)

2.8    0.815   0.807   0.801   0.798   0.799   0.807   0.823   0.851   0.901
      (0.316) (0.291) (0.265) (0.238) (0.212) (0.186) (0.163) (0.142) (0.118)
       0.042   0.095   0.157   0.228   0.309   0.400   0.503   0.623   0.774
      (0.653) (0.705) (0.721) (0.706) (0.663) (0.598) (0.515) (0.416) (0.297)

3.5    0.657   0.668   0.682   0.699   0.721   0.748   0.783   0.828   0.892
      (0.330) (0.308) (0.287) (0.266) (0.244) (0.221) (0.196) (0.167) (0.131)
       0.057   0.120   0.188   0.261   0.339   0.426   0.523   0.635   0.778
      (0.826) (0.795) (0.749) (0.692) (0.624) (0.549) (0.463) (0.379) (0.276)

4.2    0.544   0.575   0.609   0.643   0.681   0.722   0.767   0.822   0.892
      (0.444) (0.407) (0.370) (0.334) (0.299) (0.263) (0.225) (0.186) (0.138)
       0.067   0.136   0.206   0.280   0.357   0.441   0.535   0.644   0.782
      (0.932) (0.848) (0.768) (0.689) (0.611) (0.533) (0.454) (0.370) (0.274)

4.9    0.573   0.603   0.634   0.668   0.703   0.742   0.786   0.837   0.902
      (0.456) (0.415) (0.376) (0.338) (0.302) (0.265) (0.227) (0.187) (0.137)
       0.068   0.137   0.209   0.283   0.361   0.446   0.539   0.648   0.785
      (0.948) (0.867) (0.788) (0.710) (0.634) (0.557) (0.478) (0.394) (0.292)

5.6    0.749   0.754   0.762   0.773   0.789   0.811   0.838   0.874   0.924
      (0.339) (0.313) (0.288) (0.264) (0.241) (0.218) (0.194) (0.166) (0.126)
       0.057   0.121   0.191   0.267   0.348   0.437   0.535   0.647   0.786
      (0.851) (0.849) (0.823) (0.777) (0.717) (0.646) (0.563) (0.466) (0.343)

6.3    0.938   0.927   0.918   0.911   0.908   0.909   0.916   0.931   0.957
      (0.238) (0.233) (0.220) (0.200) (0.178) (0.157) (0.138) (0.122) (0.098)
       0.034   0.084   0.149   0.227   0.315   0.412   0.520   0.642   0.787
      (0.616) (0.794) (0.903) (0.948) (0.941) (0.889) (0.797) (0.665) (0.479)
--------------------------------------------------------------------
```

For the Mastery score = 3 enter N-xbar in the test mean column

Table of the Raw Agreement Index and its
S.E.*SQRT(M), the Kappa Index and its
S.E.*SQRT(M) in the Beta-binomial Model
M = Number of subjects
Number of items N = 7
Mastery score C = 6

Test Mean	KR21= .100	.200	.300	.400	.500	.600	.700	.800	.900

0.7	1.000	1.000	0.999	0.998	0.997	0.993	0.987	0.979	0.975
	(0.001)	(0.003)	(0.008)	(0.016)	(0.030)	(0.049)	(0.069)	(0.077)	(0.057)
	0.000	0.003	0.015	0.042	0.096	0.183	0.311	0.484	0.706
	(0.015)	(0.081)	(0.226)	(0.446)	(0.703)	(0.934)	(1.064)	(1.021)	(0.747)
1.4	0.998	0.997	0.994	0.990	0.984	0.975	0.963	0.951	0.949
	(0.016)	(0.027)	(0.042)	(0.061)	(0.083)	(0.104)	(0.115)	(0.105)	(0.074)
	0.002	0.011	0.032	0.072	0.136	0.230	0.356	0.518	0.721
	(0.064)	(0.175)	(0.334)	(0.515)	(0.678)	(0.785)	(0.804)	(0.715)	(0.506)
2.1	0.989	0.983	0.976	0.966	0.954	0.940	0.925	0.916	0.925
	(0.072)	(0.092)	(0.113)	(0.133)	(0.149)	(0.155)	(0.146)	(0.117)	(0.086)
	0.008	0.025	0.058	0.109	0.182	0.278	0.399	0.548	0.734
	(0.166)	(0.305)	(0.455)	(0.588)	(0.680)	(0.712)	(0.676)	(0.571)	(0.399)
2.8	0.953	0.942	0.929	0.915	0.900	0.887	0.877	0.878	0.904
	(0.181)	(0.196)	(0.205)	(0.208)	(0.201)	(0.183)	(0.155)	(0.120)	(0.100)
	0.018	0.047	0.092	0.152	0.229	0.324	0.439	0.575	0.746
	(0.322)	(0.454)	(0.565)	(0.641)	(0.672)	(0.654)	(0.589)	(0.482)	(0.338)
3.5	0.869	0.856	0.843	0.832	0.824	0.821	0.826	0.844	0.890
	(0.292)	(0.281)	(0.264)	(0.241)	(0.214)	(0.184)	(0.155)	(0.132)	(0.117)
	0.032	0.075	0.130	0.196	0.275	0.367	0.474	0.599	0.756
	(0.513)	(0.599)	(0.652)	(0.670)	(0.653)	(0.604)	(0.526)	(0.424)	(0.302)
4.2	0.728	0.726	0.727	0.731	0.741	0.757	0.783	0.821	0.884
	(0.315)	(0.287)	(0.262)	(0.238)	(0.217)	(0.197)	(0.179)	(0.161)	(0.136)
	0.048	0.103	0.166	0.237	0.316	0.404	0.504	0.620	0.766
	(0.712)	(0.727)	(0.717)	(0.685)	(0.634)	(0.566)	(0.485)	(0.392)	(0.286)
4.9	0.578	0.600	0.625	0.653	0.684	0.721	0.765	0.818	0.889
	(0.362)	(0.344)	(0.325)	(0.304)	(0.282)	(0.257)	(0.229)	(0.196)	(0.150)
	0.062	0.128	0.197	0.270	0.348	0.433	0.527	0.636	0.774
	(0.884)	(0.829)	(0.767)	(0.700)	(0.629)	(0.554)	(0.474)	(0.388)	(0.290)
5.6	0.548	0.584	0.621	0.659	0.699	0.742	0.789	0.843	0.909
	(0.513)	(0.467)	(0.423)	(0.382)	(0.341)	(0.301)	(0.259)	(0.213)	(0.153)
	0.071	0.142	0.215	0.289	0.368	0.451	0.543	0.649	0.781
	(0.990)	(0.904)	(0.822)	(0.744)	(0.668)	(0.592)	(0.513)	(0.427)	(0.323)
6.3	0.753	0.764	0.777	0.794	0.815	0.839	0.868	0.903	0.946
	(0.376)	(0.349)	(0.324)	(0.300)	(0.276)	(0.251)	(0.222)	(0.185)	(0.131)
	0.065	0.135	0.209	0.286	0.368	0.456	0.551	0.657	0.786
	(0.977)	(0.972)	(0.944)	(0.900)	(0.841)	(0.769)	(0.681)	(0.573)	(0.433)

For the Mastery score = 2 enter N-xbar in the test mean column

Table of the Raw Agreement Index and its
S.E.*SQRT(M), the Kappa Index and its
S.E.*SQRT(M) in the Beta-binomial Model
M = Number of subjects
Number of items N = 7
Mastery score C = 7

Test Mean	KR21= .100	.200	.300	.400	.500	.600	.700	.800	.900
0.7	1.000	1.000	1.000	1.000	1.000	0.999	0.996	0.990	0.981
	(0.000)	(0.000)	(0.001)	(0.002)	(0.006)	(0.014)	(0.031)	(0.057)	(0.064)
	0.000	0.000	0.003	0.012	0.036	0.088	0.184	0.347	0.604
	(0.001)	(0.014)	(0.060)	(0.168)	(0.356)	(0.616)	(0.893)	(1.068)	(0.940)
1.4	1.000	1.000	0.999	0.999	0.997	0.994	0.987	0.974	0.958
	(0.001)	(0.003)	(0.006)	(0.011)	(0.022)	(0.040)	(0.066)	(0.093)	(0.084)
	0.000	0.002	0.007	0.023	0.056	0.118	0.223	0.386	0.627
	(0.008)	(0.038)	(0.107)	(0.227)	(0.392)	(0.578)	(0.736)	(0.790)	(0.644)
2.1	0.999	0.998	0.997	0.994	0.990	0.982	0.969	0.950	0.934
	(0.009)	(0.014)	(0.023)	(0.036)	(0.055)	(0.080)	(0.108)	(0.122)	(0.091)
	0.001	0.005	0.016	0.040	0.083	0.155	0.265	0.425	0.649
	(0.030)	(0.085)	(0.179)	(0.307)	(0.453)	(0.588)	(0.672)	(0.660)	(0.508)
2.8	0.995	0.992	0.988	0.982	0.972	0.959	0.940	0.919	0.909
	(0.035)	(0.048)	(0.064)	(0.085)	(0.109)	(0.132)	(0.148)	(0.139)	(0.092)
	0.003	0.013	0.031	0.064	0.118	0.198	0.311	0.464	0.670
	(0.078)	(0.162)	(0.272)	(0.396)	(0.514)	(0.600)	(0.628)	(0.574)	(0.425)
3.5	0.979	0.972	0.963	0.951	0.936	0.918	0.898	0.880	0.886
	(0.098)	(0.117)	(0.137)	(0.157)	(0.173)	(0.181)	(0.172)	(0.138)	(0.096)
	0.009	0.025	0.054	0.098	0.160	0.246	0.358	0.502	0.690
	(0.168)	(0.271)	(0.382)	(0.486)	(0.566)	(0.604)	(0.589)	(0.510)	(0.370)
4.2	0.935	0.922	0.908	0.892	0.875	0.857	0.844	0.841	0.870
	(0.205)	(0.218)	(0.227)	(0.229)	(0.222)	(0.203)	(0.170)	(0.128)	(0.114)
	0.018	0.045	0.085	0.139	0.209	0.297	0.406	0.539	0.709
	(0.308)	(0.410)	(0.500)	(0.568)	(0.604)	(0.600)	(0.552)	(0.461)	(0.335)
4.9	0.835	0.821	0.808	0.796	0.787	0.783	0.788	0.810	0.865
	(0.309)	(0.295)	(0.275)	(0.250)	(0.219)	(0.186)	(0.157)	(0.144)	(0.148)
	0.032	0.073	0.124	0.187	0.262	0.350	0.453	0.575	0.728
	(0.501)	(0.572)	(0.620)	(0.641)	(0.632)	(0.593)	(0.524)	(0.430)	(0.318)
5.6	0.667	0.668	0.673	0.683	0.699	0.722	0.755	0.804	0.878
	(0.297)	(0.271)	(0.251)	(0.237)	(0.228)	(0.224)	(0.221)	(0.213)	(0.184)
	0.050	0.106	0.170	0.240	0.318	0.404	0.499	0.609	0.745
	(0.743)	(0.754)	(0.744)	(0.715)	(0.666)	(0.601)	(0.521)	(0.428)	(0.328)
6.3	0.536	0.573	0.611	0.653	0.697	0.744	0.796	0.853	0.919
	(0.517)	(0.504)	(0.485)	(0.459)	(0.428)	(0.389)	(0.341)	(0.278)	(0.193)
	0.072	0.145	0.219	0.295	0.374	0.456	0.543	0.641	0.761
	(1.043)	(0.985)	(0.920)	(0.848)	(0.770)	(0.687)	(0.599)	(0.504)	(0.402)

For the Mastery score = 1 enter N-xbar in the test mean column

Table of the Raw Agreement Index and its
S.E.*SQRT(M), the Kappa Index and its
S.E.*SQRT(M) in the Beta-binomial Model
M = Number of subjects
Number of items N = 8
Mastery score C = 4

Test KR21= Mean	.100	.200	.300	.400	.500	.600	.700	.800	.900
0.8	0.984	0.977	0.968	0.959	0.950	0.943	0.940	0.944	0.961
	(0.112)	(0.133)	(0.149)	(0.155)	(0.152)	(0.139)	(0.118)	(0.097)	(0.080)
	0.015	0.048	0.100	0.171	0.259	0.363	0.481	0.615	0.773
	(0.334)	(0.568)	(0.763)	(0.892)	(0.947)	(0.931)	(0.852)	(0.712)	(0.502)
1.6	0.881	0.871	0.862	0.856	0.854	0.858	0.869	0.890	0.928
	(0.290)	(0.273)	(0.251)	(0.227)	(0.202)	(0.177)	(0.154)	(0.133)	(0.107)
	0.039	0.090	0.153	0.227	0.311	0.404	0.509	0.629	0.776
	(0.627)	(0.724)	(0.770)	(0.773)	(0.741)	(0.680)	(0.595)	(0.488)	(0.350)
2.4	0.693	0.703	0.715	0.731	0.751	0.776	0.807	0.848	0.905
	(0.342)	(0.317)	(0.293)	(0.268)	(0.244)	(0.218)	(0.191)	(0.161)	(0.123)
	0.058	0.122	0.190	0.264	0.343	0.429	0.525	0.637	0.778
	(0.833)	(0.807)	(0.765)	(0.709)	(0.643)	(0.570)	(0.488)	(0.398)	(0.290)
3.2	0.549	0.581	0.615	0.649	0.686	0.726	0.771	0.824	0.892
	(0.451)	(0.409)	(0.369)	(0.331)	(0.293)	(0.256)	(0.217)	(0.177)	(0.130)
	0.067	0.136	0.206	0.279	0.356	0.439	0.532	0.640	0.778
	(0.923)	(0.838)	(0.756)	(0.677)	(0.600)	(0.522)	(0.444)	(0.360)	(0.264)
4.0	0.564	0.592	0.622	0.653	0.688	0.726	0.769	0.821	0.889
	(0.414)	(0.381)	(0.348)	(0.315)	(0.281)	(0.247)	(0.212)	(0.173)	(0.128)
	0.065	0.133	0.202	0.275	0.352	0.436	0.529	0.637	0.777
	(0.901)	(0.825)	(0.749)	(0.673)	(0.597)	(0.520)	(0.440)	(0.356)	(0.260)
4.8	0.714	0.717	0.724	0.735	0.751	0.771	0.799	0.838	0.896
	(0.324)	(0.299)	(0.275)	(0.252)	(0.229)	(0.206)	(0.181)	(0.154)	(0.120)
	0.054	0.114	0.180	0.253	0.332	0.419	0.516	0.630	0.774
	(0.777)	(0.769)	(0.739)	(0.691)	(0.630)	(0.557)	(0.474)	(0.382)	(0.275)
5.6	0.878	0.866	0.855	0.847	0.843	0.844	0.852	0.872	0.913
	(0.290)	(0.275)	(0.255)	(0.232)	(0.206)	(0.179)	(0.153)	(0.130)	(0.107)
	0.035	0.083	0.143	0.215	0.297	0.389	0.495	0.617	0.770
	(0.572)	(0.665)	(0.713)	(0.720)	(0.691)	(0.631)	(0.547)	(0.442)	(0.313)
6.4	0.971	0.962	0.951	0.939	0.928	0.918	0.912	0.915	0.937
	(0.147)	(0.165)	(0.177)	(0.181)	(0.176)	(0.161)	(0.137)	(0.109)	(0.088)
	0.017	0.049	0.098	0.164	0.248	0.348	0.464	0.600	0.764
	(0.330)	(0.507)	(0.652)	(0.745)	(0.778)	(0.753)	(0.678)	(0.557)	(0.388)
7.2	0.998	0.996	0.992	0.987	0.981	0.973	0.965	0.961	0.967
	(0.025)	(0.040)	(0.059)	(0.080)	(0.098)	(0.108)	(0.104)	(0.085)	(0.065)
	0.004	0.019	0.053	0.109	0.191	0.296	0.425	0.576	0.756
	(0.119)	(0.312)	(0.548)	(0.767)	(0.924)	(0.990)	(0.955)	(0.817)	(0.568)

For the Mastery score = 5 enter N-xbar in the test mean column

Table of the Raw Agreement Index and its
S.E.*SQRT(M), the Kappa Index and its
S.E.*SQRT(M) in the Beta-binomial Model
M = Number of subjects
Number of items N = 8
Mastery score C = 5

Test Mean	KR21=.100	.200	.300	.400	.500	.600	.700	.800	.900
0.8	0.998	0.996	0.992	0.987	0.981	0.973	0.965	0.961	0.967
	(0.025)	(0.040)	(0.059)	(0.080)	(0.098)	(0.108)	(0.104)	(0.085)	(0.065)
	0.004	0.019	0.053	0.109	0.191	0.296	0.425	0.576	0.756
	(0.119)	(0.312)	(0.548)	(0.767)	(0.924)	(0.990)	(0.955)	(0.817)	(0.568)
1.6	0.971	0.962	0.951	0.939	0.928	0.918	0.912	0.915	0.937
	(0.147)	(0.165)	(0.177)	(0.181)	(0.176)	(0.161)	(0.137)	(0.109)	(0.088)
	0.017	0.049	0.098	0.164	0.248	0.348	0.464	0.600	0.764
	(0.330)	(0.507)	(0.652)	(0.745)	(0.778)	(0.753)	(0.678)	(0.557)	(0.388)
2.4	0.878	0.866	0.855	0.847	0.843	0.844	0.852	0.872	0.913
	(0.290)	(0.275)	(0.255)	(0.232)	(0.206)	(0.179)	(0.153)	(0.130)	(0.107)
	0.035	0.083	0.143	0.215	0.297	0.389	0.495	0.617	0.770
	(0.572)	(0.665)	(0.713)	(0.720)	(0.691)	(0.631)	(0.547)	(0.442)	(0.313)
3.2	0.714	0.717	0.724	0.735	0.751	0.771	0.799	0.838	0.896
	(0.324)	(0.299)	(0.275)	(0.252)	(0.229)	(0.206)	(0.181)	(0.154)	(0.120)
	0.054	0.114	0.180	0.253	0.332	0.419	0.516	0.630	0.774
	(0.777)	(0.769)	(0.739)	(0.691)	(0.630)	(0.557)	(0.474)	(0.382)	(0.275)
4.0	0.564	0.592	0.622	0.653	0.688	0.726	0.769	0.821	0.889
	(0.414)	(0.381)	(0.348)	(0.315)	(0.281)	(0.247)	(0.212)	(0.173)	(0.128)
	0.065	0.133	0.202	0.275	0.352	0.436	0.529	0.637	0.777
	(0.901)	(0.825)	(0.749)	(0.673)	(0.597)	(0.520)	(0.440)	(0.356)	(0.260)
4.8	0.549	0.581	0.615	0.649	0.686	0.726	0.771	0.824	0.892
	(0.451)	(0.409)	(0.369)	(0.331)	(0.293)	(0.256)	(0.217)	(0.177)	(0.130)
	0.067	0.136	0.206	0.279	0.356	0.439	0.532	0.640	0.778
	(0.923)	(0.838)	(0.756)	(0.677)	(0.600)	(0.522)	(0.444)	(0.360)	(0.264)
5.6	0.693	0.703	0.715	0.731	0.751	0.776	0.807	0.848	0.905
	(0.342)	(0.317)	(0.293)	(0.268)	(0.244)	(0.218)	(0.191)	(0.161)	(0.123)
	0.058	0.122	0.190	0.264	0.343	0.429	0.525	0.637	0.778
	(0.833)	(0.807)	(0.765)	(0.709)	(0.643)	(0.570)	(0.488)	(0.398)	(0.290)
6.4	0.881	0.871	0.862	0.856	0.854	0.858	0.869	0.890	0.928
	(0.290)	(0.273)	(0.251)	(0.227)	(0.202)	(0.177)	(0.154)	(0.133)	(0.107)
	0.039	0.090	0.153	0.227	0.311	0.404	0.509	0.629	0.776
	(0.627)	(0.724)	(0.770)	(0.773)	(0.741)	(0.680)	(0.595)	(0.488)	(0.350)
7.2	0.984	0.977	0.968	0.959	0.950	0.943	0.940	0.944	0.961
	(0.112)	(0.133)	(0.149)	(0.155)	(0.152)	(0.139)	(0.118)	(0.097)	(0.080)
	0.015	0.048	0.100	0.171	0.259	0.363	0.481	0.615	0.773
	(0.334)	(0.568)	(0.763)	(0.892)	(0.947)	(0.931)	(0.852)	(0.712)	(0.502)

For the Mastery score = 4 enter N-xbar in the test mean column

Table of the Raw Agreement Index and its
S.E.*SQRT(M), the Kappa Index and its
S.E.*SQRT(M) in the Beta-binomial Model
M = Number of subjects
Number of items N = 8
Mastery score C = 6

Test Mean	KR21= .100	.200	.300	.400	.500	.600	.700	.800	.900
0.8	1.000	0.999	0.999	0.997	0.994	0.989	0.982	0.974	0.972
	(0.003)	(0.008)	(0.016)	(0.028)	(0.046)	(0.066)	(0.082)	(0.080)	(0.057)
	0.001	0.006	0.023	0.060	0.124	0.222	0.354	0.521	0.727
	(0.029)	(0.128)	(0.312)	(0.552)	(0.791)	(0.967)	(1.025)	(0.930)	(0.656)
1.6	0.996	0.992	0.988	0.981	0.972	0.960	0.948	0.939	0.945
	(0.038)	(0.055)	(0.075)	(0.097)	(0.116)	(0.123)	(0.126)	(0.105)	(0.075)
	0.005	0.019	0.050	0.100	0.175	0.275	0.400	0.553	0.740
	(0.121)	(0.270)	(0.448)	(0.615)	(0.737)	(0.788)	(0.757)	(0.642)	(0.444)
2.4	0.970	0.960	0.949	0.936	0.923	0.910	0.900	0.899	0.920
	(0.143)	(0.162)	(0.176)	(0.184)	(0.183)	(0.171)	(0.147)	(0.115)	(0.090)
	0.015	0.043	0.087	0.148	0.227	0.325	0.442	0.580	0.750
	(0.286)	(0.438)	(0.572)	(0.664)	(0.705)	(0.690)	(0.622)	(0.507)	(0.350)
3.2	0.892	0.879	0.866	0.855	0.846	0.842	0.845	0.861	0.901
	(0.275)	(0.268)	(0.254)	(0.235)	(0.210)	(0.182)	(0.153)	(0.127)	(0.106)
	0.030	0.073	0.123	0.196	0.276	0.369	0.477	0.602	0.759
	(0.497)	(0.597)	(0.659)	(0.682)	(0.665)	(0.614)	(0.533)	(0.428)	(0.299)
4.0	0.747	0.744	0.745	0.749	0.758	0.772	0.796	0.831	0.889
	(0.317)	(0.290)	(0.265)	(0.240)	(0.217)	(0.195)	(0.173)	(0.150)	(0.121)
	0.043	0.103	0.167	0.238	0.317	0.405	0.504	0.620	0.767
	(0.706)	(0.723)	(0.713)	(0.679)	(0.627)	(0.557)	(0.475)	(0.381)	(0.272)
4.8	0.583	0.609	0.633	0.660	0.691	0.726	0.767	0.818	0.886
	(0.365)	(0.342)	(0.318)	(0.294)	(0.268)	(0.240)	(0.210)	(0.175)	(0.133)
	0.062	0.127	0.196	0.268	0.346	0.430	0.523	0.633	0.772
	(0.866)	(0.808)	(0.744)	(0.675)	(0.603)	(0.527)	(0.447)	(0.362)	(0.265)
5.6	0.540	0.574	0.610	0.646	0.685	0.727	0.773	0.827	0.895
	(0.476)	(0.430)	(0.388)	(0.347)	(0.308)	(0.269)	(0.229)	(0.187)	(0.137)
	0.069	0.138	0.209	0.282	0.359	0.442	0.534	0.641	0.777
	(0.940)	(0.852)	(0.769)	(0.689)	(0.612)	(0.536)	(0.458)	(0.375)	(0.278)
6.4	0.687	0.701	0.717	0.737	0.760	0.788	0.821	0.863	0.917
	(0.370)	(0.343)	(0.316)	(0.289)	(0.263)	(0.235)	(0.206)	(0.174)	(0.129)
	0.062	0.129	0.199	0.274	0.353	0.439	0.534	0.643	0.780
	(0.889)	(0.853)	(0.805)	(0.746)	(0.680)	(0.608)	(0.528)	(0.437)	(0.323)
7.2	0.915	0.904	0.896	0.891	0.890	0.894	0.904	0.923	0.952
	(0.267)	(0.253)	(0.233)	(0.211)	(0.188)	(0.166)	(0.148)	(0.130)	(0.102)
	0.039	0.093	0.159	0.237	0.323	0.418	0.522	0.640	0.781
	(0.668)	(0.809)	(0.886)	(0.908)	(0.887)	(0.830)	(0.741)	(0.619)	(0.450)

For the Mastery score = 3 enter N-xbar in the test mean column

Table of the Raw Agreement Index and its
S.E.*SQRT(M), the Kappa Index and its
S.E.*SQRT(M) in the Beta-binomial Model
M = Number of subjects
Number of items N = 8
Mastery score C = 7

```
--------------------------------------------------------------------
Test KR21=
Mean   .100    .200    .300    .400    .500    .600    .700    .800    .900
--------------------------------------------------------------------
0.8   1.000   1.000   1.000   1.000   0.999   0.997   0.992   0.985   0.977
     (0.000) (0.001) (0.003) (0.006) (0.014) (0.029) (0.050) (0.068) (0.057)
      0.000   0.001   0.007   0.025   0.066   0.142   0.264   0.440   0.677
     (0.005) (0.036) (0.129) (0.305) (0.551) (0.815) (1.009) (1.031) (0.780)

1.6   1.000   0.999   0.998   0.996   0.992   0.985   0.975   0.961   0.953
     (0.005) (0.010) (0.019) (0.031) (0.050) (0.073) (0.096) (0.102) (0.073)
      0.001   0.005   0.018   0.048   0.101   0.187   0.311   0.478   0.695
     (0.027) (0.097) (0.222) (0.394) (0.577) (0.726) (0.792) (0.734) (0.527)

2.4   0.996   0.993   0.989   0.982   0.973   0.960   0.945   0.929   0.928
     (0.034) (0.048) (0.066) (0.088) (0.110) (0.129) (0.136) (0.119) (0.081)
      0.004   0.015   0.038   0.080   0.144   0.236   0.358   0.514   0.712
     (0.091) (0.201) (0.343) (0.493) (0.618) (0.690) (0.684) (0.591) (0.412)

3.2   0.977   0.969   0.959   0.947   0.932   0.916   0.900   0.891   0.905
     (0.112) (0.133) (0.152) (0.168) (0.177) (0.175) (0.157) (0.122) (0.090)
      0.011   0.032   0.068   0.121   0.193   0.287   0.404   0.547   0.727
     (0.212) (0.342) (0.470) (0.576) (0.641) (0.652) (0.604) (0.499) (0.345)

4.0   0.920   0.907   0.892   0.878   0.864   0.852   0.847   0.854   0.888
     (0.237) (0.242) (0.241) (0.232) (0.215) (0.189) (0.156) (0.124) (0.106)
      0.023   0.058   0.105   0.167   0.244   0.336   0.446   0.576   0.740
     (0.389) (0.499) (0.583) (0.632) (0.641) (0.610) (0.539) (0.435) (0.303)

4.8   0.798   0.788   0.781   0.776   0.775   0.780   0.795   0.824   0.879
     (0.317) (0.293) (0.266) (0.239) (0.211) (0.185) (0.162) (0.144) (0.126)
      0.039   0.088   0.146   0.214   0.292   0.381   0.483   0.602   0.752
     (0.599) (0.650) (0.671) (0.663) (0.628) (0.570) (0.490) (0.394) (0.282)

5.6   0.628   0.640   0.655   0.673   0.697   0.726   0.763   0.813   0.882
     (0.313) (0.295) (0.279) (0.263) (0.247) (0.229) (0.208) (0.183) (0.145)
      0.056   0.118   0.184   0.256   0.333   0.418   0.513   0.623   0.763
     (0.805) (0.777) (0.736) (0.682) (0.619) (0.547) (0.468) (0.380) (0.280)

6.4   0.535   0.570   0.606   0.644   0.685   0.728   0.776   0.832   0.901
     (0.482) (0.444) (0.406) (0.369) (0.332) (0.295) (0.256) (0.211) (0.154)
      0.069   0.139   0.210   0.284   0.361   0.444   0.535   0.640   0.772
     (0.956) (0.874) (0.795) (0.719) (0.645) (0.570) (0.493) (0.408) (0.309)

7.2   0.710   0.727   0.746   0.768   0.793   0.821   0.854   0.893   0.940
     (0.410) (0.379) (0.351) (0.322) (0.294) (0.265) (0.233) (0.193) (0.136)
      0.067   0.138   0.211   0.288   0.369   0.454   0.547   0.651   0.779
     (0.981) (0.952) (0.909) (0.855) (0.794) (0.723) (0.640) (0.540) (0.410)
--------------------------------------------------------------------
```

For the Mastery score = 2   enter N-xbar in the test mean column

Table of the Raw Agreement Index and its
S.E.*SQRT(M), the Kappa Index and its
S.E.*SQRT(M) in the Beta-binomial Model
M = Number of subjects
Number of items N = 8
Mastery score C = 8

Test Mean	KR21= .100	.200	.300	.400	.500	.600	.700	.800	.900
0.8	1.000	1.000	1.000	1.000	1.000	0.999	0.998	0.994	0.984
	(0.000)	(0.000)	(0.000)	(0.001)	(0.002)	(0.007)	(0.019)	(0.043)	(0.063)
	0.000	0.000	0.001	0.007	0.023	0.063	0.147	0.302	0.566
	(0.000)	(0.005)	(0.030)	(0.101)	(0.249)	(0.486)	(0.780)	(1.018)	(0.959)
1.6	1.000	1.000	1.000	1.000	0.999	0.997	0.992	0.982	0.963
	(0.000)	(0.001)	(0.002)	(0.005)	(0.011)	(0.023)	(0.046)	(0.078)	(0.086)
	0.000	0.001	0.004	0.014	0.038	0.089	0.184	0.343	0.593
	(0.003)	(0.018)	(0.062)	(0.152)	(0.297)	(0.485)	(0.671)	(0.772)	(0.660)
2.4	1.000	0.999	0.999	0.997	0.995	0.990	0.980	0.962	0.940
	(0.003)	(0.006)	(0.011)	(0.019)	(0.033)	(0.055)	(0.084)	(0.111)	(0.096)
	0.000	0.003	0.010	0.026	0.060	0.123	0.226	0.385	0.619
	(0.014)	(0.048)	(0.117)	(0.226)	(0.368)	(0.519)	(0.636)	(0.658)	(0.521)
3.2	0.998	0.996	0.994	0.990	0.983	0.973	0.956	0.933	0.914
	(0.017)	(0.025)	(0.037)	(0.054)	(0.076)	(0.103)	(0.128)	(0.137)	(0.096)
	0.002	0.007	0.020	0.046	0.091	0.164	0.273	0.427	0.644
	(0.044)	(0.105)	(0.198)	(0.317)	(0.444)	(0.554)	(0.611)	(0.581)	(0.435)
4.0	0.989	0.984	0.978	0.969	0.957	0.940	0.918	0.895	0.889
	(0.060)	(0.076)	(0.096)	(0.118)	(0.140)	(0.159)	(0.166)	(0.145)	(0.093)
	0.005	0.017	0.039	0.076	0.132	0.212	0.323	0.471	0.668
	(0.110)	(0.199)	(0.305)	(0.416)	(0.514)	(0.577)	(0.585)	(0.519)	(0.376)
4.8	0.959	0.949	0.936	0.922	0.904	0.884	0.865	0.853	0.869
	(0.152)	(0.170)	(0.187)	(0.200)	(0.206)	(0.200)	(0.177)	(0.134)	(0.102)
	0.013	0.035	0.068	0.116	0.181	0.267	0.376	0.513	0.691
	(0.230)	(0.331)	(0.429)	(0.513)	(0.570)	(0.586)	(0.554)	(0.468)	(0.335)
5.6	0.878	0.863	0.848	0.833	0.818	0.807	0.803	0.814	0.859
	(0.277)	(0.276)	(0.268)	(0.252)	(0.228)	(0.196)	(0.159)	(0.131)	(0.133)
	0.025	0.061	0.107	0.166	0.238	0.326	0.430	0.555	0.712
	(0.413)	(0.497)	(0.562)	(0.601)	(0.610)	(0.585)	(0.525)	(0.431)	(0.313)
6.4	0.713	0.708	0.706	0.708	0.715	0.730	0.756	0.798	0.869
	(0.310)	(0.281)	(0.253)	(0.228)	(0.209)	(0.197)	(0.194)	(0.193)	(0.176)
	0.044	0.096	0.156	0.224	0.300	0.386	0.483	0.594	0.733
	(0.661)	(0.691)	(0.699)	(0.684)	(0.647)	(0.590)	(0.513)	(0.420)	(0.317)
7.2	0.539	0.571	0.606	0.643	0.685	0.731	0.782	0.841	0.911
	(0.444)	(0.440)	(0.431)	(0.417)	(0.396)	(0.367)	(0.329)	(0.275)	(0.195)
	0.068	0.138	0.211	0.286	0.364	0.446	0.534	0.631	0.752
	(0.981)	(0.934)	(0.877)	(0.811)	(0.739)	(0.660)	(0.575)	(0.482)	(0.382)

For the Mastery score = 1 enter N-xbar in the test mean column

171

Table of the Raw Agreement Index and its
S.E.*SQRT(M), the Kappa Index and its
S.E.*SQRT(M) in the Beta-binomial Model
M = Number of subjects
Number of items N = 9
Mastery score C = 5

Test Mean	KR21= .100	.200	.300	.400	.500	.600	.700	.800	.900
0.9	0.996	0.993	0.988	0.982	0.974	0.966	0.958	0.955	0.964
	(0.039)	(0.058)	(0.079)	(0.099)	(0.114)	(0.119)	(0.110)	(0.088)	(0.068)
	0.006	0.025	0.063	0.124	0.208	0.314	0.440	0.585	0.758
	(0.159)	(0.367)	(0.597)	(0.791)	(0.914)	(0.949)	(0.896)	(0.758)	(0.528)
1.8	0.951	0.939	0.927	0.915	0.905	0.898	0.896	0.905	0.932
	(0.199)	(0.209)	(0.210)	(0.204)	(0.189)	(0.167)	(0.140)	(0.114)	(0.093)
	0.023	0.061	0.116	0.185	0.269	0.367	0.479	0.607	0.764
	(0.418)	(0.577)	(0.691)	(0.750)	(0.755)	(0.712)	(0.631)	(0.515)	(0.361)
2.7	0.812	0.805	0.801	0.801	0.805	0.814	0.831	0.860	0.907
	(0.315)	(0.290)	(0.264)	(0.238)	(0.213)	(0.188)	(0.164)	(0.139)	(0.110)
	0.045	0.099	0.163	0.235	0.316	0.405	0.506	0.622	0.769
	(0.676)	(0.722)	(0.730)	(0.708)	(0.660)	(0.593)	(0.509)	(0.411)	(0.293)
3.6	0.625	0.643	0.663	0.687	0.714	0.745	0.782	0.828	0.892
	(0.362)	(0.336)	(0.311)	(0.284)	(0.257)	(0.228)	(0.197)	(0.163)	(0.121)
	0.061	0.126	0.194	0.267	0.344	0.428	0.522	0.631	0.771
	(0.852)	(0.800)	(0.740)	(0.674)	(0.603)	(0.527)	(0.447)	(0.360)	(0.260)
4.5	0.534	0.568	0.603	0.639	0.677	0.718	0.764	0.817	0.886
	(0.457)	(0.412)	(0.370)	(0.331)	(0.292)	(0.253)	(0.214)	(0.172)	(0.125)
	0.067	0.136	0.205	0.278	0.354	0.436	0.527	0.634	0.772
	(0.913)	(0.824)	(0.741)	(0.661)	(0.583)	(0.506)	(0.428)	(0.345)	(0.251)
5.4	0.625	0.643	0.663	0.687	0.714	0.745	0.782	0.828	0.892
	(0.362)	(0.336)	(0.311)	(0.284)	(0.257)	(0.228)	(0.197)	(0.163)	(0.121)
	0.061	0.126	0.194	0.267	0.344	0.428	0.522	0.631	0.771
	(0.852)	(0.800)	(0.740)	(0.674)	(0.603)	(0.527)	(0.447)	(0.360)	(0.260)
6.3	0.812	0.805	0.801	0.801	0.805	0.814	0.831	0.860	0.907
	(0.315)	(0.290)	(0.264)	(0.238)	(0.213)	(0.188)	(0.164)	(0.139)	(0.110)
	0.045	0.099	0.163	0.235	0.316	0.405	0.506	0.622	0.769
	(0.676)	(0.722)	(0.730)	(0.708)	(0.660)	(0.593)	(0.509)	(0.411)	(0.293)
7.2	0.951	0.939	0.927	0.915	0.905	0.898	0.896	0.905	0.932
	(0.199)	(0.209)	(0.210)	(0.204)	(0.189)	(0.167)	(0.140)	(0.114)	(0.093)
	0.023	0.061	0.116	0.185	0.269	0.367	0.479	0.607	0.764
	(0.418)	(0.577)	(0.691)	(0.750)	(0.755)	(0.712)	(0.631)	(0.515)	(0.361)
8.1	0.996	0.993	0.988	0.982	0.974	0.966	0.958	0.955	0.964
	(0.039)	(0.053)	(0.079)	(0.099)	(0.114)	(0.119)	(0.110)	(0.088)	(0.068)
	0.006	0.025	0.063	0.124	0.208	0.314	0.440	0.585	0.758
	(0.159)	(0.367)	(0.597)	(0.791)	(0.914)	(0.949)	(0.896)	(0.758)	(0.528)

Table of the Raw Agreement Index and its
S.E.*SQRT(M), the Kappa Index and its
S.E.*SQRT(M) in the Beta-binomial Model
M = Number of subjects
Number of items N = 9
Mastery score C = 6

```
------------------------------------------------------------------
Test KR21=
Mean   .100    .200    .300    .400    .500    .600    .700    .800    .900
------------------------------------------------------------------
0.9   1.000   0.999   0.998   0.995   0.991   0.985   0.977   0.969   0.970
     (0.007) (0.014) (0.025) (0.041) (0.061) (0.080) (0.091) (0.082) (0.058)
      0.001   0.009   0.031   0.075   0.146   0.248   0.381   0.542   0.737
     (0.047) (0.174) (0.380) (0.620) (0.831) (0.961) (0.975) (0.857) (0.598)

1.8   0.990   0.985   0.978   0.968   0.957   0.945   0.934   0.929   0.940
     (0.070) (0.091) (0.112) (0.131) (0.143) (0.145) (0.132) (0.105) (0.079)
      0.008   0.029   0.067   0.125   0.205   0.306   0.428   0.572   0.748
     (0.186) (0.356) (0.530) (0.671) (0.754) (0.766) (0.708) (0.587) (0.404)

2.7   0.939   0.927   0.914   0.901   0.889   0.880   0.877   0.885   0.915
     (0.215) (0.223) (0.223) (0.215) (0.199) (0.176) (0.148) (0.118) (0.095)
      0.023   0.060   0.112   0.179   0.260   0.356   0.467   0.596   0.756
     (0.405) (0.542) (0.641) (0.693) (0.696) (0.654) (0.574) (0.462) (0.320)

3.6   0.811   0.802   0.796   0.794   0.796   0.804   0.819   0.847   0.896
     (0.314) (0.290) (0.264) (0.238) (0.212) (0.186) (0.162) (0.137) (0.110)
      0.042   0.094   0.156   0.227   0.307   0.396   0.497   0.615   0.763
     (0.640) (0.688) (0.702) (0.684) (0.640) (0.574) (0.490) (0.392) (0.276)

4.5   0.633   0.648   0.665   0.686   0.711   0.740   0.776   0.822   0.886
     (0.339) (0.317) (0.295) (0.272) (0.248) (0.222) (0.193) (0.161) (0.122)
      0.059   0.122   0.189   0.261   0.339   0.423   0.517   0.627   0.768
     (0.824) (0.782) (0.729) (0.667) (0.599) (0.524) (0.443) (0.355) (0.256)

5.4   0.534   0.568   0.603   0.639   0.677   0.718   0.764   0.818   0.887
     (0.455) (0.412) (0.371) (0.332) (0.293) (0.255) (0.216) (0.175) (0.128)
      0.067   0.135   0.205   0.278   0.354   0.436   0.527   0.634   0.772
     (0.913) (0.826) (0.743) (0.664) (0.587) (0.510) (0.432) (0.349) (0.255)

6.3   0.624   0.644   0.667   0.692   0.721   0.753   0.791   0.837   0.899
     (0.385) (0.356) (0.326) (0.297) (0.267) (0.236) (0.203) (0.168) (0.125)
      0.063   0.130   0.199   0.272   0.350   0.433   0.527   0.635   0.773
     (0.878) (0.820) (0.756) (0.689) (0.617) (0.542) (0.463) (0.377) (0.276)

7.2   0.834   0.827   0.822   0.822   0.826   0.836   0.852   0.879   0.923
     (0.311) (0.286) (0.261) (0.236) (0.211) (0.187) (0.164) (0.141) (0.111)
      0.045   0.102   0.167   0.241   0.323   0.413   0.514   0.630   0.773
     (0.700) (0.756) (0.771) (0.752) (0.707) (0.640) (0.557) (0.457) (0.330)

8.1   0.976   0.967   0.957   0.947   0.938   0.932   0.931   0.937   0.957
     (0.144) (0.161) (0.171) (0.172) (0.163) (0.145) (0.123) (0.102) (0.083)
      0.019   0.056   0.111   0.184   0.272   0.373   0.488   0.617   0.771
     (0.389) (0.610) (0.773) (0.878) (0.909) (0.880) (0.798) (0.666) (0.473)
------------------------------------------------------------------
```

For the Mastery score = 4 enter N-xbar in the test mean column

```
                  Table of the Raw Agreement Index and its
                   S.E.*SQRT(M), the Kappa Index and its
                   S.E.*SQRT(M) in the Beta-binomial Model
                          M = Number of subjects
                          Number of items N = 9
                           Mastery score C = 7
-----------------------------------------------------------------------
Test KR21=
Mean    .100    .200    .300    .400    .500    .600    .700    .800    .900
-----------------------------------------------------------------------
0.9    1.000   1.000   1.000   0.999   0.997   0.994   0.989   0.980   0.975
      (0.001) (0.002) (0.005) (0.012) (0.024) (0.042) (0.063) (0.074) (0.056)
       0.000   0.003   0.012   0.038   0.091   0.179   0.309   0.483   0.704
      (0.010) (0.062) (0.193) (0.405) (0.659) (0.886) (1.007) (0.956) (0.688)

1.8    0.999   0.997   0.995   0.991   0.985   0.975   0.963   0.951   0.948
      (0.014) (0.024) (0.038) (0.057) (0.079) (0.100) (0.112) (0.104) (0.071)
       0.002   0.010   0.031   0.071   0.137   0.232   0.360   0.520   0.720
      (0.058) (0.165) (0.324) (0.506) (0.666) (0.764) (0.769) (0.669) (0.463)

2.7    0.987   0.981   0.973   0.963   0.951   0.936   0.922   0.913   0.923
      (0.078) (0.098) (0.119) (0.139) (0.152) (0.156) (0.145) (0.116) (0.083)
       0.008   0.027   0.062   0.115   0.190   0.287   0.407   0.553   0.733
      (0.175) (0.318) (0.468) (0.596) (0.676) (0.694) (0.644) (0.530) (0.361)

3.6    0.940   0.928   0.914   0.900   0.886   0.875   0.868   0.873   0.901
      (0.207) (0.218) (0.221) (0.217) (0.205) (0.183) (0.153) (0.120) (0.096)
       0.021   0.054   0.102   0.165   0.244   0.338   0.449   0.581   0.745
      (0.363) (0.490) (0.589) (0.648) (0.661) (0.628) (0.554) (0.444) (0.304)

4.5    0.824   0.814   0.805   0.799   0.797   0.800   0.812   0.837   0.887
      (0.311) (0.289) (0.265) (0.239) (0.211) (0.184) (0.159) (0.136) (0.112)
       0.038   0.087   0.145   0.214   0.293   0.382   0.484   0.604   0.755
      (0.585) (0.644) (0.671) (0.665) (0.630) (0.570) (0.488) (0.388) (0.272)

5.4    0.651   0.660   0.673   0.690   0.711   0.737   0.771   0.817   0.882
      (0.317) (0.297) (0.277) (0.257) (0.237) (0.216) (0.192) (0.164) (0.127)
       0.056   0.116   0.182   0.254   0.331   0.416   0.511   0.622   0.763
      (0.787) (0.761) (0.720) (0.666) (0.602) (0.529) (0.449) (0.360) (0.260)

6.3    0.535   0.569   0.603   0.639   0.677   0.718   0.765   0.819   0.889
      (0.448) (0.409) (0.372) (0.336) (0.300) (0.263) (0.226) (0.185) (0.136)
       0.067   0.135   0.205   0.277   0.354   0.436   0.528   0.634   0.770
      (0.914) (0.831) (0.752) (0.675) (0.599) (0.523) (0.446) (0.364) (0.268)

7.2    0.634   0.656   0.680   0.706   0.735   0.768   0.806   0.852   0.911
      (0.410) (0.377) (0.345) (0.313) (0.281) (0.249) (0.216) (0.179) (0.131)
       0.065   0.133   0.204   0.278   0.356   0.440   0.533   0.640   0.774
      (0.911) (0.852) (0.788) (0.722) (0.652) (0.579) (0.502) (0.415) (0.308)

8.1    0.888   0.879   0.873   0.871   0.873   0.880   0.893   0.915   0.948
      (0.288) (0.267) (0.244) (0.220) (0.197) (0.176) (0.157) (0.137) (0.106)
       0.043   0.100   0.168   0.245   0.329   0.422   0.524   0.638   0.777
      (0.712) (0.820) (0.870) (0.874) (0.842) (0.782) (0.696) (0.583) (0.427)
-----------------------------------------------------------------------
For the Mastery score =  3  enter N-xbar in the test mean column
```

Table of the Raw Agreement Index and its
S.E.*SQRT(M), the Kappa Index and its
S.E.*SQRT(M) in the Beta-binomial Model
M = Number of subjects
Number of items N = 9
Mastery score C = 8

Test Mean	KR21= .100	.200	.300	.400	.500	.600	.700	.800	.900
0.9	1.000	1.000	1.000	1.000	0.999	0.998	0.996	0.989	0.980
	(0.000)	(0.000)	(0.001)	(0.002)	(0.007)	(0.016)	(0.034)	(0.057)	(0.058)
	0.000	0.000	0.004	0.015	0.045	0.109	0.222	0.398	0.648
	(0.001)	(0.015)	(0.071)	(0.203)	(0.422)	(0.697)	(0.942)	(1.029)	(0.812)
1.8	1.000	1.000	0.999	0.998	0.996	0.992	0.984	0.970	0.957
	(0.002)	(0.004)	(0.008)	(0.016)	(0.029)	(0.049)	(0.075)	(0.094)	(0.074)
	0.000	0.002	0.010	0.031	0.074	0.150	0.270	0.440	0.670
	(0.011)	(0.051)	(0.143)	(0.292)	(0.479)	(0.659)	(0.770)	(0.749)	(0.548)
2.7	0.998	0.997	0.995	0.991	0.984	0.974	0.960	0.942	0.932
	(0.015)	(0.024)	(0.037)	(0.054)	(0.076)	(0.101)	(0.120)	(0.118)	(0.081)
	0.002	0.008	0.025	0.057	0.113	0.199	0.320	0.481	0.690
	(0.048)	(0.127)	(0.251)	(0.402)	(0.549)	(0.656)	(0.685)	(0.611)	(0.427)
3.6	0.989	0.984	0.977	0.967	0.955	0.939	0.921	0.905	0.908
	(0.065)	(0.084)	(0.105)	(0.126)	(0.145)	(0.157)	(0.153)	(0.127)	(0.085)
	0.006	0.021	0.049	0.094	0.161	0.252	0.370	0.519	0.708
	(0.135)	(0.250)	(0.381)	(0.507)	(0.601)	(0.642)	(0.616)	(0.517)	(0.354)
4.5	0.952	0.941	0.928	0.913	0.897	0.881	0.868	0.865	0.888
	(0.175)	(0.191)	(0.203)	(0.208)	(0.205)	(0.189)	(0.161)	(0.124)	(0.096)
	0.016	0.043	0.084	0.141	0.214	0.307	0.419	0.554	0.725
	(0.288)	(0.407)	(0.512)	(0.588)	(0.624)	(0.613)	(0.553)	(0.448)	(0.307)
5.4	0.855	0.842	0.829	0.818	0.809	0.806	0.810	0.829	0.876
	(0.297)	(0.285)	(0.267)	(0.244)	(0.216)	(0.186)	(0.156)	(0.132)	(0.116)
	0.032	0.074	0.127	0.192	0.269	0.358	0.462	0.585	0.740
	(0.497)	(0.574)	(0.622)	(0.639)	(0.623)	(0.575)	(0.500)	(0.400)	(0.280)
6.3	0.684	0.686	0.692	0.701	0.716	0.737	0.767	0.810	0.876
	(0.305)	(0.281)	(0.259)	(0.239)	(0.222)	(0.206)	(0.189)	(0.169)	(0.139)
	0.050	0.107	0.170	0.240	0.318	0.403	0.499	0.611	0.753
	(0.725)	(0.726)	(0.705)	(0.667)	(0.614)	(0.546)	(0.467)	(0.377)	(0.274)
7.2	0.539	0.570	0.603	0.639	0.677	0.719	0.767	0.823	0.894
	(0.432)	(0.404)	(0.375)	(0.346)	(0.316)	(0.283)	(0.248)	(0.207)	(0.153)
	0.066	0.134	0.204	0.277	0.354	0.436	0.527	0.632	0.764
	(0.917)	(0.845)	(0.773)	(0.701)	(0.628)	(0.555)	(0.478)	(0.395)	(0.297)
8.1	0.671	0.694	0.718	0.744	0.773	0.805	0.841	0.883	0.934
	(0.442)	(0.407)	(0.374)	(0.342)	(0.310)	(0.277)	(0.241)	(0.199)	(0.140)
	0.069	0.140	0.213	0.289	0.368	0.452	0.544	0.647	0.773
	(0.982)	(0.935)	(0.880)	(0.821)	(0.757)	(0.686)	(0.607)	(0.513)	(0.391)

For the Mastery score = 2 enter N-xbar in the test mean column

Table of the Raw Agreement Index and its
S.E.*SQRT(M), the Kappa Index and its
S.E.*SQRT(M) in the Beta-binomial Model
M = Number of subjects
Number of items N = 9
Mastery score C = 9

Test Mean	KR21= .100	.200	.300	.400	.500	.600	.700	.800	.900
0.9	1.000	1.000	1.000	1.000	1.000	1.000	0.999	0.996	0.987
	(0.000)	(0.000)	(0.000)	(0.000)	(0.001)	(0.003)	(0.011)	(0.032)	(0.060)
	0.000	0.000	0.001	0.004	0.015	0.045	0.117	0.263	0.530
	(0.000)	(0.002)	(0.015)	(0.060)	(0.172)	(0.380)	(0.675)	(0.962)	(0.972)
1.8	1.000	1.000	1.000	1.000	0.999	0.998	0.995	0.987	0.969
	(0.000)	(0.000)	(0.001)	(0.002)	(0.005)	(0.013)	(0.031)	(0.063)	(0.085)
	0.000	0.000	0.002	0.008	0.026	0.067	0.151	0.304	0.561
	(0.001)	(0.008)	(0.035)	(0.100)	(0.222)	(0.401)	(0.605)	(0.749)	(0.675)
2.7	1.000	1.000	0.999	0.999	0.997	0.994	0.987	0.971	0.946
	(0.001)	(0.003)	(0.005)	(0.010)	(0.019)	(0.036)	(0.063)	(0.097)	(0.099)
	0.000	0.001	0.006	0.017	0.044	0.097	0.192	0.348	0.590
	(0.006)	(0.026)	(0.075)	(0.164)	(0.295)	(0.452)	(0.595)	(0.653)	(0.535)
3.6	0.999	0.998	0.997	0.994	0.990	0.982	0.968	0.946	0.920
	(0.008)	(0.013)	(0.021)	(0.033)	(0.052)	(0.077)	(0.107)	(0.129)	(0.101)
	0.001	0.004	0.013	0.033	0.071	0.135	0.239	0.394	0.619
	(0.024)	(0.067)	(0.142)	(0.249)	(0.379)	(0.505)	(0.590)	(0.585)	(0.446)
4.5	0.994	0.991	0.987	0.981	0.971	0.956	0.936	0.910	0.893
	(0.035)	(0.048)	(0.064)	(0.085)	(0.109)	(0.134)	(0.153)	(0.147)	(0.095)
	0.003	0.012	0.028	0.059	0.108	0.183	0.291	0.441	0.646
	(0.072)	(0.143)	(0.240)	(0.352)	(0.462)	(0.547)	(0.578)	(0.528)	(0.383)
5.4	0.974	0.966	0.956	0.944	0.927	0.908	0.885	0.865	0.870
	(0.108)	(0.128)	(0.148)	(0.167)	(0.183)	(0.189)	(0.179)	(0.142)	(0.095)
	0.009	0.026	0.054	0.096	0.157	0.239	0.348	0.489	0.673
	(0.170)	(0.264)	(0.365)	(0.461)	(0.534)	(0.571)	(0.555)	(0.477)	(0.339)
6.3	0.910	0.896	0.881	0.864	0.847	0.831	0.819	0.821	0.856
	(0.237)	(0.246)	(0.249)	(0.244)	(0.230)	(0.204)	(0.167)	(0.127)	(0.120)
	0.020	0.051	0.092	0.147	0.216	0.302	0.407	0.535	0.698
	(0.339)	(0.430)	(0.508)	(0.563)	(0.588)	(0.578)	(0.527)	(0.435)	(0.311)
7.2	0.757	0.747	0.739	0.735	0.735	0.742	0.760	0.795	0.862
	(0.319)	(0.292)	(0.263)	(0.233)	(0.206)	(0.184)	(0.174)	(0.174)	(0.167)
	0.039	0.086	0.143	0.208	0.283	0.369	0.467	0.580	0.722
	(0.589)	(0.635)	(0.658)	(0.656)	(0.631)	(0.582)	(0.509)	(0.417)	(0.309)
8.1	0.549	0.576	0.605	0.639	0.677	0.721	0.771	0.830	0.903
	(0.381)	(0.383)	(0.381)	(0.375)	(0.363)	(0.344)	(0.315)	(0.270)	(0.197)
	0.065	0.132	0.203	0.277	0.354	0.436	0.524	0.623	0.744
	(0.927)	(0.890)	(0.841)	(0.782)	(0.715)	(0.640)	(0.557)	(0.466)	(0.367)

For the Mastery score = 1 enter N-xbar in the test mean column

Table of the Raw Agreement Index and its
S.E.*SQRT(M), the Kappa Index and its
S.E.*SQRT(M) in the Beta-binomial Model
M = Number of subjects
Number of items N =10
Mastery score C = 5

Test Mean	KR21= .100	.200	.300	.400	.500	.600	.700	.800	.900
1.0	0.994	0.989	0.983	0.976	0.967	0.958	0.951	0.950	0.961
	(0.056)	(0.077)	(0.099)	(0.117)	(0.128)	(0.127)	(0.114)	(0.091)	(0.071)
	0.008	0.031	0.073	0.138	0.223	0.328	0.451	0.591	0.758
	(0.199)	(0.416)	(0.634)	(0.803)	(0.897)	(0.910)	(0.846)	(0.710)	(0.497)
2.0	0.924	0.912	0.900	0.889	0.882	0.878	0.881	0.895	0.927
	(0.245)	(0.243)	(0.234)	(0.218)	(0.196)	(0.171)	(0.145)	(0.120)	(0.096)
	0.029	0.073	0.132	0.203	0.286	0.381	0.489	0.612	0.764
	(0.499)	(0.632)	(0.714)	(0.745)	(0.730)	(0.676)	(0.592)	(0.482)	(0.341)
3.0	0.743	0.744	0.749	0.757	0.770	0.788	0.813	0.849	0.902
	(0.324)	(0.298)	(0.273)	(0.249)	(0.225)	(0.201)	(0.175)	(0.148)	(0.113)
	0.052	0.112	0.178	0.250	0.329	0.416	0.513	0.625	0.767
	(0.756)	(0.759)	(0.736)	(0.693)	(0.633)	(0.562)	(0.480)	(0.388)	(0.278)
4.0	0.563	0.592	0.623	0.655	0.689	0.727	0.770	0.821	0.887
	(0.421)	(0.384)	(0.349)	(0.313)	(0.278)	(0.243)	(0.206)	(0.167)	(0.122)
	0.066	0.133	0.202	0.274	0.350	0.432	0.523	0.630	0.768
	(0.889)	(0.811)	(0.735)	(0.660)	(0.585)	(0.508)	(0.430)	(0.346)	(0.250)
5.0	0.558	0.587	0.617	0.649	0.684	0.722	0.765	0.816	0.884
	(0.413)	(0.378)	(0.344)	(0.311)	(0.277)	(0.242)	(0.206)	(0.167)	(0.121)
	0.065	0.132	0.201	0.272	0.348	0.431	0.522	0.629	0.767
	(0.882)	(0.806)	(0.730)	(0.655)	(0.580)	(0.503)	(0.424)	(0.340)	(0.245)
6.0	0.722	0.724	0.730	0.739	0.753	0.772	0.798	0.835	0.892
	(0.320)	(0.295)	(0.271)	(0.248)	(0.224)	(0.201)	(0.175)	(0.147)	(0.113)
	0.052	0.111	0.176	0.248	0.326	0.412	0.509	0.621	0.764
	(0.747)	(0.744)	(0.718)	(0.673)	(0.614)	(0.541)	(0.459)	(0.367)	(0.260)
7.0	0.897	0.884	0.872	0.862	0.855	0.852	0.857	0.873	0.910
	(0.272)	(0.264)	(0.249)	(0.229)	(0.206)	(0.179)	(0.151)	(0.124)	(0.099)
	0.032	0.076	0.134	0.204	0.285	0.378	0.483	0.606	0.759
	(0.515)	(0.620)	(0.681)	(0.698)	(0.676)	(0.619)	(0.535)	(0.429)	(0.299)
8.0	0.981	0.974	0.964	0.953	0.941	0.929	0.920	0.919	0.936
	(0.109)	(0.130)	(0.149)	(0.161)	(0.164)	(0.156)	(0.136)	(0.108)	(0.082)
	0.012	0.039	0.083	0.146	0.228	0.329	0.447	0.584	0.751
	(0.256)	(0.432)	(0.590)	(0.701)	(0.751)	(0.737)	(0.665)	(0.544)	(0.375)
9.0	0.999	0.998	0.996	0.993	0.987	0.980	0.971	0.964	0.967
	(0.011)	(0.021)	(0.036)	(0.055)	(0.075)	(0.092)	(0.098)	(0.085)	(0.060)
	0.002	0.012	0.038	0.088	0.164	0.268	0.399	0.555	0.742
	(0.068)	(0.218)	(0.436)	(0.665)	(0.847)	(0.941)	(0.926)	(0.799)	(0.555)

For the Mastery score = 6 enter N-xbar in the test mean column

Table of the Raw Agreement Index and its
S.E.*SQRT(M), the Kappa Index and its
S.E.*SQRT(M) in the Beta-binomial Model
M = Number of subjects
Number of items N =10
Mastery score C = 6

```
-----------------------------------------------------------------------
Test  KR21=
Mean   .100    .200    .300    .400    .500    .600    .700    .800    .900
-----------------------------------------------------------------------
1.0   0.999   0.998   0.996   0.993   0.987   0.980   0.971   0.964   0.967
     (0.011) (0.021) (0.036) (0.055) (0.075) (0.092) (0.098) (0.085) (0.060)
      0.002   0.012   0.038   0.088   0.164   0.268   0.399   0.555   0.742
     (0.068) (0.218) (0.436) (0.665) (0.847) (0.941) (0.926) (0.799) (0.555)

2.0   0.981   0.974   0.964   0.953   0.941   0.929   0.920   0.919   0.936
     (0.109) (0.130) (0.149) (0.161) (0.164) (0.156) (0.136) (0.108) (0.082)
      0.012   0.039   0.083   0.146   0.228   0.329   0.447   0.584   0.751
     (0.256) (0.432) (0.590) (0.701) (0.751) (0.737) (0.665) (0.544) (0.375)

3.0   0.897   0.884   0.872   0.862   0.855   0.852   0.857   0.873   0.910
     (0.272) (0.264) (0.249) (0.229) (0.206) (0.179) (0.151) (0.124) (0.099)
      0.032   0.076   0.134   0.204   0.285   0.378   0.483   0.606   0.759
     (0.515) (0.620) (0.681) (0.698) (0.676) (0.619) (0.535) (0.429) (0.299)

4.0   0.722   0.724   0.730   0.739   0.753   0.772   0.798   0.835   0.892
     (0.320) (0.295) (0.271) (0.248) (0.224) (0.201) (0.175) (0.147) (0.113)
      0.052   0.111   0.176   0.248   0.326   0.412   0.509   0.621   0.764
     (0.747) (0.744) (0.718) (0.673) (0.614) (0.541) (0.459) (0.367) (0.260)

5.0   0.558   0.587   0.617   0.649   0.684   0.722   0.765   0.816   0.884
     (0.413) (0.378) (0.344) (0.311) (0.277) (0.242) (0.206) (0.167) (0.121)
      0.065   0.132   0.201   0.272   0.348   0.431   0.522   0.629   0.767
     (0.882) (0.806) (0.730) (0.655) (0.580) (0.503) (0.424) (0.340) (0.245)

6.0   0.563   0.592   0.623   0.655   0.689   0.727   0.770   0.821   0.887
     (0.421) (0.384) (0.349) (0.313) (0.278) (0.243) (0.206) (0.167) (0.122)
      0.066   0.133   0.202   0.274   0.350   0.432   0.523   0.630   0.768
     (0.889) (0.811) (0.735) (0.660) (0.585) (0.508) (0.430) (0.346) (0.250)

7.0   0.743   0.744   0.749   0.757   0.770   0.788   0.813   0.849   0.902
     (0.324) (0.298) (0.273) (0.249) (0.225) (0.201) (0.175) (0.148) (0.113)
      0.052   0.112   0.178   0.250   0.329   0.416   0.513   0.625   0.767
     (0.756) (0.759) (0.736) (0.693) (0.633) (0.562) (0.480) (0.388) (0.278)

8.0   0.924   0.912   0.900   0.889   0.882   0.878   0.881   0.895   0.927
     (0.245) (0.243) (0.234) (0.218) (0.196) (0.171) (0.145) (0.120) (0.096)
      0.029   0.073   0.132   0.203   0.286   0.381   0.489   0.612   0.764
     (0.499) (0.632) (0.714) (0.745) (0.730) (0.676) (0.592) (0.482) (0.341)

9.0   0.994   0.989   0.983   0.976   0.967   0.958   0.951   0.950   0.961
     (0.056) (0.077) (0.099) (0.117) (0.128) (0.127) (0.114) (0.091) (0.071)
      0.008   0.031   0.073   0.138   0.223   0.328   0.451   0.591   0.758
     (0.199) (0.416) (0.634) (0.803) (0.897) (0.910) (0.846) (0.710) (0.497)
-----------------------------------------------------------------------
```

For the Mastery score = 5 enter N-xbar in the test mean column

178

Table of the Raw Agreement Index and its
S.E.*SQRT(M), the Kappa Index and its
S.E.*SQRT(M) in the Beta-binomial Model
M = Number of subjects
Number of items N =10
Mastery score C = 7

Test Mean	KR21= .100	.200	.300	.400	.500	.600	.700	.800	.900
1.0	1.000	1.000	0.999	0.998	0.996	0.992	0.985	0.976	0.972
	(0.002)	(0.004)	(0.010)	(0.019)	(0.034)	(0.054)	(0.073)	(0.078)	(0.056)
	0.000	0.004	0.017	0.050	0.110	0.206	0.339	0.508	0.717
	(0.017)	(0.091)	(0.251)	(0.480)	(0.722)	(0.908)	(0.977)	(0.891)	(0.627)
2.0	0.997	0.994	0.990	0.984	0.976	0.964	0.952	0.941	0.944
	(0.030)	(0.044)	(0.063)	(0.085)	(0.105)	(0.121)	(0.123)	(0.105)	(0.073)
	0.004	0.016	0.044	0.092	0.166	0.265	0.391	0.544	0.731
	(0.098)	(0.235)	(0.410)	(0.581)	(0.709)	(0.764)	(0.732)	(0.616)	(0.421)
3.0	0.972	0.962	0.951	0.938	0.925	0.911	0.901	0.899	0.918
	(0.136)	(0.156)	(0.171)	(0.180)	(0.181)	(0.170)	(0.147)	(0.115)	(0.086)
	0.014	0.041	0.084	0.145	0.225	0.322	0.438	0.575	0.743
	(0.271)	(0.422)	(0.556)	(0.650)	(0.689)	(0.672)	(0.601)	(0.485)	(0.329)
4.0	0.883	0.870	0.858	0.847	0.839	0.836	0.841	0.857	0.897
	(0.281)	(0.271)	(0.256)	(0.235)	(0.210)	(0.182)	(0.153)	(0.126)	(0.101)
	0.032	0.075	0.131	0.199	0.279	0.371	0.476	0.599	0.753
	(0.506)	(0.599)	(0.654)	(0.670)	(0.648)	(0.593)	(0.510)	(0.405)	(0.279)
5.0	0.714	0.716	0.720	0.729	0.742	0.761	0.788	0.826	0.885
	(0.316)	(0.291)	(0.267)	(0.244)	(0.222)	(0.199)	(0.176)	(0.149)	(0.115)
	0.051	0.109	0.173	0.244	0.322	0.408	0.504	0.616	0.760
	(0.730)	(0.729)	(0.705)	(0.663)	(0.605)	(0.534)	(0.452)	(0.359)	(0.254)
6.0	0.555	0.583	0.613	0.645	0.680	0.718	0.762	0.814	0.883
	(0.405)	(0.373)	(0.341)	(0.310)	(0.278)	(0.244)	(0.209)	(0.170)	(0.125)
	0.065	0.131	0.200	0.271	0.347	0.430	0.521	0.628	0.765
	(0.878)	(0.804)	(0.730)	(0.656)	(0.582)	(0.506)	(0.427)	(0.343)	(0.248)
7.0	0.573	0.602	0.632	0.664	0.698	0.736	0.778	0.828	0.893
	(0.431)	(0.392)	(0.355)	(0.319)	(0.284)	(0.248)	(0.211)	(0.172)	(0.125)
	0.066	0.134	0.203	0.276	0.352	0.435	0.526	0.632	0.768
	(0.900)	(0.823)	(0.747)	(0.672)	(0.598)	(0.523)	(0.446)	(0.362)	(0.265)
8.0	0.783	0.781	0.783	0.789	0.799	0.815	0.837	0.869	0.917
	(0.323)	(0.296)	(0.271)	(0.246)	(0.222)	(0.198)	(0.174)	(0.148)	(0.114)
	0.051	0.111	0.178	0.252	0.332	0.420	0.517	0.629	0.770
	(0.758)	(0.779)	(0.768)	(0.732)	(0.677)	(0.609)	(0.527)	(0.433)	(0.315)
9.0	0.965	0.955	0.944	0.935	0.926	0.922	0.922	0.931	0.953
	(0.175)	(0.187)	(0.191)	(0.185)	(0.171)	(0.151)	(0.128)	(0.107)	(0.087)
	0.023	0.063	0.121	0.195	0.282	0.382	0.493	0.618	0.768
	(0.441)	(0.643)	(0.786)	(0.862)	(0.875)	(0.836)	(0.753)	(0.628)	(0.449)

For the Mastery score = 4 enter N-xbar in the test mean column

Table of the Raw Agreement Index and its
S.E.*SQRT(M), the Kappa Index and its
S.E.*SQRT(M) in the Beta-binomial Model
M = Number of subjects
Number of items N =10
Mastery score C = 8

```
---------------------------------------------------------------------
Test KR21=
Mean   .100    .200    .300    .400    .500    .600    .700    .800    .900
---------------------------------------------------------------------
1.0   1.000   1.000   1.000   1.000   0.999   0.997   0.993   0.985   0.978
     (0.000) (0.001) (0.002) (0.005) (0.012) (0.025) (0.046) (0.065) (0.056)
      0.000   0.001   0.006   0.024   0.065   0.143   0.268   0.446   0.681
     (0.003) (0.029) (0.115) (0.289) (0.535) (0.794) (0.973) (0.974) (0.719)

2.0   1.000   0.999   0.998   0.996   0.992   0.985   0.975   0.961   0.952
     (0.005) (0.010) (0.018) (0.031) (0.050) (0.073) (0.094) (0.100) (0.071)
      0.001   0.005   0.019   0.049   0.105   0.194   0.321   0.488   0.700
     (0.026) (0.096) (0.226) (0.402) (0.586) (0.725) (0.771) (0.693) (0.482)

3.0   0.995   0.991   0.987   0.979   0.969   0.956   0.940   0.926   0.927
     (0.039) (0.055) (0.074) (0.096) (0.118) (0.134) (0.137) (0.117) (0.079)
      0.004   0.017   0.043   0.087   0.156   0.250   0.373   0.526   0.717
     (0.102) (0.221) (0.370) (0.519) (0.634) (0.687) (0.661) (0.554) (0.374)

4.0   0.968   0.958   0.947   0.933   0.918   0.903   0.890   0.885   0.904
     (0.141) (0.160) (0.176) (0.186) (0.188) (0.178) (0.155) (0.120) (0.089)
      0.014   0.039   0.079   0.136   0.212   0.307   0.422   0.560   0.731
     (0.255) (0.389) (0.512) (0.604) (0.648) (0.638) (0.574) (0.462) (0.311)

5.0   0.883   0.869   0.856   0.844   0.834   0.829   0.831   0.846   0.886
     (0.278) (0.271) (0.258) (0.238) (0.214) (0.185) (0.155) (0.127) (0.104)
      0.029   0.071   0.124   0.189   0.267   0.358   0.464   0.588   0.744
     (0.472) (0.564) (0.623) (0.646) (0.632) (0.583) (0.503) (0.399) (0.274)

6.0   0.718   0.717   0.720   0.726   0.737   0.754   0.780   0.818   0.879
     (0.312) (0.286) (0.262) (0.239) (0.217) (0.197) (0.175) (0.152) (0.121)
      0.049   0.104   0.167   0.237   0.315   0.400   0.497   0.610   0.754
     (0.701) (0.709) (0.693) (0.657) (0.604) (0.536) (0.454) (0.362) (0.257)

7.0   0.554   0.581   0.611   0.643   0.677   0.716   0.760   0.814   0.884
     (0.394) (0.367) (0.340) (0.312) (0.282) (0.251) (0.218) (0.180) (0.134)
      0.064   0.130   0.199   0.271   0.347   0.429   0.520   0.627   0.763
     (0.875) (0.806) (0.736) (0.664) (0.591) (0.517) (0.439) (0.356) (0.261)

8.0   0.591   0.619   0.649   0.680   0.714   0.751   0.793   0.842   0.905
     (0.445) (0.405) (0.368) (0.331) (0.295) (0.259) (0.223) (0.183) (0.133)
      0.067   0.136   0.206   0.280   0.357   0.439   0.530   0.636   0.769
     (0.921) (0.847) (0.774) (0.702) (0.630) (0.557) (0.482) (0.399) (0.296)

9.0   0.860   0.853   0.850   0.851   0.856   0.866   0.882   0.907   0.944
     (0.303) (0.279) (0.254) (0.230) (0.207) (0.186) (0.166) (0.144) (0.110)
      0.048   0.107   0.175   0.251   0.335   0.425   0.525   0.637   0.773
     (0.749) (0.827) (0.855) (0.844) (0.805) (0.742) (0.660) (0.553) (0.409)
---------------------------------------------------------------------
```

For the Mastery score = 3 enter N-xbar in the test mean column

Table of the Raw Agreement Index and its
S.E.*SQRT(M), the Kappa Index and its
S.E.*SQRT(M) in the Beta-binomial Model
M = Number of subjects
Number of items N =10
Mastery score C = 9

Test Mean	KR21= .100	.200	.300	.400	.500	.600	.700	.800	.900
1.0	1.000	1.000	1.000	1.000	1.000	0.999	0.997	0.993	0.983
	(0.000)	(0.000)	(0.000)	(0.001)	(0.003)	(0.009)	(0.022)	(0.046)	(0.058)
	0.000	0.000	0.002	0.009	0.031	0.083	0.186	0.359	0.620
	(0.000)	(0.006)	(0.039)	(0.132)	(0.317)	(0.586)	(0.867)	(1.017)	(0.840)
2.0	1.000	1.000	1.000	0.999	0.998	0.995	0.989	0.977	0.962
	(0.001)	(0.001)	(0.003)	(0.007)	(0.016)	(0.031)	(0.056)	(0.083)	(0.076)
	0.000	0.001	0.006	0.020	0.054	0.120	0.233	0.404	0.646
	(0.004)	(0.027)	(0.090)	(0.212)	(0.389)	(0.587)	(0.737)	(0.757)	(0.570)
3.0	0.999	0.999	0.998	0.995	0.991	0.984	0.971	0.953	0.937
	(0.006)	(0.011)	(0.019)	(0.032)	(0.050)	(0.075)	(0.101)	(0.113)	(0.083)
	0.001	0.005	0.016	0.040	0.088	0.166	0.284	0.449	0.669
	(0.024)	(0.079)	(0.178)	(0.319)	(0.478)	(0.614)	(0.677)	(0.627)	(0.443)
4.0	0.995	0.992	0.987	0.980	0.970	0.956	0.938	0.918	0.912
	(0.036)	(0.050)	(0.068)	(0.090)	(0.113)	(0.133)	(0.143)	(0.129)	(0.084)
	0.004	0.014	0.035	0.073	0.133	0.220	0.338	0.492	0.691
	(0.084)	(0.178)	(0.302)	(0.437)	(0.554)	(0.625)	(0.623)	(0.535)	(0.365)
5.0	0.972	0.963	0.953	0.939	0.923	0.906	0.888	0.877	0.890
	(0.122)	(0.142)	(0.161)	(0.176)	(0.185)	(0.182)	(0.164)	(0.127)	(0.090)
	0.011	0.032	0.066	0.117	0.187	0.278	0.392	0.532	0.710
	(0.208)	(0.325)	(0.442)	(0.540)	(0.601)	(0.612)	(0.566)	(0.463)	(0.313)
6.0	0.898	0.884	0.870	0.855	0.842	0.831	0.827	0.836	0.874
	(0.259)	(0.260)	(0.254)	(0.241)	(0.219)	(0.191)	(0.158)	(0.126)	(0.108)
	0.025	0.061	0.109	0.170	0.245	0.335	0.442	0.568	0.728
	(0.405)	(0.501)	(0.572)	(0.612)	(0.615)	(0.581)	(0.511)	(0.408)	(0.282)
7.0	0.739	0.733	0.731	0.732	0.739	0.751	0.773	0.809	0.872
	(0.313)	(0.286)	(0.259)	(0.234)	(0.211)	(0.191)	(0.173)	(0.157)	(0.133)
	0.044	0.096	0.156	0.225	0.301	0.387	0.485	0.599	0.743
	(0.648)	(0.673)	(0.675)	(0.653)	(0.610)	(0.548)	(0.470)	(0.377)	(0.270)
8.0	0.555	0.581	0.609	0.641	0.675	0.714	0.760	0.815	0.888
	(0.377)	(0.359)	(0.339)	(0.317)	(0.294)	(0.268)	(0.238)	(0.202)	(0.152)
	0.063	0.129	0.198	0.269	0.346	0.428	0.519	0.624	0.757
	(0.874)	(0.815)	(0.752)	(0.686)	(0.617)	(0.545)	(0.469)	(0.386)	(0.288)
9.0	0.637	0.664	0.692	0.722	0.755	0.790	0.829	0.874	0.928
	(0.470)	(0.430)	(0.393)	(0.357)	(0.322)	(0.286)	(0.248)	(0.204)	(0.143)
	0.070	0.141	0.214	0.289	0.367	0.450	0.540	0.642	0.768
	(0.980)	(0.919)	(0.857)	(0.793)	(0.727)	(0.657)	(0.581)	(0.491)	(0.375)

For the Mastery score = 2 enter N-xbar in the test mean column

Table of the Raw Agreement Index and its
S.E.*SQRT(M), the Kappa Index and its
S.E.*SQRT(M) in the Beta-binomial Model
M = Number of subjects
Number of items N =10
Mastery score C =10

Test Mean	KR21= .100	.200	.300	.400	.500	.600	.700	.800	.900
1.0	1.000	1.000	1.000	1.000	1.000	1.000	0.999	0.997	0.989
	(0.000)	(0.000)	(0.000)	(0.000)	(0.000)	(0.002)	(0.006)	(0.023)	(0.055)
	0.000	0.000	0.000	0.002	0.009	0.032	0.093	0.229	0.497
	(0.000)	(0.001)	(0.007)	(0.036)	(0.118)	(0.294)	(0.579)	(0.901)	(0.981)
2.0	1.000	1.000	1.000	1.000	1.000	0.999	0.997	0.991	0.973
	(0.000)	(0.000)	(0.000)	(0.001)	(0.003)	(0.007)	(0.020)	(0.049)	(0.082)
	0.000	0.000	0.001	0.005	0.017	0.050	0.124	0.269	0.530
	(0.000)	(0.004)	(0.020)	(0.066)	(0.164)	(0.329)	(0.541)	(0.721)	(0.687)
3.0	1.000	1.000	1.000	0.999	0.999	0.997	0.991	0.978	0.952
	(0.000)	(0.001)	(0.002)	(0.005)	(0.011)	(0.023)	(0.046)	(0.082)	(0.100)
	0.000	0.001	0.003	0.011	0.032	0.076	0.162	0.314	0.563
	(0.003)	(0.014)	(0.047)	(0.117)	(0.234)	(0.390)	(0.551)	(0.642)	(0.548)
4.0	1.000	0.999	0.998	0.997	0.994	0.989	0.977	0.957	0.927
	(0.004)	(0.007)	(0.012)	(0.020)	(0.034)	(0.056)	(0.087)	(0.118)	(0.106)
	0.000	0.003	0.009	0.023	0.054	0.111	0.209	0.363	0.595
	(0.013)	(0.042)	(0.100)	(0.194)	(0.319)	(0.456)	(0.565)	(0.587)	(0.458)
5.0	0.997	0.995	0.992	0.988	0.980	0.969	0.950	0.923	0.899
	(0.021)	(0.030)	(0.042)	(0.060)	(0.082)	(0.109)	(0.136)	(0.145)	(0.101)
	0.002	0.008	0.020	0.045	0.088	0.157	0.262	0.413	0.626
	(0.046)	(0.102)	(0.187)	(0.295)	(0.412)	(0.513)	(0.567)	(0.535)	(0.393)
6.0	0.984	0.978	0.970	0.960	0.946	0.927	0.903	0.879	0.872
	(0.076)	(0.093)	(0.114)	(0.136)	(0.157)	(0.173)	(0.175)	(0.149)	(0.093)
	0.006	0.019	0.043	0.080	0.135	0.214	0.322	0.465	0.656
	(0.124)	(0.209)	(0.308)	(0.410)	(0.498)	(0.553)	(0.554)	(0.486)	(0.344)
7.0	0.935	0.922	0.908	0.891	0.873	0.853	0.836	0.829	0.854
	(0.197)	(0.212)	(0.223)	(0.228)	(0.224)	(0.208)	(0.175)	(0.130)	(0.109)
	0.016	0.042	0.079	0.129	0.195	0.280	0.386	0.517	0.685
	(0.277)	(0.371)	(0.457)	(0.526)	(0.566)	(0.570)	(0.529)	(0.441)	(0.312)
8.0	0.795	0.783	0.771	0.762	0.756	0.757	0.767	0.795	0.856
	(0.317)	(0.297)	(0.272)	(0.243)	(0.212)	(0.182)	(0.162)	(0.157)	(0.158)
	0.034	0.078	0.130	0.193	0.267	0.352	0.451	0.567	0.712
	(0.524)	(0.582)	(0.619)	(0.631)	(0.617)	(0.576)	(0.508)	(0.416)	(0.304)
9.0	0.564	0.585	0.610	0.639	0.673	0.714	0.762	0.821	0.896
	(0.333)	(0.335)	(0.337)	(0.336)	(0.331)	(0.320)	(0.299)	(0.263)	(0.198)
	0.061	0.126	0.195	0.268	0.345	0.427	0.516	0.615	0.737
	(0.877)	(0.850)	(0.810)	(0.758)	(0.696)	(0.624)	(0.544)	(0.454)	(0.354)

For the Mastery score = 1 enter N-xbar in the test mean column

References

Algina, J., and Noe, M. J. 1978. A study of the accuracy of Subkoviak's single-administration estimate of the coefficient of agreement using two true-score estimates. *Journal of Educational Measurement* 15:101-10.

Brennan, R. L., and Kane, M. T., 1977a. An index of dependability for mastery tests. *Journal of Educational Measurement* 14:277-89.

———. 1977b. Signal/noise ratios for domain-referenced tests. *Psychometrika* 42:609-25; 1978 Errata, 43:289.

Carver, R. P. 1970. Special problems in measuring change with psychometric devices. In *Evaluative research: Strategies and methods.* Pittsburgh, Pa.: American Institutes for Research. Pp. 48-63.

Cohen, J. 1960. A coefficient of agreement for nominal scales. *Educational and Psychological Measurement* 20:37-46.

———. 1968. Weighted kappa: Nominal scale agreement with provision for scaled disagreement of partial credit. *Psychological Bulletin* 70:213-30.

Fleiss, J. L.; Cohen, J.; and Everitt, B. S. 1969. Large sample standard errors of kappa and weighted kappa. *Psychological Bulletin* 72:323-27.

Goodman, L. A., and Kruskal, W. H. 1954. Measures of association for cross classifications. *Journal of the American Statistical Association* 49:732-64.

Gupta, S. S. 1963. Probability integrals of multivariate normal and multivariate t. *Annals of Mathematical Statistics* 34:792-828.

Hambleton, R. K. 1974. Testing and decision-making procedures for selected individualized instruction programs. *Review of Educational Research* 44: 371-400.

Hambleton, R. K., and Novick, M. R. 1973. Toward an integration of theory and method for criterion-referenced tests. *Journal of Educational Measurement,* 10:159-70.

Hambleton, R. K.; Swaminathan, H.; Algina, J.; and Coulson, D. B. 1978. Criterion-referenced testing and measurement: A review of technical issues and developments. *Review of Educational Research* 48:1-47.

Harris, C. A. 1972. An interpretation of Livingston's reliability coefficient for criterion-referenced tests. *Journal of Educational Measurement* 9:27-29.

Hubert, L. J. 1977. Kappa revisited. *Psychological Bulletin* 84:289-97.

Huynh, H. 1976. On the reliability of decisions in domain-referenced testing. *Journal of Educational Measurement* 13:253-64.

———. 1977a. The kappamax reliability index for decisions in domain-referenced testing. Paper presented at the annual meeting of the American Educational Research Association, April 1977, New York.

———. 1977b. Statistical inference for the kappa and kappamax reliability indices based on the beta-binomial model. Paper presented at the annual meeting of the Psychometric Society, June 1977, Chapel Hill.

———. 1978. *Computation and inference for two reliability indices in mastery testing based on the beta-binomial model.* Publication Series in Mastery Testing, Research Memorandum 78-1. Columbia, S.C.: College of Education, University of South Carolina.

Huynh, H., and Saunders, J. C. 1979. *Accuracy of two procedures for estimating reliability of mastery tests.* Publication Series in Mastery Testing, Research Memorandum 79-1. Columbia, S.C.: College of Education, University of South Carolina.

Kane, M. T., and Brennan, R. L. In press. Agreement coefficients as indices of dependability for domain-referenced tests. *Applied Psychological Measurement.*

Keats, J. A., and Lord, F. M. 1962. A theoretical distribution for mental test scores. *Psychometrika* 27:59-72.

LaValle, I. H. 1970. *An introduction to probability, decision, and inference.* New York: Holt, Rinehart and Winston.

Livingston, S. A. 1972a. Criterion-referenced applications of classical test theory. *Journal of Educational Measurement* 9:13-26.

_____. 1972b. A reply to Harris' "An interpretation of Livingston's reliability coefficient for criterion-referenced tests." *Journal of Educational Measurement* 9:31.

_____. 1972c. Reply to Shavelson, Block and Ravitch's "Criterion-referenced testing: Comments on reliability." *Journal of Educational Measurement* 9:139-40.

_____. 1978. Reliability of tests used to make pass/fail decisions: Answering the right questions. Paper presented at the annual meeting of the National Council on Measurement in Education, March 1978, Toronto.

Lord, F. M. 1965. A strong true score theory, with applications. *Psychometrika* 30:239-70.

_____. 1969. Estimating true score distributions in psychological testing (An empirical Bayes estimation problem). *Psychometrika* 34:259-99.

Marshall, J. L., and Haertel, E. H. 1976. The mean split-half coefficient of agreement: A single administration index of reliability for mastery tests. Manuscript, University of Wisconsin.

Marshall, J. L., and Serlin, R. C. 1979. Characteristics of four mastery test reliability indices: Influence of distribution shape and cutting score. Paper presented at the annual meeting of the American Educational Research Association, April 1979, San Francisco.

Mellenbergh, G. J., and van der Linden, W. J. 1978. The internal and external optimality of decisions based on tests. Manuscript, Twente University, Enschede, Netherlands.

Novick, M. R.; Lewis, C.; and Jackson, P. H. 1973. The estimation of proportions in *m* groups. *Psychometrika* 38:19-45.

Peng, C.-Y. 1979. An investigation of Huynh's normal approximation procedure for estimating criterion-referenced reliability. Paper presented at the annual meeting of the American Educational Research Association, April 1979, San Francisco.

Reid, J. B., and Roberts, D. M. 1978. A Monte Carlo comparison of phi and kappa as measures of criterion-referenced reliability. Paper presented at the annual meeting of the American Educational Research Association, March 1978, Toronto.

Shavelson, R. J.; Block, J. H.; and Ravitch, M. M. 1972. Criterion-referenced testing: Comments on reliability. *Journal of Educational Measurement* 9: 133–37.

Subkoviak, M. J. 1975. *Estimating reliability from a single administration of a mastery test.* Occasional Paper no. 15. Madison, Wis.: Laboratory of Experimental Design, University of Wisconsin.

———. 1976. Estimating reliability from a single administration of a mastery test. *Journal of Educational Measurement* 13:265–76.

———. 1977a. *Evaluation of criterion-referenced reliability coefficients.* Final Report, Grant NIE-G-76-0088. Washington, D.C.: National Institute of Education.

———. 1977b. Further comments on reliability for mastery tests. Manuscript, University of Wisconsin.

———. 1978. Empirical investigation of procedures for estimating reliability for mastery tests. *Journal of Educational Measurement* 15:111–16.

Subkoviak, M. J., and Wilcox, R. R. 1978. Estimating the probability of correct classification in mastery testing. Paper presented at the annual meeting of the American Educational Research Association, March 1978, Toronto.

Swaminathan, H.; Hambleton, R. K.; and Algina, J. 1974. Reliability of criterion-referenced tests: A decision-theoretic formulation. *Journal of Educational Measurement* 11:263–67.

Tables of the binomial probability distribution. 1949. Washington, D.C.: U.S. Government Printing Office.

Tables of the bivariate normal distribution function and related functions. 1959. Washington, D.C.: U.S. Government Printing Office.

Wilcox, R. R. 1977. Estimating the likelihood of false-positive and false-negative decisions in mastery testing: An empirical Bayes approach. *Journal of Educational Statistics* 2:289–307.

———. 1978. Estimating true score in the compound binomial error model. *Psychometrika* 43:245–58.

6

APPLICATIONS OF GENERALIZABILITY THEORY

Robert L. Brennan

Introduction

The approach to reliability issues that is reviewed and discussed in this chapter is based primarily upon the fundamental principles of generalizability theory, as documented by Cronbach, Gleser, Nanda, and Rajaratnam (1972) and reviewed by Brennan (1977a) and Brennan and Kane (in press). Many aspects of this approach can be found in Brennan (1977b, 1978), Brennan and Kane (1977a, 1977b) and Kane and Brennan (in press). Indeed, this chapter may be viewed, in part, as an integrated summary of much of the work reported in these publications. As such, this chapter provides an introduction to, and review of, a specific psychometric theory for criterion-referenced testing. From another perspective, in terms of the Hambleton, Swaminathan, Algina, and Coulson (1978) trichotomy of types of criterion-referenced reliability, this chapter treats one approach to issues involving the "reliability of criterion-referenced test scores" and, to some extent, the "reliability of domain score estimates."

Since Popham and Husek (1969) challenged the appropriateness of correlation coefficients as indices of reliability for criterion-referenced,

Appreciation is extended to Dr. Michael T. Kane, who participated in most of the research reviewed here and who offered many insightful comments about drafts of this chapter. This research was partially supported by contracts between the American College Testing Program and the Navy Personnel Research and Development Center, Contract Nos. N00123-77-C-0739 and N00123-78-C-1206.

domain-referenced, and mastery tests, considerable effort has been devoted to developing more appropriate indices. Most of these indices have been proposed as measures of *reliability*; in this chapter, however, the more generic term *dependability* will be used to avoid unwarranted associations with classical reliability coefficients.

Probably the most important results of the approach discussed here center around the definition of error variance for domain-referenced interpretations. It is this error variance that principally distinguishes this approach from others that have been proposed, and it is this error variance that is incorporated in the indices of dependability developed and discussed here.

Review of Generalizability Theory Approach

Classical test theory provides a very simple structural model of the relationship between observed, true, and error scores. However, the simplicity of the model necessitates some rather restrictive assumptions if the model is to be applied to real data. Generalizability theory liberalizes and extends classical test theory in several important respects. For example, the theory of generalizability does not necessitate the classical test theory assumption of "parallel" tests; rather, generalizability theory employs the weaker assumption of "randomly parallel" tests. Also, classical test theory assumes that errors of measurement are sampled from an undifferentiated univariate distribution. By contrast, generalizability theory allows for the existence of multiple types and sources of error through the application of analysis of variance procedures or, more specifically, through the application of the general linear model to the dependability of measurement. Consequently, generalizability theory is applicable to a broad range of testing and evaluation studies that arise in education and psychology. The subject of this chapter—namely, the dependability of domain-referenced tests—is only one such application.

Since generalizability theory is unfamiliar to many practitioners, the review provided below is intentionally didactic to some extent. In general, the text provides an outline, without proofs, of the development of theoretical results, with emphasis placed upon the interpretation of such results. For the most part, formulas for estimating results are provided in tables and illustrative examples are reported in sufficient detail to enable the reader to verify calculations. Also, relationships between results for norm-referenced and domain-referenced interpretations are treated to a limited extent. Finally, major emphasis is placed upon results for the simple persons-crossed-with-items design, but a limited treatment of some other designs is provided, too.

Model, Assumptions, and Variance Components for the p × i Design.
Let us assume that the data for a particular test are derived from a
random sample of n_p persons from an infinite population of persons
and a random sample of n_i items from an infinite universe (or domain)
of items. The observed score for any person p on any item i can be
represented by the linear model

$$X_{pi} = \mu + \mu_p\tilde{} + \mu_i\tilde{} + \mu_{pi}\tilde{} + e ,$$

where μ = grand mean in the population of persons and the universe
of items,

$\mu_p\tilde{}$ = score effect for person p,

$\mu_i\tilde{}$ = score effect for item i,

$\mu_{pi}\tilde{}$ = score effect for the interaction of person p and item i, and

e = experimental error.

Usually there is only one observation for each person-item combination,
which implies that the $\mu_{pi}\tilde{}$ and e effects are completely confounded.
Cronbach, Gleser, Nanda, and Rajaratnam (1972) represent this confounding with the notation (pi, e). Here, in accordance with the notational conventions in Brennan (1977a), this confounding will not be
indicated explicitly, and this equation may be written as

$$X_{pi} = \mu + \mu_p\tilde{} + \mu_i\tilde{} + \mu_{pi}\tilde{}. \tag{1}$$

The basic assumptions underlying the model in equation 1 are the
typical analysis of variance (or general linear model) assumptions that
are well documented by Cronbach, Gleser, Nanda, and Rajaratnam
(1972) and by most experimental design texts. Briefly, these assumptions are that all effects in the model are assumed to be sampled independently, and the expected value of each effect over the population
of persons and the universe of items is set equal to zero. Given these
assumptions, equation 1 is the random effects model for the persons-
crossed-with-items design, $p \times i$. It is particularly important to note
that this model does *not* require any assumptions about the distributional form for the observed scores or any score effects.

Score Effects and Mean Scores. Equation 1 provides a decomposition
of the observed score for person p on item i in terms of score effects, or
components. In a similar manner, the *average* observed score for person
p on a *sample* of items (i.e., a test) can be represented as

$$X_{pI} = \mu + \mu_p\tilde{} + \mu_I\tilde{} + \mu_{pI}\tilde{}, \tag{2}$$

where I denotes the average score for a particular sample of n_i items and, as in equation 1, $\mu_{pI}{}^{\sim}$ is completely confounded with experimental error.

Following the terminology of generalizability theory, the *universe score* for person p is denoted μ_p and defined as the expected value of the observed score over the *universe* of items. Therefore, using equation 1

$$\mu_p = \mathcal{E}_i X_{pi} = \mu + \mu_p{}^{\sim}, \tag{3}$$

or, equivalently, using equation 2

$$\mu_p = \mathcal{E}_I X_{pI} = \mu + \mu_p{}^{\sim},$$

where the expectation is taken over all possible samples of size n_i from the universe of items.

Similarly, the population mean for item i is

$$\mu_i = \mathcal{E}_p X_{pi} = \mu + \mu_i{}^{\sim}, \tag{4}$$

and the population mean for a test, or set of items, I, is

$$\mu_I = \mathcal{E}_p X_{pI} = \mu + \mu_I{}^{\sim}. \tag{5}$$

Equations 4 and 5, respectively, imply that μ_i is the item difficulty level for the population of persons and that μ_I is the test mean in terms of the proportion of items correct.

In classical test theory, the assumption of parallel tests requires that $\mu_I = \mu_J$, where I and J are two different sets of items, or tests. Here, however, it is *not* assumed that tests are *classically* parallel. Rather, in generalizability theory the assumption of *classically* parallel tests is replaced by the weaker assumption of *randomly* parallel tests. Two tests are randomly parallel if they both consist of random samples of the same number of items from the same universe, or domain, of items.

Defining and Interpreting Variance Components. For each of the score effects, or components, in equation 1, there is an associated *variance component*. For example, the variance component for persons is denoted $\sigma^2(p)$ and defined as

$$\sigma^2(p) = \mathcal{E}_p(\mu_p - \mu)^2 = \mathcal{E}_p(\mu_p{}^{\sim})^2. \tag{6}$$

Similarly,

$$\sigma^2(i) = \mathcal{E}_i(\mu_i - \mu)^2 = \mathcal{E}_i(\mu_i{}^{\tilde{}})^2 \tag{7}$$

and

$$\sigma^2(pi) = \mathcal{E}_p\,\mathcal{E}_i(X_{pi} - \mu_p - \mu_i + \mu)^2 = \mathcal{E}_p\,\mathcal{E}_i(\mu_{pi}{}^{\tilde{}})^2. \tag{8}$$

These variance components are called *random effects* variance components, because they are derived from the random effects model in equation 1. The sum of these variance components equals the total observed score variance, denoted $\sigma^2(X_{pi})$, which should *not* be confused with the *expected* observed score variance discussed later. Note especially that these variance components are associated with score effects for *single* observations. If, for example, items are scored dichotomously, then the maximum value of any of the variance components in equations 6–8 is 0.25.

The variance component, $\sigma^2(p)$, assumes a particularly important role here, in that it is the universe score variance, that is, the variance over persons of the universe scores defined in equation 3. In generalizability theory, the universe score variance plays a role like that of the true score variance in classical test theory. Similarly, $\sigma^2(pi)$ is analogous to the usual error variance, for a *single*-item test, in classical test theory. Classical test theory, however, has no quantity analogous to $\sigma^2(i)$, which is by definition the variance of the mean scores for all items in the universe, where each mean is based upon the population of persons. As shown later, $\sigma^2(i)$ plays an especially important role in distinctions between norm-referenced and domain-referenced interpretations of test scores.

By substituting I for i everywhere in equations 6–8, one can obtain the definitions of the variance components associated with equation 2. It is evident that $\sigma^2(p)$, the universe score variance, remains unchanged, and it is easily shown that

$$\sigma^2(I) = \sigma^2(i)/n_i \tag{9}$$

and

$$\sigma^2(pI) = \sigma^2(pi)/n_i. \tag{10}$$

Recall that I denotes an *average* score for a particular sample of n_i items. This is the usual convention in generalizability theory, but if one prefers *total* score variance components, they are obtained by multiplying all variance components by $n_i{}^2$.

In equation 10, $\sigma^2(pI)$ is the usual error variance in classical test theory for a test of length n_i. However, $\sigma^2(I)$ in equation 9 is not analogous to any quantity in classical test theory. Indeed, the assumption of parallel tests in classical test theory necessitates that $\sigma^2(I)$ be zero. To appreciate this fact, recall that the assumption of parallel tests requires that, for two different sets of items, I and J, the population means be equal, that is, $\mu_I = \mu_J$ (see equation 5). When this assumption is extended to multiple sets of items (tests of length n_i), it is evident that the assumption is met only if $\sigma^2(I) = 0$. Again, generalizability theory assumes randomly parallel, not classically parallel, tests.

Estimating Variance Components. In generalizability theory, variance components assume central importance. They are the building blocks that provide a crucial foundation for all subsequent results. From a practical point of view, therefore, the estimation and interpretation of variance components is a matter of considerable importance. In understanding variance components, the defining equations 6–8 are useful, but they cannot be used directly to estimate variance components because these equations are expressed in terms of model parameters, not estimates.

Rather, one usually estimates variance components through an analysis of variance, such as that provided in table 6.1 for the $p \times i$ design. It is evident from table 6.1 that $\sigma^2(p)$, $\sigma^2(i)$, and $\sigma^2(pi)$ are estimated using mean squares and sample sizes only; once these variance components have been estimated, equations 9 and 10 can be used to estimate $\sigma^2(I)$ and $\sigma^2(pI)$. (For present purposes, the reader should disregard all references in table 6.1 to G study and D study, as well as the primes attached to some sample sizes.) Since variance components are unfamiliar statistics for many readers, the lower third of table 6.1 provides equations for some relatively common statistics in terms of variance components.

Variance components can also be estimated using Venn diagrams. More importantly, however, Venn diagrams provide a useful visual aid to understanding variance components as well as other aspects of generalizability analyses. Figure 6.1 provides the general form of a Venn diagram for the $p \times i$ design, as well as the relationships among areas of a Venn diagram and certain equations frequently encountered in analysis of variance and/or generalizability theory. As indicated in figures 6.1A, 6.1B, and 6.1C, circles and their intersections can be interpreted as mean squares, while parts of circles can be interpreted as variance components or simple functions of them. These relationships provide a visual procedure for estimating variance components. From figures 6.1B and 6.1D, it is evident that subtracting $MS(pi)$ from $MS(p)$, and dividing by n_i, provides an estimate of $\sigma^2(p)$, the universe score variance.

TABLE 6.1. ANOVA for Estimating Variance Components for the Random Effects or $p \times i$ Design

Effect, Component, or Source	df	SS	MS	Estimated G Study Variance Component	D Study Sampling Frequency	Estimated D Study Variance Component
Persons (p)	$n_p - 1$	$SS(p)$	$MS(p)$	$\hat{\sigma}^2(p)$	1	$\hat{\sigma}^2(p)$
Items (i)	$n_i - 1$	$SS(i)$	$MS(i)$	$\hat{\sigma}^2(i)$	n_i'	$\hat{\sigma}^2(I)$
Interaction (pi)	$(n_p - 1)(n_i - 1)$	$SS(pi)$	$MS(pi)$	$\hat{\sigma}^2(pi)$	n_i'	$\hat{\sigma}^2(pI)$

$$\hat{\sigma}^2(p) = [MS(p) - MS(pi)]/n_i$$
$$\hat{\sigma}^2(i) = [MS(i) - MS(pi)]/n_p$$
$$\hat{\sigma}^2(pi) = MS(pi)$$

$$\hat{\sigma}^2(I) = \hat{\sigma}^2(i)/n_i'$$
$$\hat{\sigma}(pI) = \hat{\sigma}^2(pi)/n_i'$$

Variance of Observed Person Mean Scores: $\hat{S}_p^2(X_{pI}) = \hat{\sigma}^2(p) + \hat{\sigma}^2(pi)/n_i$

Variance of Observed Item Difficulty Levels: $\hat{S}_i^2(X_{Pi}) = \hat{\sigma}^2(i) + \hat{\sigma}^2(pi)/n_p$

Sum of Observed Item Variances: $\sum_i \hat{S}_p^2(X_{pi}) = \hat{\sigma}^2(p) + \hat{\sigma}^2(pi) = \sum_i X_{Pi}(1 - X_{Pi})$ for dichotomous items

NOTE: Upper case P and I represent mean scores, *not* total scores.

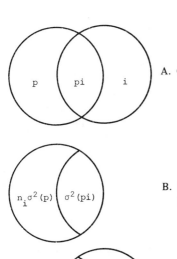

A. General Form of Venn Diagram for $p \times i$ Design

B. Expected Value of the Mean Square for the Effect $\mu_p \sim$: $EMS(p) = \sigma^2(pi) + n_i\sigma^2(p)$

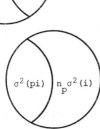

C. Expected Value of the Mean Square for the Effect $\mu_i \sim$: $EMS(i) = \sigma^2(pi) + n_p\sigma^2(i)$

D. Expected Value of the Mean Square for the Effect $\mu_{pi} \sim$: $EMS(pi) = \sigma^2(pi)$

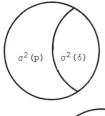

E. Expected Observed Score Variance:
$$\mathcal{E}\sigma^2(X) = \sigma^2(p) + \sigma^2(\delta)$$
$$= \sigma^2(p) + \sigma^2(pI)$$

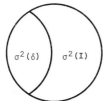

F. $\sigma^2(\Delta) = \sigma^2(\delta) + \sigma^2(I)$
$$= \sigma^2(pI) + \sigma^2(I)$$

FIGURE 6.1. Venn diagram representation of mean squares and variance components for $p \times i$ design

To clarify further the estimation and interpretation of variance components, as well as the notational conventions used here, consider the synthetic data in table 6.2, which have been studied extensively by Guilford (1954) from the perspective of classical test theory. These data are introduced, not because they are illustrative of any ideal characteristics of a test, but rather because they can be studied in their entirety by the reader, without encountering either trivial results or extensive computational complexity. In particular, using the equations in table 6.1 and the data in table 6.2, it is easy to verify the numerical values of the estimated variance components in table 6.3. It is evident that, for these data, the estimated universe score variance, $\sigma^2(p)$, is slightly less than estimated variance among item mean scores, $\sigma^2(i)$, but neither of these variance components is nearly as large as $\sigma^2(pi)$.

The Error Variance $\sigma^2(\Delta)$ and Domain-Referenced Interpretations. One of the distinct advantages of generalizability theory over classical test theory is that generalizability theory allows one to distinguish clearly between two different types of error, denoted σ and Δ. As argued below, σ and its associated variance, $\sigma^2(\delta)$, are appropriate for norm-referenced interpretations, while Δ and its variance, $\sigma^2(\Delta)$, are generally appropriate for domain-referenced interpretations. For the approach developed here to domain-referenced issues of dependability of measurement, this distinction is of crucial importance. Indeed, this approach suggests that classical test theory is generally incapable of distinguishing between norm-referenced and domain-referenced interpretations. I shall begin with a discussion of $\sigma^2(\delta)$ to enable subsequent comparisons of $\sigma^2(\Delta)$ with $\sigma^2(\delta)$.

The Error Variance $\sigma^2(\delta)$. In norm-referenced testing, interest is focused on "the relative ordering of individuals with respect to their test performance, for example, whether student A can solve his problems more quickly than student B" (Glaser 1963, p. 519) or "the adequacy of the measuring procedure for making *comparative* decisions" (Cronbach et al. 1972, p. 95). In this situation, the error for a given person, as defined by Cronbach, Gleser, Nanda, and Rajaratnam (1972), is

$$\delta_p = (X_{pI} - \mu_I) - (\mu_p - \mu). \tag{11}$$

In equation 11, μ represents the reference point for making statements about μ_p, and μ_I represents the reference point for making statements about X_{pI}. That is, the raw score, X_{pI}, carries no inherent meaning for a norm-referenced test. It is the deviation score, $X_{pI} - \mu_I$, that

TABLE 6.2. Synthetic Data Reported by Guilford (1954, p. 381)

Person	Item 1	2	3	4	5	6	7	8	9	10	11	12	Total	X_{pI}
1	1	0	1	0	0	0	0	0	0	0	0	0	2	0.1667
2	1	1	1	0	0	1	0	0	0	0	0	0	4	0.3333
3	1	1	1	1	0	0	0	0	0	0	0	0	4	0.3333
4	1	1	0	1	1	0	0	1	0	0	0	0	5	0.4167
5	1	1	1	1	1	0	0	0	0	0	0	0	5	0.4167
6	1	1	1	0	1	1	1	0	0	0	0	0	6	0.5000
7	1	1	1	1	1	1	1	0	0	0	0	0	7	0.5833
8	1	1	1	1	0	1	1	1	1	1	0	0	9	0.7500
9	1	1	1	1	1	1	1	1	1	1	1	0	11	0.9167
10	1	1	1	1	1	1	1	1	1	1	1	1	12	1.0000
Total	10	9	9	7	6	6	5	4	3	3	2	1		
X_{Pi}	1.0	0.9	0.9	0.7	0.6	0.6	0.5	0.4	0.3	0.3	0.2	0.1		$X_{PI} = 0.5417$

$X_{PI}(1 - X_{PI}) = 0.2483$ $\qquad \sum_i X_{Pi}(1 - X_{Pi}) = 2.03$ $\qquad \hat{S}_i^2(X_{Pi}) = 0.0863$ $\qquad \hat{S}_p^2(X_{pI}) = 0.0729$

Coefficient α = KR-20 = 0.856 $\qquad$ KR-21 = 0.747 $\qquad S_p^2(X_{pI}) = 0.0656$

Note: Upper case *P* and *I* represent mean scores, *not* total scores.

TABLE 6.3. G Study and D Study for Random Effects $p \times i$ Design Using Guilford Data and Assuming $n_i = n_i{'} = 12$

Effect, Component, or Source	df	SS	MS	Estimated G Study Variance Component	D Study Sampling Frequency	Estimated D Study Variance Component
Persons (p)	9	7.875	0.8750	$\hat{\sigma}^2(p) = 0.0625$	1	$\hat{\sigma}^2(p) = 0.0625$
Items (i)	11	9.492	0.8629	$\hat{\sigma}^2(i) = 0.0737$	12	$\hat{\sigma}^2(I) = 0.0061$
Interaction (pi)	99	12.425	0.1255	$\hat{\sigma}^2(pi) = 0.1255$	12	$\hat{\sigma}^2(pI) = 0.0105$

$$\hat{\varepsilon\rho}^2 = 0.856 \ (5.95)$$
$$\hat{\Phi} = 0.790 \ (3.77)$$

$\hat{\sigma}^2(\delta) = 0.0105$
$\hat{\sigma}^2(\Delta) = 0.0166$
$X_{PI} = 0.5417$
$\hat{\sigma}^2(X_{PI}) = 0.0134$

$\hat{\Phi}(\lambda = 0.4) = 0.807(4.17)$ $\hat{\Phi}(\lambda = 0.7) = 0.817(4.47)$
$\hat{\Phi}(\lambda = 0.5) = 0.754(3.06)$ $\hat{\Phi}(\lambda = 0.8) = 0.875(6.98)$
$\hat{\Phi}(\lambda = 0.6) = 0.760(3.16)$ $\hat{\Phi}(\lambda = 0.9) = 0.915(10.69)$

$$\hat{\Phi}(\lambda = X_{PI}) = 0.747(2.96)$$

NOTE: Numbers in parentheses following values for $\hat{\Phi}(\lambda)$ are the estimated signal/noise ratios. All estimates of $\hat{\sigma}^2(X_{PI})$ and $\Phi(\lambda)$ assume $n_p = n_p{'} = 10$.

carries the meaning, and this deviation score is to be interpreted as an estimate of $\mu_p - \mu$.

When X_{pI}, μ_p, and μ_I are expressed in terms of score effects (see equations 2, 3, and 5), one obtains

$$\delta_p = \mu_{pI} \tilde{} \tag{12}$$

with variance

$$\sigma^2(\delta) = \sigma^2(pI). \tag{13}$$

This is the error variance for norm-referenced interpretations of test data, and it is identical to the error variance incorporated in coefficients such as a KR-20 and Cronbach's (1951) α, although the derivation of $\sigma^2(\delta)$ is based upon generalizability theory, not classical test theory.

From table 6.3, for illustrative data, one can see that the estimate of $\sigma^2(\delta)$ is $\hat{\sigma}(pI) = 0.0105$. It is well known that the error variance in classical test theory is obtained by multiplying the observed variance by $1 - r$, where r is the reliability of the test. From table 6.2, for these data, the observed variance is 0.0729, KR-20 is 0.856 and, therefore, the error variance is $0.0729(1 - 0.856) = 0.0105$, which is identical to $\sigma^2(\delta)$.

The Error Variance $\sigma^2(\Delta)$. In norm-referenced testing, then, our interest is in observed *deviation* scores, $X_{pI} - \mu_I$, which are to be interpreted relative to universe *deviation* scores, $\mu_p - \mu$. In domain-referenced testing, however, our interest is in "the degree to which the student has attained criterion performance" (Glaser 1963, p. 519), independent of the performance of other students. That is, we are *not* primarily interested in the relative ordering of examinees' universe scores; rather, we are interested in the difference between each examinee's universe score and some absolute standard. In this case, the error for a given examinee is

$$\Delta_{pI} = (X_{pI} - \lambda) - (\mu_p - \lambda) = X_{pI} - \mu_p, \tag{14}$$

where λ is some reference point. Here, no restrictions are placed upon the value of λ except that it be expressed as a proportion of items correct, to be consistent with the previously adopted convention of using mean scores rather than total scores. Usually λ is defined by the user, a priori, and in such cases it is common to speak about *mastery* interpretations, where λ is the mastery cut-off score. However, it will be shown that λ

might also be expressed as a population parameter or sample statistic, for certain more general domain-referenced interpretations.

When X_{pI} and μ_p in equation 14 are expressed in terms of score effects (see equations 2 and 3), one obtains

$$\Delta_{pI} = \mu_I\tilde{\ } + \mu_{pI}\tilde{\ } \tag{15}$$

with variance

$$\sigma^2(\Delta) = \sigma^2(I) + \sigma^2(pI). \tag{16}$$

This is the error variance for domain-referenced interpretations.

It is evident from equations 13 and 16 that $\sigma^2(\Delta)$ is always at least as large as $\sigma^2(\delta)$. For example, for the illustrative data $\hat{\sigma}^2(\Delta) = 0.0061 + 0.0105 = 0.0166$, which is greater than $\hat{\sigma}^2(\delta) = 0.0105$. Indeed, the difference between $\sigma^2(\Delta)$ and $\sigma^2(\delta)$ is simply $\sigma^2(I)$. Therefore, the two-error variances are equal only when μ_I is a constant for all instances of the testing procedure. The variance component for the main effect for items, $\sigma^2(I)$, reflects differences in the mean score (in the population) for different samples of items. If one is interested only in differences among examinee universe scores, as in norm-referenced testing, then any effect that is a constant for all examinees does not contribute to the error variance. However, for domain-referenced testing, we are interested in the absolute magnitude of examinee universe scores, or the magnitude compared to some externally defined cut-off score. In this case, fluctuations in mean scores for samples of items *do* contribute to error variance.

From another point of view, since all persons take all items for the $p \times i$ design, the effect $\mu_I\tilde{\ }$ in equation 2 contributes to all examinees' observed scores in the same way. For domain-referenced testing, however, this does not eliminate the item effect as a source of error. For example, if one happens to select an especially easy set of items from the universe of items, the estimates of μ_p and $\mu_p - \lambda$ will tend to be too high. This component of error is taken into account in $\sigma^2(\Delta)$, but not in $\sigma^2(\delta)$.

Although $\sigma^2(\Delta)$ cannot be obtained directly from classical test theory, Brennan and Kane (1977*b*) have shown that, for dichotomous data, $\hat{\sigma}^2(\Delta)$ is related to Lord's (1957) formula for the standard error of measurement for a person's score, which in my notation is

$$\hat{\sigma}(\Delta \mid X_{pI}) = \sqrt{\frac{X_{pI}(1 - X_{pI})}{n_i - 1}} . \tag{17}$$

In effect, $\hat{\sigma}^2(\Delta)$ is the average over persons of the square of Lord's standard error of measurement. The reader can verify this result for the data in table 6.2. It is also possible to show that $\hat{\sigma}^2(\Delta)$ is an estimate of the generic error variance discussed in Lord and Novick (1968).

Confidence Intervals. $\sigma^2(\Delta)$ and $\sigma^2(\delta)$ are discussed extensively by Cronbach, Gleser, Nanda, and Rajartnam (1972), but they do not directly consider $\sigma^2(\Delta)$ in the context of domain-referenced *mastery* testing. Rather, they state:

> Classical theory, assuming uniform condition means ($\mu_I = \mu$), ignores the distinction between Δ and δ. Lord (1962) pointed out that condition means are unlikely to be equal when tests are not carefully equated. Lord showed that the variance of the within-person error Δ, over nonequivalent tests, differs from the error variance calculated by classical formulas. ... A confidence interval of the conventional sort has to be defined in terms of $\sigma(\Delta)$, not $\sigma(\delta)$; only if all tests (or other procedures) yield strictly equal means is it appropriate to use $\sigma(\delta)$. (P. 82)

When Cronbach, Gleser, Nanda, and Rajaratnam (1972) speak of a "confidence interval of the conventional sort," they are speaking in the context of using the observed score, X_{pI}, as an estimate of the universe score, μ_p. In this context it is clear from equation 14 that the error variance for a confidence interval is indeed $\sigma^2(\Delta)$. More generally, $\sigma^2(\Delta)$ is the appropriate error variance for a confidence interval when $X_{pI} - \lambda$ is used as an estimate of $\mu_p - \lambda$, independent of the value of λ. However, if the observed score under consideration is the *deviation* score, $X_{pI} - \mu_I$, which is used as an estimate of $\mu_p - \mu$, then $\sigma^2(\delta)$ is the appropriate error variance for a confidence interval. One might say, therefore, that for the score of a *single* examinee on a test, $\sigma^2(\Delta)$ is the appropriate error variance for confidence intervals involving domain-referenced interpretations, whereas $\sigma^2(\delta)$ is the appropriate error variance for confidence intervals involving norm-referenced interpretations.

For the illustrative data in tables 6.2 and 6.3, a 68 percent confidence interval for the eighth examinee with a score of 0.75 would extend from $[0.75 - \hat{\sigma}(\Delta)]$ to $[0.75 + \hat{\sigma}(\Delta)]$. Since $\hat{\sigma}^2(\Delta)$ is 0.0166, $\hat{\sigma}(\Delta)$ equals 0.1288, and this confidence interval is approximately 0.62 to 0.88. Alternatively, one could use Lord's standard error of measurement in equation 17 to establish a confidence interval for any examinee with a score of 0.75. Using equation 17, $\hat{\sigma}(\Delta \mid X_{PI}) = \sqrt{(0.75 \, (0.25)/11}$ $= 0.1306$, and a 68 percent confidence interval again extends from 0.62 to 0.88, approximately. In this case, the confidence interval based upon Lord's standard error of measurement is virtually identical to the interval based upon $\hat{\sigma}(\Delta)$. In general, however, the length of such intervals will differ somewhat, because Lord's standard error of measurement varies for examinees with different scores.

It should be noted that in order to attach a probability statement to a confidence interval, it is necessary to make some distributional assumption. For such purposes, it is traditional to assume a normal distribution, although binomial and compound binomial assumptions are sometimes made, especially in domain-referenced testing. As pointed out previously, these distributional assumptions are not an integral part of generalizability theory, although they are required for the use of error variances in establishing confidence intervals.

The line of reasoning discussed above for identifying the appropriate error variance for a confidence interval for a single examinee's score can be extended to a consideration of confidence intervals for the difference between the scores for two different examinees on two different tests, the difference between the scores for the *same* examinee on two different tests, and the difference between the scores for two different examinees, on the *same* test. Table 6.4 summarizes results reported by Brennan (1978) for each of these three cases and for the two different types of error, Δ and δ.

The reader is cautioned *not* to infer from table 6.4 that all such comparisons are always meaningful or useful. Also, if a measure of change is required, simple difference scores are seldom appropriate (see Cronbach et al. 1972). However, table 6.4 does highlight one important fact, namely, that $2\ \sigma^2(\delta)$ [*not* $2\ \sigma^2(\Delta)$] is the appropriate estimate of error variance for two different examinees on the *same* test, even when an *individual* examinee's score is to be interpreted in a domain-referenced manner. This result may seem anomalous, but it is consistent with a similar result reported by Lord and Novick (1968, pp. 180–84), who refer to $\sigma^2(\Delta)$ as "generic" error variance. Furthermore, this result is quite reasonable when one realizes that the magnitude of this difference score reflects the *relative* standing of two examinees on the same test.

TABLE 6.4. Error Variances for Simple Difference Scores

Examinees	Tests[a]	Error is Δ for an Individual Examinee's Score	Error is δ for an Individual Examinee's Score
Different	Different	$2\sigma^2(\Delta)$	$2\sigma^2(\delta)$
Same	Different	$2\sigma^2(\Delta)$	$2\sigma^2(\delta)$
Different	Same	$2\sigma^2(\delta)$	$2\sigma^2(\delta)$

[a]Different tests are, more specifically, different random samples of the same number of items from the same universe of items.

Indeed, such a comparison is *not* properly a domain-referenced consideration.

Indices of Dependability for Domain-Referenced Tests. Using generalizability theory it is possible to define two indices of dependability for domain-referenced tests. These indices can be given interpretations that have some similarities with interpretations of classical reliability coefficients and generalizability coefficients. However, since indices of dependability for domain-referenced tests are indeed different from analogous indices for norm-referenced tests, I always refer to domain-referenced indices as "indices of dependability" and to norm-referenced indices as "reliability coefficients" (based on classical test theory) or "generalizability coefficients" (based on generalizability theory). A principal difference is that the domain-referenced indices discussed below incorporate $\sigma^2(\Delta)$, while the norm-referenced coefficients incorporate $\sigma^2(\delta)$. I shall begin with a brief discussion of norm-referenced coefficients to enable subsequent comparisons of indices of dependability with such coefficients.

Norm-Referenced Coefficients. Cronbach, Gleser, Nanda, and Rajaratnam (1972) define a generalizability coefficient for the $p \times i$ design as

$$\mathcal{E}\rho^2 = \frac{\mathcal{E}_p(\mu_p - \mu)^2}{\mathcal{E}_I\,\mathcal{E}_p(X_{pI} - \mu_I)^2}. \tag{18}$$

The numerator is simply the universe score variance, $\sigma^2(p)$, and the denominator is called the *expected* observed score variance (see figure 6.1E):

$$\mathcal{E}\sigma^2(X_{pI}) = \sigma^2(p) + \sigma^2(\delta).$$

In terms of variance components, therefore,

$$\mathcal{E}\rho^2 = \frac{\sigma^2(p)}{\sigma^2(p) + \sigma^2(\delta)}. \tag{19}$$

Technically, $\mathcal{E}\rho^2$ is an intraclass correlation coefficient.

The generalizability coefficient in equation 19 is approximately equal to the expected value of the correlation between randomly selected instances of the testing procedure, where the scores correlated are *deviation* scores of the form $X_{pI} - \mu_I$. (Recall that such deviation scores are inherent in the definition of δ in equation 11.) Also, it is well known that, when the variance components in equation 19 are replaced by their estimates, $\mathcal{E}\rho^2$ is identical to Cronbach's (1951) coefficient α, and to KR-20 when items are scored dichotomously. Therefore, this simple generalizability coefficient is interpretable in much the same way as these classical estimates of reliability, even though the derivation of $\mathcal{E}\rho^2$ is based on the model equation 2, *not* the classical test theory model.

The generalizability coefficient, $\mathcal{E}\rho^2$, can also be expressed as a simple function of the signal/noise ratio:

$$\psi(g) = S(g)/N(g) = \sigma^2(p)/\sigma^2(\delta), \tag{20}$$

where g is used to distinguish this ratio from corresponding ratios for domain-referenced interpretations discussed later. Given equation 20, it is easy to show that

$$\mathcal{E}\rho^2 = \psi(g)/[1 + \psi(g)].$$
$$= S(g)/[S(g) + N(g)].$$

The signal/noise ratio $\psi(g)$ is itself a useful alternative coefficient for norm-referenced interpretations. The concept arises naturally in discussing communication systems where the "signal to noise ratio compares the strength of the transmission to the strength of the interference" (Cronbach and Gleser 1964, p. 468). The signal is intended to characterize the magnitude of the desired discriminations. Noise characterizes the effect of extraneous variables in blurring these discriminations. If the signal is large compared to the noise, the intended discriminations are easily made. If the signal is weak compared to the noise, the intended discriminations may be completely lost. In norm-referenced testing, the signal, $\sigma^2(p)$, is a function of the magnitude of the intended discriminations, $\mu_p - \mu$. These intended discriminations reflect the tolerance or sensitivity requirements that must be met if the measurement procedure is to achieve its intended purpose. The noise, $\sigma^2(\delta)$, reflects the *degree of precision*, or the magnitude of the errors that arise in the testing procedure. The signal/noise ratio is, therefore, a measure of the *relative precision* of the testing procedure.

An Index of Dependability for Domain-Referenced Mastery Interpretations. In my treatment of error variance for domain-referenced interpretations, I noted that the differences we want to detect are of the form $\mu_p - \lambda$, and the observed differences are of the form $X_{pI} - \lambda$, where λ is a reference point, or mastery cut-off score. As shown above, for a norm-referenced test the corresponding differences $\mu_p - \mu$ and $X_{pI} - \mu_I$ provide a basis for defining the generalizability coefficient, $\mathcal{E}\rho^2$, equation 19. In a similar manner, an index of dependability for domain-referenced mastery testing can be defined by substituting λ for μ and μ_I in equation 19. The resulting index is

$$\Phi(\lambda) = \frac{\mathcal{E}_p(\mu_p - \lambda)^2}{\mathcal{E}_I \, \mathcal{E}_p(X_{pI} - \lambda)^2},\tag{21}$$

and in terms of variance components

$$\Phi(\lambda) = \frac{\sigma^2(p) + (\mu - \lambda)^2}{\sigma^2(p) + (\mu - \lambda)^2 + \sigma^2(\Delta)}.\tag{22}$$

Equation 22 was first derived by Brennan and Kane (1977a), who denoted this index "M(C)." Since the derivation is rather involved, it will not be repeated here. I simply note that the derivation relies heavily on the fact that the numerator and denominator of equation 21 are expected squared deviations, rather than variances. In this sense, the derivation of $\Phi(\lambda)$ in terms of variance components is similar to the derivation of Livingston's (1972) coefficient. Indeed, it can be shown that equation 21 is identical to Livingston's coefficient when $\sigma^2(\Delta)$ equals $\sigma^2(\delta)$—i.e., when $\sigma^2(I)$ is zero. This is consistent with the fact that Livingston's coefficient is based on the assumption of classically parallel tests, which precludes distinguishing between $\sigma^2(\Delta)$ and $\sigma^2(\delta)$. By contrast, the development of $\Phi(\lambda)$ is based on the assumption of *randomly parallel* tests.

Several characteristics of $\Phi(\lambda)$ are evident from equation 22. First and most importantly, $\Phi(\lambda)$ incorporates the error variance $\sigma^2(\Delta)$, rather than the error variance $\sigma^2(\delta)$ in $\mathcal{E}\rho^2$ (equation 19). Second, $\Phi(\lambda)$ will be different for different values of λ. Third, $\Phi(\lambda)$ has an upper limit of one. Fourth, the numerator of $\Phi(\lambda)$ is dependent upon both the universe score variance, $\sigma^2(p)$, *and* the squared distance of the population mean, μ, from the reference point or cut-off score, λ. Clearly $\Phi(\lambda)$ can be positive even when there is *no* variance among examinee universe scores. Suppose, for example, that $\sigma^2(\Delta)$ is positive and all examinees have identical "high" universe scores relative to λ. In this case, $\Phi(\lambda)$ will be positive, reflecting the fact that it is relatively easy to determine correctly whether or not examinees are above the cut-off score. By contrast, in this case, $\mathcal{E}p^2$ would be zero.

$\Phi(\lambda)$ can be interpreted in terms of signal and noise concepts in a manner analogous to one interpretation of $\mathcal{E}\rho^2$ discussed previously. In particular, Brennan and Kane (1977b) show that the signal/noise ratio for domain-referenced interpretations, d, is

$$\psi(d) = S(d)/N(d) = [\sigma^2(p) + (\mu - \lambda)^2]/\sigma^2(\Delta),\tag{23}$$

and, in terms of this ratio,

$$\Phi(\lambda) = \psi(d)/[1 + \psi(d)]$$
$$= S(d)/[S(d) + N(d)].$$

Note, in particular, that for domain-referenced interpretations the noise is $\sigma^2(\Delta)$, *not* $\sigma^2(\delta)$, and, when such interpretations are made with respect to a mastery cut-off score, λ, the signal is $\sigma^2(p) + (\mu - \lambda)^2$.

It is clear from equation 23 that the signal/noise ratio for a domain-referenced mastery test, $\psi(d)$, can be large, even if $\sigma^2(p)$ is zero, provided $(\mu - \lambda)^2$ is large relative to $\sigma^2(\Delta)$. In other words, this signal/noise ratio will be relatively large whenever the detection of the signal, $\mu_p - \lambda$, is relatively easy, or, equivalently, whenever it is easy to make correct classifications of randomly selected persons. In short, the signal/noise ratio, $\psi(d)$, is a measure of the *relative precision* of a domain-referenced mastery testing procedure, and the index $\Phi(\lambda)$ is a simple monotonic function of $\psi(d)$.

Since $\Phi(\lambda)$ and $\psi(d)$ are monotonically related, the choice between them (if such a choice is required) should be made on the basis of convenience or interpretability. In this regard, the reader should note that, unlike $\Phi(\lambda)$, the signal/noise ratio $\psi(d)$ does not have an upper limit of one. For example, when $\Phi(\lambda)$ is 0.85, $\psi(d)$ is $0.85/0.15$, or 5.67. Whether or not this characteristic of $\psi(d)$, and other signal/noise ratios, is desirable depends upon one's perspective.

A General-Purpose Index of Dependability for Domain-Referenced Interpretations. It is evident from equation 21 that $\Phi(\lambda)$ achieves its lower limit when λ equals μ, the grand mean in the *population* of persons and the *universe* of items. That is, the lower limit of $\Phi(\lambda)$ is simply

$$\Phi = \frac{\sigma^2(p)}{\sigma^2(p) + \sigma^2(\Delta)} . \tag{24}$$

In comparing Φ with $\mathcal{E}\rho^2$ one can see that, since $\sigma^2(\Delta)$ is always at least as large as $\sigma^2(\delta)$, the index of dependability (Φ) must also be less than or equal to the generalizability coefficient $\mathcal{E}\rho^2$. Intuitively, this is a reasonable characteristic of Φ, since domain-referenced interpretations of "absolute" scores are more "stringent" than norm-referenced interpretations of "relative" scores.

The index Φ can also be interpreted in terms of signal/noise concepts in a matter analogous to the interpretation of $\Phi(\lambda)$. For Φ, the noise is still $\sigma^2(\Delta)$, but the signal is $\sigma^2(p)$, resulting in the signal/noise ratio $\sigma^2(p)/\sigma^2(\Delta)$. In this case, the signal reflects universe score differences among persons, independent of any cut-off score. The reasonableness of such a definition of signal for a domain-referenced test may be clarified by the following argument:

> In some cases, a person's score on a domain-referenced test may be used as a descriptive statistic. In other cases, the test may be designed to serve several types of decisions. Under either of these cases, it would be useful to have a general index of the precision of the test, in addition to any indices associated with specific decision procedures. If a particular decision procedure is not specified, the value to be assigned to the signal, or tolerance, must be somewhat vague. However, a natural and useful definition is provided by the magnitudes of the differences that do exist in the population with which the instrument is used. There is strong precedent for this choice in the traditions of physical measurement. General-purpose instruments for measuring length, for example, are typically evaluated by their ability to detect differences of the order of magnitude of those encountered in some area of practice. Thus, rulers are used in carpentry and verniers are used in machine shops. (Brennan & Kane 1977*b*, pp. 616–17)

The Indices $\Phi(\lambda)$ *and* Φ *As Agreement Statistics.* Previous sections have discussed various distinctions between the domain-referenced indices of dependability, $\Phi(\lambda)$ and Φ, as well as distinctions between these indices and more traditional norm-referenced coefficients. A framework for interpreting $\Phi(\lambda)$ and Φ, and for identifying similarities and differences among these indices and others, has been provided by Kane and Brennan (in press). They discuss two general agreement coefficients, one of which involves a correction for chance agreement. These two general coefficients are

$$\theta = \frac{A}{A_m} \tag{25}$$

and

$$\theta_c = \frac{A - A_c}{A_m - A_c} \tag{26}$$

where A is observed agreement, A_m is maximum agreement, and A_c is chance agreement. Under very weak assumptions about A, A_m, and A_c, it is possible to show that both coefficients have an upper limit of one.

In general, θ indicates how closely the scores for any examinee can be expected to agree on randomly sampled instances of a testing procedure. by contrast, θ_c indicates how closely such scores can be expected to agree when the contribution of chance agreement is removed. To specify either of these coefficients completely, however, one must define an appropriate agreement function.

For domain-referenced interpretations, one such agreement function is

$$d = (X_{pI} - \lambda)(X_{qJ} - \lambda),$$

where p and q are persons and I and J are sets of items or tests. Briefly, expected agreement (A) is defined by Kane and Brennan (in press) as the expected value of d when p equals q; maximum agreement (A_m) is defined as the expected value of d when p equals q *and* I equals J; and chance agreement (A_c) is defined as the expected value of d for different persons (p and q) *and* for different samples of items (I and J). Given these definitions, Kane and Brennan (in press) derive the results presented in table 6.5. Note in particular that the agreement coefficient $\theta(d)$ is *identical* to $\Phi(\lambda)$ and the agreement coefficient corrected for chance, $\theta_c(d)$, is *identical* to Φ.

These results imply that the two indices, $\Phi(\lambda)$ and Φ, address different questions about dependability. In general, $\Phi(\lambda)$ indicates how closely, in terms of the agreement function (d), the scores for any examinee can be expected to agree. Φ indicates how closely (again, in terms of the agreement function, d) the two scores for an examinee can be expected to agree, with the contribution of chance agreement *removed*. The index, $\Phi(\lambda)$, therefore, characterizes the dependability of decisions, or estimates, based on the testing procedure. The magnitude of $\Phi(\lambda)$ depends, in part, on chance agreement; it may be greater than zero even when decisions based on the testing procedure are no more dependable than the decisions based on marginal probabilities in the population. The index, Φ, characterizes the contribution of the testing procedure to the dependability of the decisions, over what would be expected on the basis of chance agreement. $\Phi(\lambda)$ provides an estimate of the dependability of the decisions based on the testing procedure; Φ provides an estimate of the *contribution* of the testing procedure to the dependability of such decisions. The two indices provide answers to different questions. The issue is not which of these indices is best, but rather which is appropriate in a given context.

Table 6.5 also indicates that the loss, defined in general as

$$L = A_m - A,$$

is $\sigma^2(\Delta)$, for the domain-referenced agreement function d. In effect, therefore, depending upon the perspective one chooses, for domain-

TABLE 6.5. Coefficients for Different Agreement Functions

Agreement Function	Parameters	Agreement Coefficients
Domain-Referenced: $d = (X_{pI} - \lambda)(X_{qJ} - \lambda)$	$A(d) = (\mu - \lambda)^2 + \sigma^2(p)$ $A_m(d) = (\mu - \lambda)^2 + \sigma^2(p) + \sigma^2(\Delta)$ $A_c(d) = (\mu - \lambda)^2$ $L(d) = \sigma^2(\Delta)$	$\theta(d) = \dfrac{(\mu - \lambda)^2 + \sigma^2(p)}{(\mu - \lambda)^2 + \sigma^2(p) + \sigma^2(\Delta)}$ $\theta_c(d) = \dfrac{\sigma^2(p)}{\sigma^2(p) + \sigma^2(\Delta)}$
Norm-Referenced: $g = (X_{pI} - \mu_I)(X_{qJ} - \mu_J)$	$A(g) = \sigma^2(p)$ $A_m(g) = \sigma^2(p) + \sigma^2(\delta)$ $A_c(g) = 0$ $L(g) = \sigma^2(\delta)$	$\theta(g) = \theta_c(g) = \dfrac{\sigma^2(p)}{\sigma^2(p) + \sigma^2(\delta)}$
Threshold: $t = 1$ if X_{pI} and X_{qJ} result in same classification; 0 otherwise	$A(t) = \sum \pi_{ii}$ $A_m(t) = 1$ $A_c(t) = \sum \pi_i^2$ $L(t) = \sum \pi_{ii} \ (i \neq j)$	$\theta(t) = \sum \pi_{ii}$ $\theta_c(t) = \dfrac{\sum \pi_{ii} - \sum \pi_i^2}{1 - \sum \pi_i^2}$

NOTE: Here p and q are different persons; I and J are different random samples of items.

referenced interpretations $\sigma^2(\Delta)$ can be interpreted in terms of error, noise, or loss in the measurement procedure.

The approach outlined above can also be applied to other agreement functions. For example, table 6.5 shows that, for the agreement function

$$g = (X_{pI} - \mu_I)(X_{qJ} - \mu_J),$$

both θ and θ_c are identical to the generalizability coefficient, $\mathcal{E}\rho^2$, with the loss, L, being $\sigma^2(\delta)$. In effect, $\mathcal{E}\rho^2$ incorporates its own correction for chance agreement, and $\sigma^2(\delta)$ can be interpreted in terms of error, noise, or loss in a norm-referenced measurement procedure.

Both the d and g agreement functions are consistent with squared-error loss approaches to measurement error. Others have suggested using a threshold loss, or agreement, function for domain-referenced interpretations (see Subkoviak, chapter 5). As indicated in table 6.5, for the threshold agreement function, t, the coefficient θ is simply

$$\theta(t) = \Sigma\pi_{ii},$$

the proportion of persons consistently classified as masters or non-masters on two randomly selected instances of the testing procedure. When a correction-for-chance agreement is incorporated, the resulting coefficient is

$$\theta_c(t) = \frac{\Sigma\pi_{ii} - \Sigma\pi_i^2}{1 - \Sigma\pi_i^2}$$

where $\Sigma\pi_i^2$ is the sum of the squared marginal proportions of masters and nonmasters in the population. Under the assumption of randomly parallel tests, $\theta_c(t)$ is identical to Cohen's (1960) coefficient kappa. From this perspective, therefore, the choice between Φ and Cohen's kappa as indices of dependability is primarily a choice between two different agreement functions. This issue is discussed more fully later.

Perspectives on Indices of Dependability. Table 6.6 summarizes three perspectives that have been discussed as a basis for defining and/or interpreting indices of dependability for domain-referenced tests. One perspective involves defining these indices in a manner analogous to the definition of a generalizability coefficient; another is based upon a consideration of agreement coefficients; the third uses signal/noise concepts. Each of these perspectives has two principal features in common. First, the error variance, noise power, or squared-error loss is always $\sigma^2(\Delta)$.

TABLE 6.6. Indices of Dependability for Domain-Referenced Interpretations Given Random Effects $p \times i$ Design

Approach	Indices	Parameters
Generalizability Theory	$\Phi(\lambda) = \dfrac{\mathcal{E}_p(\mu_p - \lambda)^2}{\mathcal{E}_I\mathcal{E}_p(X_{pI} - \lambda)^2}$ $\Phi = \dfrac{\mathcal{E}_p(\mu_p - \mu)^2}{\mathcal{E}_I\mathcal{E}_p(X_{pI} - \mu)^2}$	$\mathcal{E}_p(\mu_p - \lambda)^2 = \sigma^2(p) + (\mu - \lambda)^2$ $\mathcal{E}_I\mathcal{E}_p(X_{pI} - \lambda)^2 = \sigma^2(p) + (\mu - \lambda)^2 + \sigma^2(\Delta)$ $\mathcal{E}_p(\mu_p - \mu)^2 = \sigma^2(p)$ $\mathcal{E}_I\mathcal{E}_p(X_{pI} - \mu)^2 = \sigma^2(p) + \sigma^2(\Delta)$
Agreement Function: $(X_{pI} - \lambda)(X_{qJ} - \lambda)$	$\theta(d) = \dfrac{A(d)}{A_m(d)}$ $\theta_c(d) = \dfrac{A(d) - A_c(d)}{A_m(d) - A_c(d)}$	$A(d) = \sigma^2(p) + (\mu - \lambda)^2$ $A_m(d) = \sigma^2(p) + (\mu - \lambda)^2 + \sigma^2(\Delta)$ $A_c(d) = (\mu - \lambda)^2$ $L(d) = A_m(d) - A(d) = \sigma^2(\Delta)$
Signal/Noise Ratios	$\psi(d) = \dfrac{S(d)}{N(d)}$ $\psi_c(d) = \dfrac{S_c(d)}{N(d)}$	$S(d) = \sigma^2(p) + (\mu - \lambda)^2$ $S_c(d) = \sigma^2(p)$ $N(d) = \sigma^2(\Delta)$

NOTE: $\Phi(\lambda) = \theta(d) = \psi(d)/[1 + \psi(d)]$; $\Phi = \theta_c(d) = \psi_c(d)/[1 + \psi_c(d)]$; and $\sigma^2(\Delta) = L(d) = N(d)$.

Second, there are *two* distinct indices that can be derived and interpreted, and these two indices address different issues of measurement dependability for domain-referenced tests. In the terminology used by Hambleton, Swaminathan, Algina, and Coulson (1978) to describe their trichotomy of types of reliability, the index $\Phi(\lambda)$ addresses the "reliability of criterion-referenced test scores," and index Φ is associated with the "reliability of domain score estimates."

Estimating Indices of Dependability for Domain-Referenced Tests.
The previous section discussed definitions and interpretations of the two indices of dependability for domain-referenced tests, $\Phi(\lambda)$ in equation 22 and Φ in equation 24. In this section I will consider *estimates* of these indices.

The $p \times i$ Design. Brennan (1979) provides a computer program for performing generalizability analysis with the $p \times i$ design. This program is quite general in that it provides, among other things, estimates of variance components and indices of dependability for models involving sampling of items from either an infinite or a finite universe of items. Here, however, interest is restricted to a consideration of the random effects model, which assumes sampling from an essentially infinite universe of items. For this model, the formulas in table 6.1 can be used to estimate variance components, and using these estimates, the formulas in table 6.7 can be used to estimate indices of dependability.

For the most part, the *estimation* of the two indices of dependability for domain-referenced tests, $\Phi(\lambda)$ and Φ, involves a straightforward replacement of variance components with their estimates, as indicated in the first two columns of table 6.7. There is, however, one exception to this rule. An unbiased estimate of $(\mu - \lambda)^2$ is *not* obtained by replacing μ, the grand mean, with X_{PI}, the mean over the *sample* of n_p persons and n_i items. Rather, Brennan and Kane (1977a) show that an unbiased estimate of $(\mu - \lambda)^2$ is $(X_{PI} - \lambda)^2 - \hat{\sigma}^2(X_{PI})$, where $\hat{\sigma}^2(X_{PI})$ is the estimated variability of the sample mean. In terms of variance components,

$$\hat{\sigma}^2(X_{PI}) = \hat{\sigma}^2(p)/n_p' + \hat{\sigma}^2(i)/n_i' + \hat{\sigma}^2(pi)/n_p'n_i'.$$

Table 6.7 also reports the estimate for $\mathcal{E}\rho^2$ in terms of variance components, as well as formulas in terms of sample statistics, when items are scored dichotomously. I have already pointed out that KR-20 estimates $\mathcal{E}\rho^2$ when items are scored dichotomously. By contrast, table 6.7 indicates that KR-21 estimates $\Phi(\lambda)$ when λ equals X_{PI}, the mean for the sample of n_p persons and n_i items. This relationship is proved and discussed extensively by Brennan (1977b). The proof is quite long, but

TABLE 6.7. Estimates of Indices of Dependability

Estimate	In Terms of Estimated Variance Components	In Terms of Sample Statistics for a Full-Length Test of Dichotomously Scored Items
$\hat{\Phi}(\lambda) = \dfrac{\hat{\sigma}^2(p) + (X_{PI} - \lambda)^2 - \hat{\sigma}^2(X_{PI})}{\hat{\sigma}^2(p) + (X_{PI} - \lambda)^2 - \hat{\sigma}^2(X_{PI}) + \hat{\sigma}^2(\Delta)}$		$= 1 - \dfrac{1}{n_i - 1}\left[\dfrac{X_{PI}(1 - X_{PI}) - S^2(X_{pI})}{(X_{PI} - \lambda)^2 + S^2(X_{pI})}\right]$
$\hat{\Phi}(\lambda = X_{PI}) = \dfrac{\hat{\sigma}^2(p) - \hat{\sigma}^2(X_{PI})}{\hat{\sigma}^2(p) - \hat{\sigma}^2(X_{PI}) + \hat{\sigma}^2(\Delta)}$		$= \text{KR-21} = 1 - \dfrac{1}{n_i - 1}\left[\dfrac{X_{PI}(1 - X_{PI}) - S^2(X_{pI})}{S^2(X_{pI})}\right]$
$\hat{\Phi} = \dfrac{\hat{\sigma}^2(p)}{\hat{\sigma}^2(p) + \hat{\sigma}^2(\Delta)}$		
$\widehat{\mathcal{E}\rho^2} = \dfrac{\hat{\sigma}^2(p)}{\hat{\sigma}^2(p) + \hat{\sigma}^2(\delta)}$		$= \text{KR-20} = 1 - \dfrac{1}{n_i - 1}\left[\dfrac{\sum\limits_i (X_{Pi})(1 - X_{Pi})/n_i - S^2(X_{pI})}{S^2(X_{pI})}\right]$

Note: $\hat{\sigma}^2(X_{PI}) = \hat{\sigma}^2(p)/n_p' + \hat{\sigma}^2(i)/n_i' + \hat{\sigma}^2(pi)/n_p'n_i'$

the reader can verify the equality of the two formulas for $\hat{\Phi}(\lambda = X_{PI})$ for the data reported in tables 6.2 and 6.3. In effect, when items are scored dichotomously, $\hat{\Phi}(\lambda)$ can be no less than KR-21. This fact provides a useful basis for considering the domain-referenced dependability of scores on tests that have been documented with classical reliability estimates only. Similarly, when only sample statistics are available, one can use the second formula in the first row to estimate $\Phi(\lambda)$, for any cut-off score λ. For reasons discussed later, however, it is strongly suggested that whenever possible one report variance components, and estimate indices of dependability, in terms of variance components.

Using the formulas in table 6.7, the reader can verify the numerical results for the indices of dependability reported in table 6.3, based on the illustrative data in table 6.2. For example, using the estimated variance components in table 6.3 with the first formula for $\hat{\Phi}(\lambda)$ in table 6.7, and assuming that λ is 0.7, one obtains

$$\hat{\Phi}(\lambda = 0.7) = \frac{0.0625 + (0.5417 - 0.7)^2 - 0.0134}{0.0625 + (0.5417 - 0.7)^2 - 0.0134 + 0.0166}$$

$$= 0.817.$$

Alternatively, since the data in table 6.2 are dichotomous, one can use the second formula in table 6.7 with the sample statistics reported in table 6.2 to obtain

$$\hat{\Phi}(\lambda = 0.7) = 1 - \frac{1}{11}\left[\frac{0.5417(1 - 0.5417) - 0.0656}{(0.5417 - 0.7)^2 + 0.0656}\right]$$

$$= 0.817.$$

In a similar manner, the reader can use either of the formulas in the second row of table 6.7 to verify that $\hat{\Phi}(\lambda = X_{PI})$ is 0.747, the value of KR-21 reported by Guilford (1954) for the data in table 6.2. Also, using the formula for $\hat{\Phi}$ in table 6.6, one obtains

$$\hat{\Phi} = \frac{0.0625}{0.0625 + 0.0166}$$

$$= 0.790,$$

and using the formula for $\mathcal{E}\rho^2$ one obtains

$$\widehat{\mathcal{E}\rho^2} = \frac{0.0625}{0.0625 + 0.0105}$$

$$= 0.856.$$

These results illustrate that

$$\hat{\Phi}(\lambda = X_{PI}) \leq \hat{\Phi} \leq \widehat{\mathcal{E}\rho^2},$$

or, when items are scored dichotomously, as they are in this case,

$$\text{KR-21} \leq \hat{\Phi} \leq \text{KR-20}.$$

Table 6.3 also indicates that $\hat{\Phi}(\lambda)$ decreases as λ moves from zero to the sample mean and increases as λ moves from the sample mean to one. This fact is displayed graphically by the dashed line in figure 6.2. Figure 6.2 also reports estimated values of $\Phi(\lambda)$ for $n_i{}' = 5$, 10, 15, and 20 items. In effect, figure 6.2 graphically suggests one of the distinctions in generalizability theory between a G study and a D study. For these illustrative data one can view the G study (or "generalizability" study) in terms of the actual $n_i = 12$ items in table 6.2. Some decision maker, however, may be interested in a D study (or "decision" study) involving generalization to a different sample of $n_i{}'$ items, where $n_i{}'$ need not equal n_i. It is for this reason that table 6.1 distinguishes between n_i and $n_i{}'$.

Figure 6.2 was developed using the G study and D study variance components and other results reported in table 6.8. From table 6.8 and figure 6.2 it is evident that increasing the number of items sampled, $n_i{}'$, has no effect on the universe score variance, $\hat{\sigma}^2(p)$, but increasing $n_i{}'$ results in decreasing $\hat{\sigma}^2(I)$, $\hat{\sigma}^2(pI)$, $\hat{\sigma}^2(\delta)$, and $\hat{\sigma}^2(\Delta)$. Furthermore, these decreases in $\sigma^2(\Delta)$ cause the indices of dependability $\hat{\Phi}(\lambda)$ and $\hat{\Phi}$ to increase.

The i:p Design. Another way in which G studies and D studies can differ is in terms of the data collection design. Until now, we have implicitly assumed that both the G study and the D study use the crossed design, $p \times i$. We will continue to assume that variance components have been *estimated* from the crossed design, but now we will assume that the D study employs a design in which each person is administered a different random sample of $n_i{}'$ items. This design is denoted $i:p$, where the colon is read "nested within."

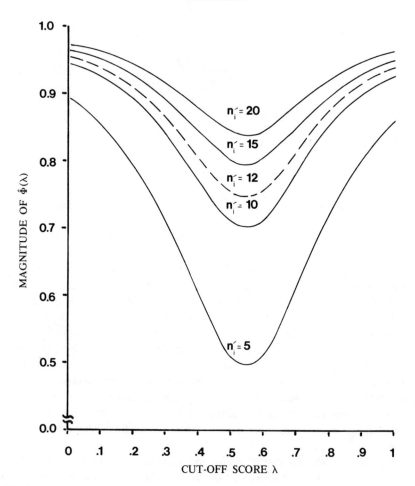

FIGURE 6.2. Estimates of $\Phi(\lambda)$ for various numbers of items based on Guilford (1954) data

Suppose, for example, that as a result of some G study, estimated variance components are available for the $p \times i$ design, but decisions are to be made based upon administering different random samples of $n_i{}'$ items to each examinee. This frequently occurs in computer-assisted test construction (Lippey 1974) or computer-generated repeatable testing (Lord 1977). Under these circumstances, the linear model for item scores in the D study is

$$X_{i:p} = \mu + \mu_p{}^{\sim} + \mu_{i:p}{}^{\sim},\tag{27}$$

where experimental error is confounded with the item effect $\mu_{i:p}{}^{\sim}$. The model for mean scores over n_i' items is obtained by substituting I for i everywhere in equation 27. Cronbach, Gleser, Nanda, and Rajaratnam (1972) discuss the $i{:}p$ D study design extensively, and Kane and Brennan (1977) extend their discussion to considerations in domain-referenced testing. Here, I simply summarize some of the more important results.

In comparing the $i{:}p$ design in equation 27 with the $p \times i$ design in equation 1, one can see that the effect for items nested within persons, $\mu_{i{:}p}{}^{\sim}$, in the $i{:}p$ design represents the confounding of $\mu_i{}^{\sim}$ and $\mu_{pi}{}^{\sim}$ in the $p \times i$ design. Also, the expected value, over persons, of the observed score for the $i{:}p$ design equals μ, the grand mean in the *universe* of items, but for the $p \times i$ design, this expected value equals μ_I, the mean for the *sample* of n_i items.

Figure 6.3 provides a Venn diagram representation of the variance components and mean squares for the $i{:}p$ design. From figure 6.3, one can see that for the $i{:}p$ design, *both* $\sigma^2(\delta)$ and $\sigma^2(\Delta)$ equal $\sigma^2(I{:}p)$. Furthermore, it is easy to show that

$$\sigma^2(I{:}p) = \sigma^2(I) + \sigma^2(pI),$$

where variance components to the right of the equality are for the $p \times i$ design (see equations 9 and 10). Clearly, then, given estimates of $\sigma^2(I)$ and $\sigma^2(pI)$ for a G study employing the $p \times i$ design, one can easily

TABLE 6.8. D Studies for Random Effects $p \times i$ Design Using Guilford Data for $n_i' = 5$, 10, 15, 20

Effect, Component, or Source	Estimated G Study Variance Component	D Study Variance Component			
		$n_i' = 5$	$n_i' = 10$	$n_i' = 15$	$n_i' = 20$
Persons (p)	0.0625	0.0625	0.0625	0.0625	0.0625
Items (i)	0.0737	0.0147	0.0074	0.0049	0.0037
Interaction (pi)	0.1255	0.0251	0.0126	0.0084	0.0063
$X_{PI} = 0.5417$	$\hat{\sigma}^2(\delta) = 0.0251$	0.0126	0.0084	0.0063	
	$\hat{\sigma}^2(\Delta) = 0.0398$	0.0200	0.0133	0.0100	
	$\hat{\sigma}^2(X_{PI}) = 0.0235$	0.0149	0.0120	0.0106	
	$\widehat{\mathcal{E}\rho^2} = 0.714$	0.832	0.882	0.908	
	$\hat{\Phi} = 0.611$	0.758	0.825	0.862	
	$\hat{\Phi}(\lambda = X_{PI}) = 0.495$	0.704	0.792	0.838	
	$\hat{\Phi}(\lambda = 0.7) = 0.617$	0.784	0.850	0.885	
	$\hat{\Phi}(\lambda = 0.8) = 0.727$	0.851	0.898	0.922	
	$\hat{\Phi}(\lambda = 0.9) = 0.808$	0.898	0.931	0.948	

NOTE: All estimates of $\sigma^2(X_{PI})$ and $\Phi(\lambda)$ assume $n_p = n_p' = 10$.

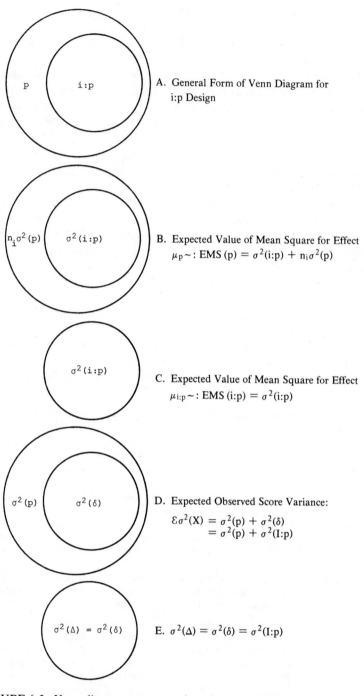

A. General Form of Venn Diagram for $i{:}p$ Design

B. Expected Value of Mean Square for Effect
$\mu_p{\sim}$: EMS $(p) = \sigma^2(i{:}p) + n_i\sigma^2(p)$

C. Expected Value of Mean Square for Effect
$\mu_{i{:}p}{\sim}$: EMS $(i{:}p) = \sigma^2(i{:}p)$

D. Expected Observed Score Variance:
$$\mathcal{E}\sigma^2(X) = \sigma^2(p) + \sigma^2(\delta)$$
$$= \sigma^2(p) + \sigma^2(I{:}p)$$

E. $\sigma^2(\Delta) = \sigma^2(\delta) = \sigma^2(I{:}p)$

FIGURE 6.3. Venn diagram representation of mean squares and variance components for $i : p$ design

estimate $\sigma^2(\delta) = \sigma^2(\Delta)$ for a D study employing the $i{:}p$ design. Furthermore, so long as items are sampled from the same universe, the universe score variance, $\sigma^2(p)$, is identical for both designs. It follows that the domain-referenced indices of dependability for the nested design are identical to those for the crossed design, and the generalizability coefficient, $\mathcal{E}\rho^2$, for the nested design is identical to Φ for the crossed design.

These results imply that the dependability of a domain-referenced testing procedure is not affected by whether the D study uses the crossed design, $p \times i$, or the nested design, $i{:}p$. The aim of domain-referenced testing is to provide point estimates of examinee universe scores rather than to make comparisons among examinees. The dependability of each examinee's score is determined by the number of items administered to that examinee, not by how many items or which items are administered to other examinees. Administering the same items to all examinees, in any instance of the testing procedure, improves the dependability of norm-referenced interpretations but does not improve the dependability of domain-referenced interpretations. Furthermore, the use of different samples of items for different examinees will tend to improve estimates of group means. If, therefore, domain-referenced tests are to be used for program evaluation, the selection of independent samples of items for different examinees provides *more* dependable estimates of group means without any loss in the dependability of estimates of examinees' universe scores.

An Example with Considerations of Extensions to Other Designs. In previous sections a simple set of synthetic data have been used primarily to illustrate computational procedures and results for the $p \times i$ design, with some consideration given to the $i{:}p$ design. Here, the theoretical framework discussed above will be applied to a large real data base for one of the instruments in the Adult Performance Level (APL) Program. The APL Program is an objectives-based assessment program, administered by the American College Testing Program (ACT) and designed to measure the life skills proficiency of adults. Rather than emphasizing purely academic knowledge, the APL Program focuses on functional competency as manifested in basic tasks that are relevant to everyday living.

The APL Program consists of six instruments: the APL Survey (ACT 1976) and five Content Area Measures, or CAMs (ACT 1977). All items in all instruments are scored dichotomously (correct $= 1$, incorrect $= 0$). The data base analyzed here is for the adult version of the APL Survey only, and this data base consists of the responses of 2,432 adults to each of the $n_i = 8$ items in each of the five content area subtests of the

APL Survey. These subtests are in the areas of Community Resources, Occupational Knowledge, Consumer Economics, Health, and Government and Law. Actually, the 2,432 examinees are only a subset of the entire data base, and the analyses reported here are only illustrative of a number of analyses of these data (see Brennan 1978). For these reasons, these analyses should not be interpreted as a validation of the APL Program.

Table 6.9 reports mean squares and estimated variance components for the $p \times i$ design, for each of the five content area subtests of the APL Survey. From table 6.9 it is evident, for example, that there is considerably less variability among items in the Health Content area than in the other areas. Table 6.10 reports variance components, error variances, summary statistics, and indices of dependability for each of these subtests, when the number of items in any subtest is $n_i' = 8$ or $n_i' = 20$.

Consider, for example, the last row of table 6.10, which provides estimates of $\Phi(\lambda)$ when the criterion level is 0.75, in terms of the proportion of items correct. For the APL Survey with $n_i' = 8$ items, the values of $\hat{\Phi}(\lambda = 0.75)$ are somewhat low by conventional standards, suggesting that domain-referenced decisions based on the eight items and a criterion level of 0.75 may not be very dependable for these subtests. For this reason, ACT has developed the five Content Area Measures (CAMs) referenced above, which are considerably longer versions of each of the five subtests in the APL Survey. ACT (1977) reports, for each CAM, estimates of $\Phi(\lambda = 0.75)$ that exceed 0.90.

Now, suppose one wanted to consider constructing a 100-item version of the APL Survey. It would be of interest to estimate error variances and indices of dependability for the five subtests in this new version of the survey. These estimates are also provided in table 6.10 under the columns headed $n_i' = 20$. The last row of table 6.10 indicates that $\Phi(\lambda = 0.75)$ is estimated to be in the 0.80s for each content area subtest.

The discussion above has been couched in terms of indices of dependability. In my opinion, it is especially important to consider also the error variances, $\hat{\sigma}^2(\Delta)$, for each of these subtests, which are reported in the fifth row of table 6.10. The square root of these error variances, or the standard errors, are the estimates used in establishing confidence intervals about the examinees' proportion-correct scores. For $n_i' = 8$ items, these standard errors range from 0.13 to 0.16, approximately; and for $n_i' = 20$ items, the range is about 0.08 to 0.10.

It is important to note that the above discussion does *not* address domain-referenced issues of dependability for the *entire* forty-item APL Survey. Thus far, I have considered such issues for each subtest or

TABLE 6.9. G Studies for the Five Subtests of the APL Survey Using the $p \times i$ Design

Effect	df	Mean Squares					Estimated G Study Variance Components				
		$s_1 =$ CR	$s_2 =$ OK	$s_3 =$ CE	$s_4 =$ H	$s_5 =$ GL	$s_1 =$ CR	$s_2 =$ OK	$s_3 =$ CE	$s_4 =$ H	$s_5 =$ GL
p	2431	.38121	.52279	.50769	.65299	.54843	.0322	.0459	.0440	.0631	.0477
i	7	50.74109	62.34850	79.60269	18.03560	84.19510	.0208	.0256	.0327	.0074	.0346
pi	17017	.12371	.15540	.15548	.14858	.16689	.1237	.1554	.1555	.1486	.1669

NOTE: The five subtests are as follows: $s_1 =$ Community Resources (CR); $s_2 =$ Occupational Knowledge (OK); $s_3 =$ Consumer Economics (CE); $s_4 =$ Health (H); and $s_5 =$ Government and Law (GL).

TABLE 6.10. D Studies for the Five APL Content Areas Using the $p \times i$ Design with $n_i' = 8, 20$

	Community Resources (CR)		Occupational Knowledge (OK)		Consumer Economics (CE)		Health (H)		Government and Law (GL)	
Effect	$n_i' = 8$	$n_i' = 20$	$n_i' = 8$	$n_i' = 20$	$n_i' = 8$	$n_i' = 20$	$n_i' = 8$	$n_i' = 20$	$n_i' = 8$	$n_i' = 20$
p	.0322	.0322	.0459	.0459	.0440	.0440	.0631	.0621	.0477	.0477
i	.0026	.0010	.0032	.0013	.0041	.0016	.0009	.0004	.0043	.0017
pi	.0155	.0062	.0194	.0078	.0194	.0078	.0186	.0074	.0209	.0084
$\hat{\sigma}^2(\delta)$	.0155	.0062	.0194	.0078	.0194	.0078	.0186	.0074	.0209	.0084
$\hat{\sigma}^2(\Delta)$	.0181	.0072	.0226	.0091	.0235	.0094	.0195	.0078	.0252	.0101
$\hat{\mathcal{E}}\rho^2$	.675	.839	.703	.855	.694	.849	.772	.895	.695	.850
$\hat{\Phi}$	.640	.817	.670	.835	.652	.824	.764	.890	.654	.825
X_{PI}	.7753	.7753	.6615	.6615	.6472	.6472	.6780	.6780	.5694	.5694
$\hat{\sigma}^2(X_{PI})$	.0026	.0010	.0032	.0013	.0041	.0016	.0009	.0004	.0043	.0017
$\hat{\Phi}(\lambda = X_{PI})$	.620	.812	.654	.831	.629	.819	.761	.889	.633	.820
$\hat{\Phi}(\lambda = .50)$	.853	.937	.753	.886	.724	.872	.824	.924	.657	.834
$\hat{\Phi}(\lambda = .75)$	.625	.816	.691	.852	.682	.849	.776	.897	.751	.886

NOTE: All estimates of $\sigma^2(X_{PI})$ and $\Phi(\lambda)$ assume $n_p = n_p' = 2432$.

content area only. By analogy with classical approaches, one might conduct a $p \times i$ analysis in which all forty items in the survey were *not* differentiated by content area. To do so, however, would confound certain estimates and induce some ambiguities, because such an approach fails to reflect the fact that items are *nested* within subtests in the universe. Classical test theory cannot directly take into account such nesting, but generalizability theory can. Furthermore, the approach to domain-referenced interpretations discussed above has been extended by Brennan (1978) to such designs.

Specifically, for the entire forty-item APL Survey and the data base discussed above, each person responded to every one of the $n_i = 8$ items in each of the $n_s = 5$ subtests. This design is denoted $p \times (i{:}s)$, where, as before, the colon is to be interpreted as "nested within." Figure 6.4 provides the Venn diagram and structural model for this design, along with formulas for the estimated random effects G study variance components. Note that for this design there are five independently esti-

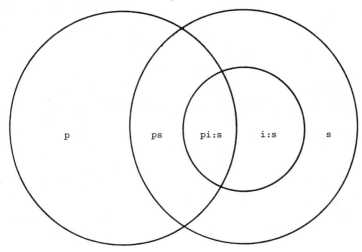

Model:

$$X_{pi{:}s} = \mu + \mu_p{\sim} + \mu_s{\sim} + \mu_{i{:}s}{\sim} + \mu_{ps}{\sim} + \mu_{pi{:}s}{\sim}$$

where experimental error is confounded with $\mu_{pi{:}s}{\sim}$.

Estimated Random Effects G Study Variance Components:

$$\hat{\sigma}^2(p) = [MS(p) - MS(ps)]/n_i n_s$$
$$\hat{\sigma}^2(i{:}s) = [MS(i{:}s) - MS(pi{:}s)]/n_p$$
$$\hat{\sigma}^2(s) = [MS(s) - MS(i{:}s) - MS(ps) + MS(pi{:}s)]/n_p n_i$$
$$\hat{\sigma}^2(ps) = [MS(ps) - MS(pi{:}s)]/n_i$$
$$\hat{\sigma}^2(pi{:}s) = MS(pi{:}s)$$

FIGURE 6.4. Venn diagram, model, and estimated random effects G study variance components for $p \times (i : s)$ design

mable sources of variance, whereas for the $p \times i$ design there are only three. A principal advantage of the $p \times (i{:}s)$ design is that it enables one to distinguish effects due to items *within* subtests from effects due to subtest means.

Table 6.11 reports results for four different D studies of the entire APL Survey using the $p \times (i{:}s)$ design. The reader interested in a detailed consideration of procedures for obtaining these results can refer to Brennan (1977a, 1978). Here, I simply consider some of the more important aspects of these results. Basically, Table 6.11 reports four different D studies: two in which the five subtests are considered random with $n_i' = 8$ and 20 and two in which the subtests are considered fixed with $n_i' = 8$ and 20. To say that these five subtests are random is to imply that we are interested in generalizing to some essentially infinite universe of potential subtests. (See Brennan 1977a for considerations in sampling from a *finite* universe.) By contrast, if subtests are considered fixed, then our interest is only in the actual subtests in the APL Survey. Table 6.11 illustrates that when subtests are considered fixed, indices of dependability are larger and error variances are smaller than when subtests are considered random. This is not to say that subtests here *should* be considered fixed. Such a decision is generally not a psychometric issue; it is a judgment that must be made by a decision maker with a particular universe of generalization in mind.

Recall that the estimates of $\Phi(\lambda)$ for each subtest with a criterion level of 0.75 and eight items were somewhat low by conventional standards (see table 6.10). From the last row of table 6.11, however, one can see that for the entire 40-item APL Survey, $\hat{\Phi}(\lambda = 0.75)$ is 0.89 or 0.92, depending upon whether subtests are considered random or fixed, respectively, and for a 100-item version of the survey these estimates are on the order of 0.95. Again, I suggest that such results be used in conjunction with the estimates of the error variance of $\sigma^2(\Delta)$. From table 6.11, it is evident that these estimates are relatively small.

Suggestions for Future Research

In considering suggestions for future research, it is desirable first to summarize some of the more salient features of the approach reviewed in previous sections. Basically, this approach may be viewed as an extension of generalizability theory to domain-referenced interpretations. As such, it is applicable to numerous data collection designs including the simple $p \times i$ design, and it enables one to make concrete and meaningful distinctions between norm-referenced and domain-referenced interpretations—distinctions that resolve a number of ambiguities in other approaches. To a large extent, such distinctions are made possible by, and indeed the approach is based upon, differentiating between two

TABLE 6.11. D Studies for APL Survey Using Design $p \times (i{:}s)$

			Subtests Random $(n_s' = 5)$		Subtests Fixed $(n_s' = 5)$	
Effect[a]	MS	G Study Variance Component	$n_i' = 8$	$n_i' = 20$	$n_i' = 8$	$n_i' = 20$
p (2432)	1.84829	.0414	.0414	.0414	.0414	.0414
s (5)	106.02210	.0024	.0005	.0005		
$i{:}s$ (8)	58.98439	.0242	.0006	.0002	.0006	.0002
ps	.19105	.0053	.0011	.0011	.0011	.0011
$pi{:}s$	.14857	.1486	.0037	.0015	.0037	.0015
		$\hat{\sigma}^2(\delta) =$	.0048	.0026	.0037	.0015
		$\hat{\sigma}^2(\Delta) =$	.0059	.0033	.0043	.0017
		$\hat{\sigma}^2(\tau)^b =$	.0414	.0414	.0425	.0425
		$\hat{\mathcal{E}}\rho^2 =$	.896	.941	.920	.966
		$\hat{\Phi} =$	.875	.926	.908	.962
		$X_{PI{:}S} =$	.6663	.6663	.6663	.6663
		$\sigma^2(X_{PI{:}S}) =$	.0011	.0007	.0006	.0002
		$\hat{\Phi}(\lambda = X_{PI{:}S}) =$	.872	.925	.907	.961
		$\hat{\Phi}(\lambda = .50) =$	.920	.954	.942	.976
		$\hat{\Phi}(\lambda = .75) =$	.889	.935	.919	.967

[a] Numbers in parentheses are G study sample sizes; i.e., $n_p = 2432$, $n_s = 5$, $n_i = 8$.

[b] $\hat{\sigma}^2(\tau)$ is the universe score variance, which is identical to $\hat{\sigma}^2(p)$ when subtests are random, and equals $\hat{\sigma}^2(p) + \hat{\sigma}^2(pS)$ when subtests are fixed.

different types of error variance. There are, nevertheless, a number of issues that remain to be researched. Some of these are summarized below.

Distributional Assumptions. It has been argued that one of the advantages of generalizability theory is that it is distribution free. That is, the error variances and indices of dependability discussed above can be defined and estimated without any assumptions about the form of the distribution of universe, observed, or error scores. Nevertheless, for some purposes, such as establishing confidence intervals, distributional assumptions are required. For classical norm-referenced interpretations, it is traditional to assume that errors of measurement are normally distributed. It has been pointed out by many, however, that for domain-referenced interpretations such an assumption may not be optimal. In particular, the binomial or compound binomial distribution may be a better choice for domain-referenced interpretations. However, as yet, this distributional assumption has not been extensively studied in the context of the approach to domain-referenced interpretations discussed above.

Loss Functions. The approach to domain-referenced interpretations suggested here explicitly incorporates a squared-error loss function. It has been noted previously that other researchers have suggested using a threshold loss function (see Subkoviak, chapter 5). Some issues involved in choosing a loss function for domain-referenced interpretations have been discussed by Kane and Brennan (1977). Briefly, they argue that the threshold loss function is appropriate whenever the only distinction that can be made usefully is a *qualitative* distinction between masters and nonmasters. If, however, different degrees of mastery and non-mastery exist to an appropriate extent, the threshold loss function is not appropriate because it ignores such differences.

In many (but *not* all) educational contexts, differences between masters and nonmasters are not purely qualitative. Rather, the attribute that is measured is conceptualized as an ordinal or interval scale, and the examinees may possess the attribute to varying degrees even though a single cut-off score is used to define mastery. In this context it is important that examinees who are far above or below the cut-off score be classified correctly. The misclassification of such examinees is likely to cause serious losses. The misclassification of examinees whose level of ability is close to the cut-off score will involve much less serious losses. Current techniques for setting the cut-off score are not very precise, and the choice of a cut-off score is, to some extent, arbitrary. It is, therefore, relatively less important that the testing procedure correctly classify examinees whose level of skill is close to the specified cut-off score. The domain-referenced indices suggested in this chapter reflect these considerations.

This is *not* to say that squared-error loss is always preferable to threshold loss, or vice versa. Indeed, in some contexts both seem some-what inappropriate; therefore, one potential line of research involves examining the applicability of other loss (or utility) functions. To do so, however, is by no means trivial in theory or in practice.

Cut-off Scores. Hambleton (chapter 4) treats some procedures that have been proposed for establishing a cut-off score, λ. A number of issues encountered in the application of such procedures have yet to be studied extensively. One such issue involves the effect of disagreement among cut-off score "setters" on the dependability of domain-referenced interpretations. More specifically, most procedures for establishing a cut-off score necessitate some type of subjective judgment(s) by experts. The validity and practical utility of such procedures may rest heavily upon the extent to which the experts agree in their judgments. Moreover, when λ is defined as the average of the experts' judgments, Brennan and Lockwood (in press) have suggested that some types of measurement dependability are affected by the extent to which experts disagree.

The Brennan and Lockwood (in press) study is based upon an application of generalizability theory to the Angoff (1971) and Nedelsky (1954) cut-off score procedures. To examine the effect of rater disagreement on measurement dependability they developed a modification of the index $\Phi(\lambda)$, which incorporates a term reflecting disagreement among raters. They found that $\Phi(\lambda)$ generally decreases as rater disagreement increases. The Brennan and Lockwood study is a preliminary attempt to combine, in a systematic manner, some issues associated with cut-off score procedures and measurement dependability for domain-referenced tests. Such issues need to be examined more thoroughly.

Other Issues. There are a number of issues in generalizability theory that have not been studied extensively, including alternative procedures for estimating variance components, especially for nonorthogonal designs, and issues of validity viewed from the perspective of generalizability theory. Since the approach to domain-referenced interpretations discussed above is based, in part, on generalizability theory, it follows that studying these issues may shed additional light on domain-referenced interpretations.

Also, the approach to dependability discussed above has not yet been extended to a consideration of multiple cut-off scores used simultaneously in a single instance of a testing procedure. To address this issue *may* necessitate some multivariate considerations of considerable complexity.

Guidelines for Practitioners

If the previous section provides suggestions for those who might extend the approach described in this chapter, then this section is addressed to those who would apply the approach as it currently exists. Of course, these two audiences overlap to some extent—perhaps to a considerable extent. Indeed, practitioners frequently generate the questions that lead to research topics, and sometimes the same people answer these questions. In any case, any set of guidelines for practitioners is likely to raise questions while it proposes suggestions. Also, the viability of such suggestions depends upon the role of the practitioners, to some extent, and certainly on the context within which the practitioner exists.

Finally, in considering the applicability of a set of guidelines, it is useful to consider the perspective of the person making the suggestions. The first two subsections below expand upon two issues that seem important to me, when one views issues of measurement dependability for domain-referenced tests, in the context of generalizability theory.

Nature of a Domain of Items and Parallel Tests Assumptions. In previous sections, no assumptions have been made about the nature of the domain, or universe, of items except that it is sufficiently well defined that one can reasonably consider the items in a test to be a sample from the domain. In particular, for the approach suggested and reviewed in this paper, there is no requirement that the item mean scores, or difficulty levels in the population, have any particular distributional form, and there is no requirement that $\mu_I = \mu_J$ for two different tests, or sets of items, I and J. In short, I have assumed randomly parallel, as opposed to classically parallel, tests.

Clearly, if all items in the universe are homogeneous in difficulty levels, then certain simplifications of results will occur. However, it is not necessary to require such conditions. Indeed, for domain-referenced testing (and many would argue for norm-referenced testing, too) the domain of items should be specified by content matter specialists, and these specialists should *not* be constrained to include items in the domain only if they have a constant difficulty level in some population. Now, when the items in a domain vary in difficulty, it is impossible for all tests (i.e., random samples of the same number of items) to be classically parallel. Therefore, it can be argued that the assumption of classically parallel tests is not only unnecessary but it is also frequently unreasonable, at least for domain-referenced testing.

Some object to the assumption of randomly parallel tests in that tests are not usually built by a strict process of random sampling from a domain of items. Even so, the assumption of randomly parallel tests is a useful idealization. Although the items of a particular test may not have been drawn at random, one can usually conceive of a universe of items from which the test items might have been drawn (see Cronbach et al. 1972, pp. 359-60, 366-70, for further details).

The discussion above has been couched in terms of random sampling from an undifferentiated domain of items. This is the simplest case to consider, but it is by no means the only possibility. For example, items may be randomly sampled from a stratified universe, as illustrated in the previous discussion of the $p \times (i{:}s)$ design. In such cases, analyses are more involved, but the argument is essentially unchanged.

Score Interpretations and Domain Specification. From the point of view of generalizability theory, a test is simply a random sample of items from some domain. Therefore, the existence of a domain (or universe of generalization) does not provide a clear basis for distinguishing between norm-referenced and domain-referenced testing. Rather, in my opinion, the fundamental distinction between norm-referenced and domain-referenced testing is a distinction in score use and interpretation. To avoid verbal complexity, it is common to speak of "tests" rather than "interpretations, or uses, or scores"; however, the distinction should be kept in mind.

Some writers differentiate between norm-referenced and domain-referenced tests in terms of the procedures used for constructing items. Such procedures affect domain specification. Suppose a group of test developers uses one procedure to construct items for what they call a "domain-referenced test" and a different procedure to construct items for what they call a "norm-referenced test." Even if both tests are for the same *general* content area, the domain of items will almost certainly be different for the two tests. In such a case, differences in test content are attributable to differences in the two *domains*, or universes of generalization, not to any inherent differences in norm-referenced and domain-referenced interpretations per se. Indeed, in such a case, one could provide norm-referenced and domain-referenced interpretations for scores on tests sampling either domain.

Also, a number of researchers and practitioners have suggested differential criteria for identifying "acceptable" items for norm-referenced and domain-referenced tests (see Berk, chapter 3). It is not my purpose here to evaluate such criteria, but it is clear that different criteria will usually produce different tests, or sets of "acceptable" items. To be more specific, once one changes the criteria for item acceptability, the domain, or universe of generalization, is likely to change. Consequently, when the criteria for item acceptability differ, the differences in the tests themselves are most directly attributable to differences in the specification of the universe of generalization. To summarize, in my opinion, differences between norm-referenced and domain-referenced testing are best thought of as differences in score interpretation, while different procedures for item construction and different criteria for item acceptability usually imply different domains, or universes of generalization. Once a universe of generalization is specified and items are sampled from it to form a test, then the scores on the test can be given either a norm-referenced or a domain-referenced interpretation. It may well be that practitioners find certain universes of generalization interesting or useful primarily for domain-referenced interpretations, while they find other universes interesting or useful primarily for norm-referenced interpretations. Even so, it seems best to differentiate between norm-referenced and domain-referenced testing *principally* in terms of score interpretation. Otherwise, one is likely to confound differences in score interpretations with differences in universes of generali-

zation, which result from different item construction and/or identification procedures. This is *not* to mitigate, in any way, the importance
of such procedures. The point here is that such procedures affect the
universe of generalization and do not necessarily imply a distinction
between norm-referenced and domain-referenced interpretations *per se*.

Indices of Dependability. I have considered two indices of dependability, $\Phi(\lambda)$ and Φ, for domain-referenced interpretations, as well as
two corresponding signal/noise ratios. As discussed previously, indices
of dependability and signal/noise ratios are monotonically related by
simple equations. From a technical perspective, therefore, it is of little
importance whether one emphasizes indices of dependability or signal/
noise ratios. However, $\Phi(\lambda)$ and Φ have characteristics that are more
familiar to most practitioners; therefore, the following discussion will be
couched in terms of indices of dependability.

Basically, three different approaches have been discussed for defining
and interpreting $\Phi(\lambda)$ and Φ. These approaches are based upon developing these indices in three ways: (*a*) in a manner somewhat analogous to the development of a generalizability coefficient, (*b*) through
signal/noise concepts, and (*c*) as special cases of two general agreement
coefficients. In terms of interpretability, I suggest that the "agreement"
approach may be the easiest for most practitioners. However, interpretations in terms of signal/noise concepts may be more informative
for people familiar with measurement procedures in the physical sciences. Finally, people familiar with generalizability theory may find
the first approach to be the most straightforward.

No matter which approach practitioners prefer in interpreting $\Phi(\lambda)$
and Φ, it is crucial that practitioners differentiate between $\Phi(\lambda)$ and Φ.
These two indices address *different* questions about the dependability of
decisions based on the testing procedure. $\Phi(\lambda)$ indicates the dependability of decisions based on the testing procedure, while Φ characterizes the
contribution of the testing procedure to the dependability of such decisions. Therefore, both indices should be reported, and practitioners
should be careful not to confuse them.

Actually, of course, there are an infinite number of possible values for
$\Phi(\lambda)$, depending upon the cut-off score, λ. For many domain-referenced
tests, therefore, it is best to report as many values of $\Phi(\lambda)$ as there are
cut-off scores that might be used in particular contexts. Better still, one
might report a $\Phi(\lambda)$ "curve" (see, for example, figure 6.2). Indeed,
several curves might be reported if the number of items, in any given
instance of the testing procedure, can be altered.

In interpreting the magnitudes of any specific values of $\Phi(\lambda)$ and Φ,
practitioners should keep in mind that $\Phi(\lambda)$ is dependent upon the

universe score variance, $\sigma^2(p)$, the error variance, $\sigma^2(\Delta)$, and the quantity, $(\mu - \lambda)^2$; and Φ is dependent upon $\sigma^2(p)$ and $\sigma^2(\Delta)$. Interpretations based solely upon the magnitude of $\Phi(\lambda)$ or Φ seldom provide a sufficient basis for good decision making.

Variance Components. In previous sections, considerably more space has been devoted to indices of dependability than to variance components. Such indices have practical as well as theoretical value. However, variance components and associated error variances are likely to be the most important results, because they frequently provide the most important basis for making decisions. Therefore, the central role that variance components play, in domain-referenced interpretations, should not be overlooked. Indeed, according to the *Standards for Educational and Psychological Tests* (APA/AERA/NCME 1974): "the estimation of clearly labeled components of score variance is the most informative outcome of a reliability study, both for the test developer wishing to improve the reliability of his instrument and for the user desiring to interpret test scores with maximum understanding" (p. 49).

For these reasons, it is recommended that variance components, and especially the error variance, $\sigma^2(\Delta)$, be reported in documenting the technical characteristics of a domain-referenced test. Furthermore, it is recommended that users give at least as much consideration to variance components as they give to indices of dependability in making judgments about the applicability of domain-referenced tests in specific contexts, for specific purposes. Finally, it is recommended that test developers carefully consider variance components, and especially error variance, in their deliberations about the optimal length of a domain-referenced test. Minimizing error variance is by no means the only relevant consideration in defining test length, but it is one important consideration.

Other Issues. Decisions about the appropriateness of particular loss functions cannot be made on the basis of a test *per se*. Such decisions are intimately involved with a consideration of the purpose and context of the testing procedure. For this reason, it is impossible to make a statement about the universal applicability of either squared-error loss functions or threshold loss functions, for domain-referenced interpretations. Prudence would suggest, therefore, that when ambiguity exists with respect to choice of a loss function, practitioners should interpret results cautiously. Indeed, it is sometimes advisable to report and interpret results based upon more than one loss function when ambiguity in choice of loss function exists.

In previous sections, an effort has been made to demonstrate relationships between sample statistics and other well-known quantities on one hand and $\Phi(\lambda)$, Φ, and $\sigma^2(\Delta)$ on the other. For example, table 6.7 illustrates that $\hat{\Phi}(\lambda = X_{PI})$ equals KR-21. Such relationships are not of fundamental theoretical importance, but they can be used advantageously as a "rough and ready" way to estimate dependability for some domain-referenced interpretations. Indeed, this is the principal reason why such results have been reported here. Again, however, it is strongly recommended that whenever possible one report variance components, and estimate indices of dependability, in terms of variance components.

Appendix

GLOSSARY OF SYMBOLS

Symbol	Definition
$\times$	"Crossed with"
$:$	"Nested within"
p, i, s	A person, item, or subtest
P, I, S	A *set* of persons, items, or subtests
n	G study sample size
n'	D study sample size
MS	Mean square
SS	Sum of squares
X_{PI}	Observed mean score over persons *and* items, expressed as a proportion of items correct
$\mathcal{E}$	Expected value
Σ	Summation
λ	Cut-off score
μ	Grand mean in population and universe
μ_p	Universe score for person p; expected value of observed score for person p, over universe of items
μ_i	Population mean for item i; expected value of observed score for item i, over the population of persons
$\sigma^2(p)$	Universe score variance, or random effects variance component for persons
$\sigma^2(i)$	Random effects variance components for items
$\sigma^2(pi)$	Random effects variance components for the interaction of persons and items
$\sigma^2(\Delta)$	Variance of differences between observed scores and universe scores
$\sigma^2(\delta)$	Variance of differences between observed deviation scores and universe scores expressed in deviation form

$\mathcal{E}\rho^2$	Generalizability coefficient
$\Phi(\lambda)$	Index of dependability for domain-referenced mastery interpretations
Φ	General-purpose index of dependability for domain-referenced interpretations
θ	Agreement coefficient *not* corrected for chance agreement
θ_c	Agreement coefficient corrected for chance agreement
ψ	Signal/noise ratio *not* corrected for chance
ψ_c	Signal/noise ratio corrected for chance
A	Expected agreement
A_c	Chance agreement
A_m	Maximum expected agreement
L	Loss or expected disagreement
d	Domain-referenced agreement function
g	Norm-referenced agreement function

References

American College Testing Program. 1976. *User's guide: Adult APL survey.* Iowa City, Iowa: American College Testing Program.

_____. 1977. *Technical supplement: APL content area measures.* Iowa City, Iowa: American College Testing Program.

Angoff, W. H. 1971. Scales, norms, and equivalent scores. In *Educational measurement,* ed. R. L. Thorndike. 2nd ed. Washington, D.C.: American Council on Education. Pp. 508–600.

APA/AERA/NCME Committee. 1974. *Standards for educational and psychological tests.* Rev. ed. Washington, D.C.: American Psychological Association.

Brennan, R. L. 1977a. *Generalizability analyses: Principles and procedures.* ACT Technical Bulletin no. 26. Iowa City, Iowa: American College Testing Program.

_____. 1977b. *KR-21 and lower limits of an index of dependability for mastery tests.* ACT Technical Bulletin no. 27. Iowa City, Iowa: American College Testing Program.

_____. 1978. *Extensions of generalizability theory to domain-referenced testing.* ACT Technical Bulletin no. 30. Iowa City, Iowa: American College Testing Program.

_____. 1979. GAPID: *A FORTRAN IV computer program for generalizability analyses with single-facet designs.* ACT Technical Bulletin no. 34. Iowa City, Iowa: American College Testing Program.

Brennan, R. L., and Kane, M. T. 1977a. An index of dependability for mastery tests. *Journal of Educational Measurement* 14: 277–89.

_____. 1977b. Signal/noise ratios for domain-referenced tests. *Psychometrika* 42: 609–25; 1978 Errata, 43: 289.

_____. In press. Generalizability theory: A review of basic concepts, issues, and procedures. In *New directions in testing and measurement*, ed. R. E. Traub. San Francisco: Jossey-Bass.

Brennan, R. L., and Lockwood, R. E. In press. A comparison of two cutting score procedures using generalizability theory. *Applied Psychological Measurement*.

Cohen, J. 1960. A coefficient of agreement for nominal scales. *Educational and Psychological Measurement* 20: 37–46.

Cronbach, L. J. 1951. Coefficient alpha and the internal structure of tests. *Psychometrika* 16: 292–334.

Cronbach, L. J., and Gleser, G. C. 1964. The signal/noise ratio in the comparison of reliability coefficients. *Educational and Psychological Measurement* 24: 467–80.

Cronbach, L. J.; Gleser, G. C.; Nanda, H.; and Rajaratnam, N. 1972. *The dependability of behavioral measurements: Theory of generalizability for scores and profiles*. New York: Wiley.

Glaser, R. 1963. Instructional technology and the measurement of learning outcomes: Some questions. *American Psychologist* 18: 519–21.

Guilford, J. P. 1954. *Psychometric methods*. 2nd ed. New York: McGraw-Hill.

Hambleton, R. K.; Swaminathan, H.; Algina, J.; and Coulson, D. B. 1978. Criterion-referenced testing and measurement: A review of technical issues and developments. *Review of Educational Research* 48: 1–47.

Kane, M. T., and Brennan, R. L. In press. Agreement coefficients as indices of dependability for domain-referenced tests. *Applied Psychological Measurement*.

Lippey, G., ed. 1974. *Computer-assisted test construction*. Englewood Cliffs, N.J.: Educational Technology Publications.

Livingston, S. A. 1972. Criterion-referenced applications of classical test theory. *Journal of Educational Measurement* 9: 13–26.

Lord, F. M. 1957. Do tests of the same length have the same standard error of measurement? *Educational and Psychological Measurement* 17: 510–21.

_____. 1962. Test reliability: A correction. *Educational and Psychological Measurement* 22: 511–12.

_____. 1977. Some item analysis and test theory for a system of computer-assisted test construction for individualized instruction. *Applied Psychological Measurement* 1: 447–55.

Lord, F. M., and Novick, M. R. 1968. *Statistical theories of mental test scores*. Reading, Mass.: Addison-Wesley.

Nedelsky, L. 1954. Absolute grading standards for objective tests. *Educational and Psychological Measurement* 14: 3–19.

Popham, W. J., and Husek, T. R. 1969. Implications of criterion-referenced measurement. *Journal of Educational Measurement* 6: 1–9.

BIOGRAPHICAL NOTES

RONALD A. BERK is Associate Professor of Education and Director of the annual Johns Hopkins University National Symposium on Educational Research. He received his Ph.D. degree from the University of Maryland in 1973. Prior to assuming a teaching position at Johns Hopkins, he taught elementary school in the District of Columbia from 1968 to 1972 and served as an evaluator in the Montgomery County (Md.) School System from 1973 to 1976. Dr. Berk has developed over sixty tests and scales and has published more than thirty articles in psychometrics, evaluation, and computer applications. He has also been a reviewer for several journals and publishing companies.

ROBERT L. BRENNAN is Director of Measurement Research for the American College Testing Program in Iowa City. He received his Ed.D. degree from Harvard University in 1970. He was Research Associate at Harvard from 1968 to 1971 and Assistant Professor of Education at SUNY at Stony Brook from 1971 to 1976. Dr. Brennan's research on generalizability theory and criterion-referenced measurement has been published in numerous journals. He has served as a reviewer for various measurement journals and as advisory editor to *Journal of Educational Measurement*. He has also directed American Educational Research Association training sessions on generalizability theory and applications.

RONALD K. HAMBLETON is Professor of Education and Psychology and Director of the Laboratory of Psychometric and Evaluative Research at the University of Massachusetts, Amherst. He received his Ph.D. degree from the University of Toronto in 1969. He has authored over 100 research papers, articles, book reviews, and computer programs in educational and psychological measurement. Dr. Hambleton has served as a frequent reviewer for numerous journals and publishing companies and as advisory editor to *Journal of Educational Measurement* (1973–present) and *Applied Psychological Measurement* (1977–present). He has directed American Educational Research Association training sessions on criterion-referenced testing for the past three years.

JASON MILLMAN is Professor of Educational Research Methodology at Cornell University. He is also the current president of the National Council on Measurement in Education. He received his Ph.D. degree from the University of Michigan in 1960. Prior to assuming a teaching position at Cornell, Dr. Millman taught junior-senior high school from 1955 to 1956. He has published over fifty articles, two books, and several edited volumes and has served as editor-in-chief of *Educational Researcher* (1964-1968) and *Journal of Educational Measurement* (1968-1971). He has also conducted numerous workshops on educational research design, statistics, and measurement and evaluation, including a few on criterion-referenced measurement sponsored by the American Educational Research Association.

W. JAMES POPHAM is Professor of Education at the University of California, Los Angeles, and Director of the Instructional Objectives Exchange (IOX). He received his Ed.D. degree from Indiana University in 1958. He taught at Kansas State College from 1958 to 1960 and San Francisco State College from 1960 to 1962. Dr. Popham is a past president of the American Educational Research Association and California Educational Research Association. He has authored over 100 research papers, articles, and monographs, fourteen books, and twenty filmstrip-tape programs for preservice and inservice teacher education. He has also received numerous awards for excellence in teaching and research and, in 1978, he was appointed founding editor of the AERA journal *Educational Evaluation and Policy Analysis*.

MICHAEL J. SUBKOVIAK is Professor and Chairman of the Department of Educational Psychology at the University of Wisconsin, Madison. He received his Ph.D. degree from SUNY at Buffalo in 1972. Previously, he was Director of Psychological Testing and Chief Statistician for the U.S. Army in Vietnam from 1970 to 1972 and Director of Testing and Evaluation Services at the University of Wisconsin from 1977 to 1979. Dr. Subkoviak has published extensively in the areas of educational evaluation and psychometric theory, particularly multidimensional scaling. He has also served as a reviewer for numerous measurement and research journals.

Library of Congress Cataloging in Publication Data

Johns Hopkins University National Symposium on
  Educational Research, 1st, Washington, D.C., 1978.
  Criterion-referenced measurement.

  Bibliography:
  1. Criterion-referenced tests—Congresses.
I. Berk, Ronald A.   II. Title.
LB3060.32.C74J63 1978   371.2'6 ⬦   79-18194
ISBN 0-8018-2264-5